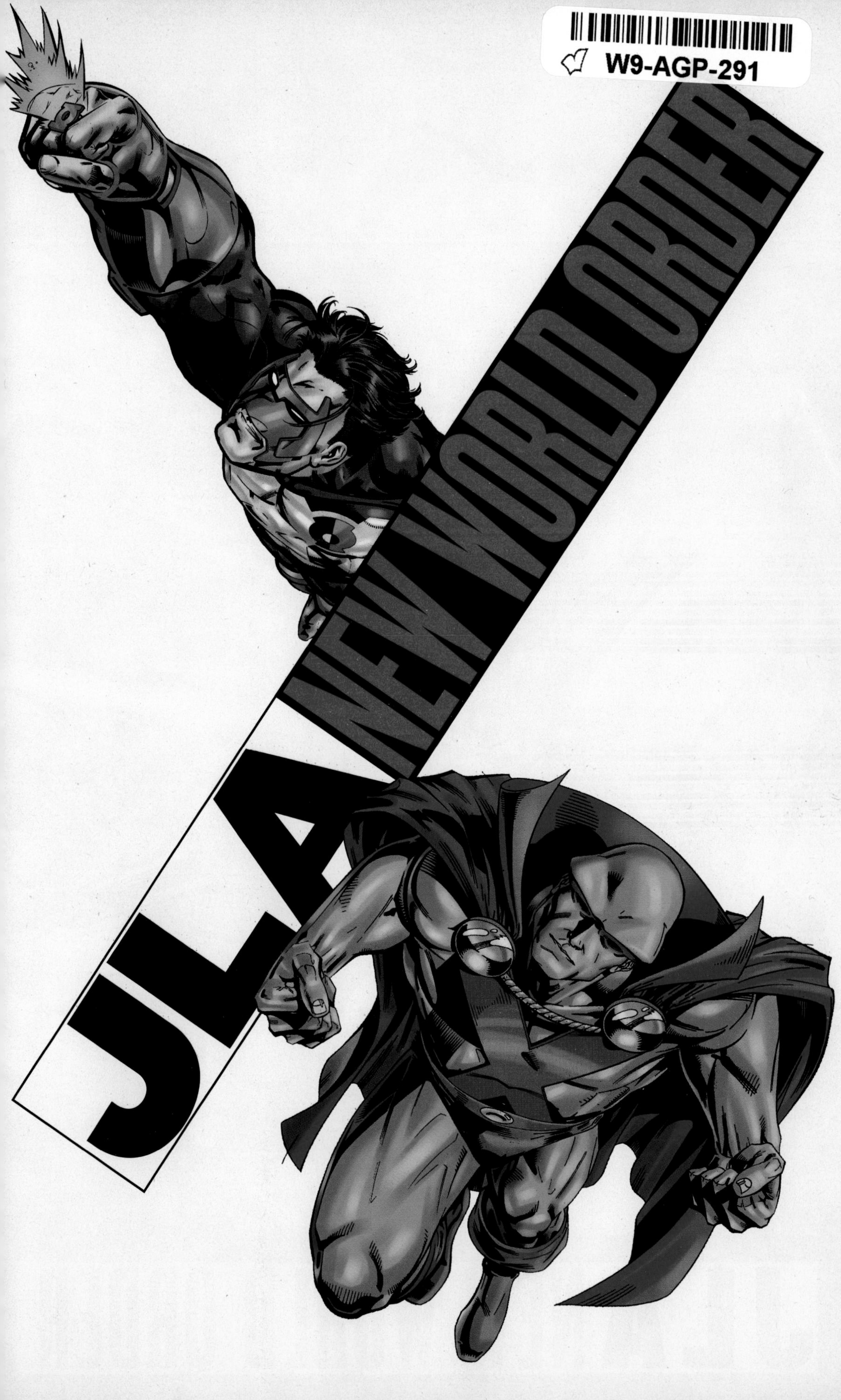
JLA
NEW WORLD ORDER

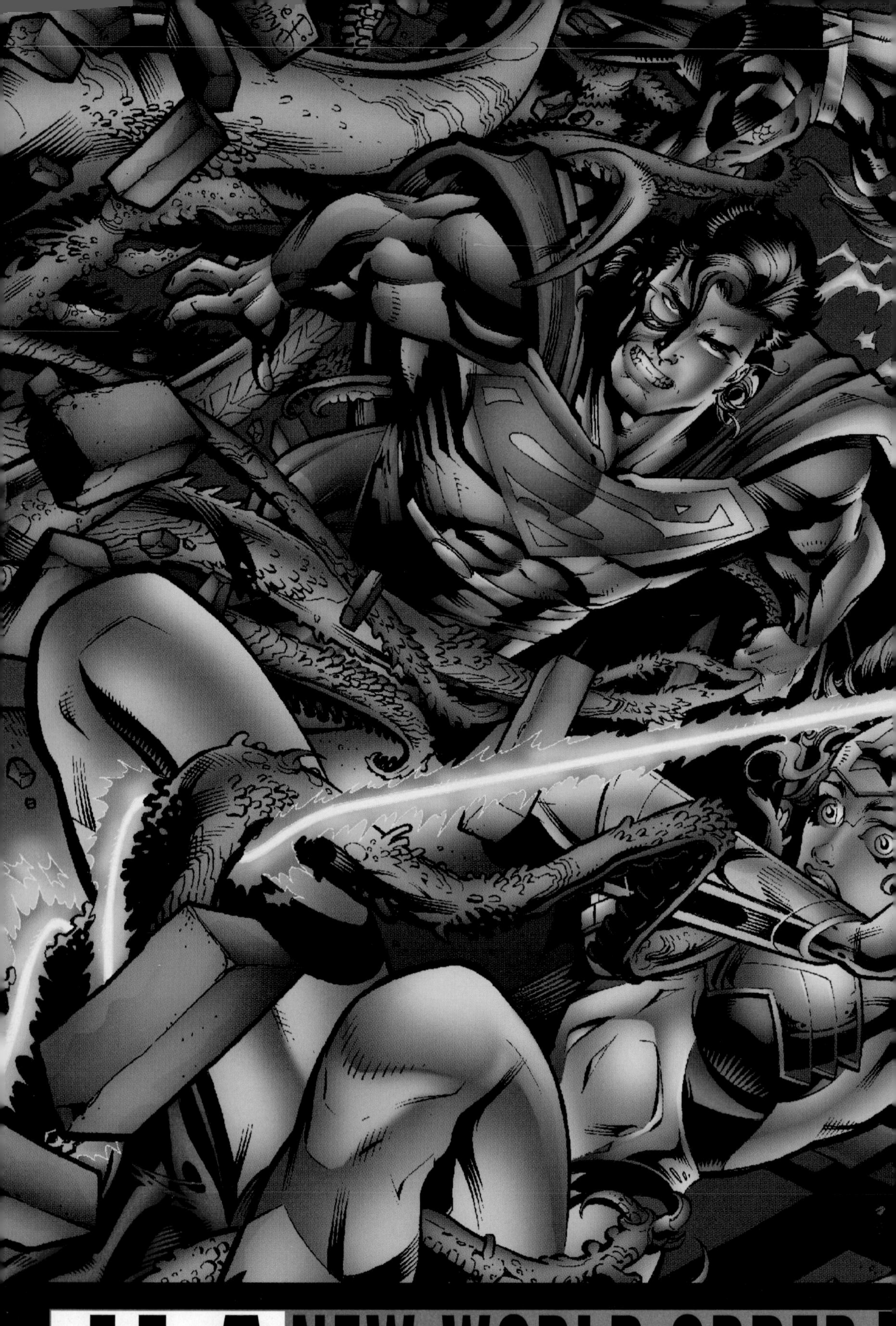

JLA NEW WORLD ORDER

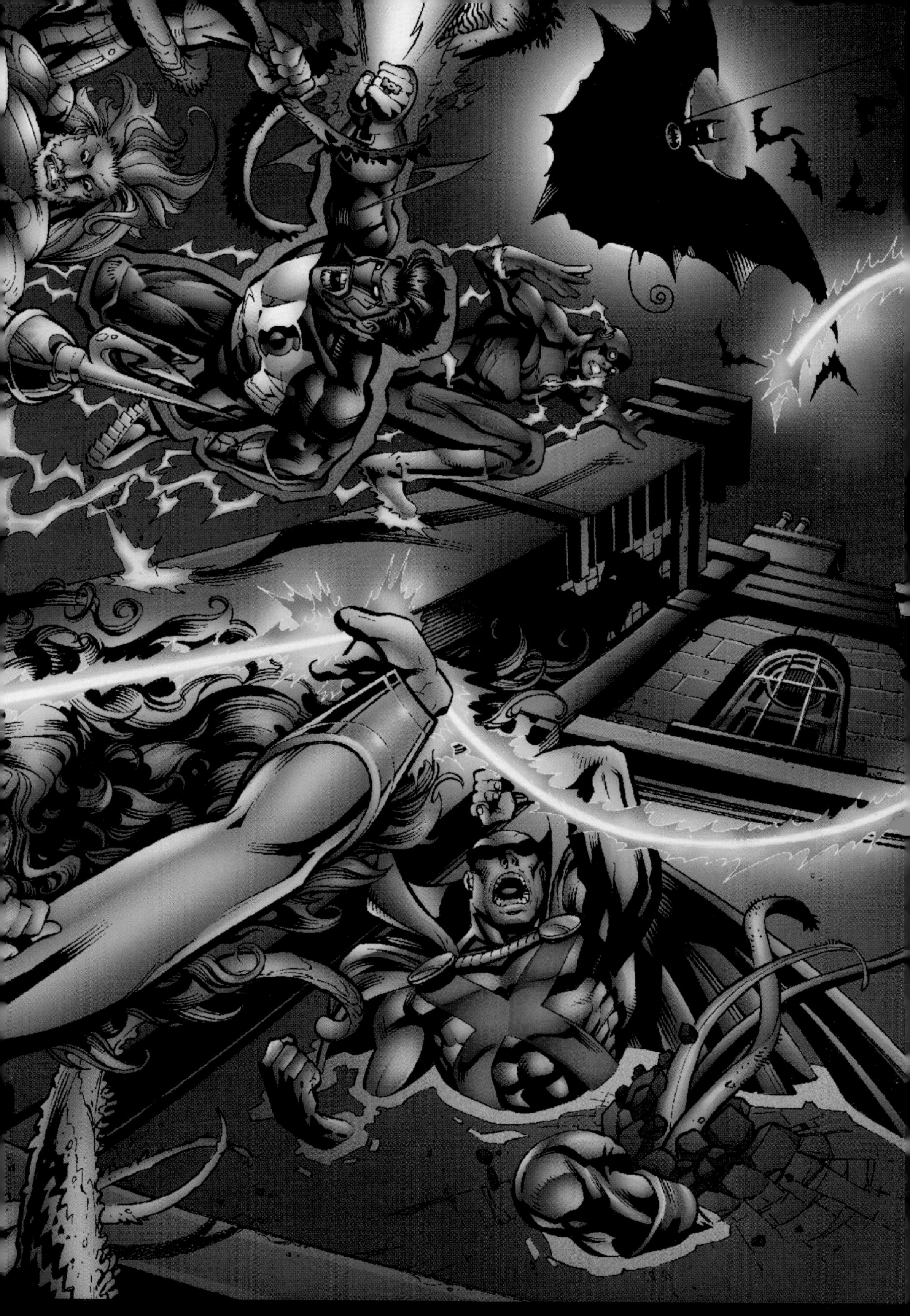

Grant Morrison **Writer** Howard Porter **Penciller** John Dell **Inker** Pat Garrahy **Colorist** Ken Lopez **Letterer** SUPERMAN created by Jerry Siegel and Joe Shuster BATMAN created by Bob Kane W[illegible]NDER WOMAN created by William Moulton Marston AQUAMAN

Dan DiDio — VP-Editorial

Ruben Diaz — Editor-original series

Bob Kahan — Editor-collected edition

Robbin Brosterman — Senior Art Director

Paul Levitz — President & Publisher

Georg Brewer — VP-Design & Retail Product Development

Richard Bruning — Senior VP-Creative Director

Patrick Caldon — Senior VP-Finance & Operations

Chris Caramalis — VP-Finance

Terri Cunningham — VP-Managing Editor

Alison Gill — VP-Manufacturing

Rich Johnson — VP-Book Trade Sales

Hank Kanalz — VP-General Manager, WildStorm

Lillian Laserson — Senior VP & General Counsel

Jim Lee — Editorial Director-WildStorm

David McKillips — VP- Advertising & Custom Publishing

John Nee — VP-Business Development

Gregory Noveck — Senior VP-Creative Affairs

Cheryl Rubin — VP-Brand Management

Bob Wayne — VP-Sales & Marketing

JLA

Superman: The last son of the doomed planet Krypton, Kal-El uses his incredible powers of flight, super-strength, and invulnerability to fight for truth and justice on his adopted planet, Earth.

Batman: Dedicated to ridding the world of crime since the brutal murder of his parents, billionaire Bruce Wayne dons the cape and cowl of the Dark Knight to battle evil from the shadows of Gotham City.

Wonder Woman: Born an Amazonian princess, Diana was chosen to serve as her people's ambassador of peace in the World of Man. Armed with the Lasso of Truth and indestructible bracelets, she directs her gods-given abilities of strength and speed toward the betterment of mankind.

The Flash: A member of the Teen Titans when he was known as Kid Flash, Wally West now takes the place of the fallen Flash, Barry Allen, as the speedster of the Justice League.

Green Lantern: After the destruction of the Green Lantern Corps, Kyle Rayner was chosen to be the one true Green Lantern. The powers of his ring are limited only by the imagination of its bearer — a strong suit of Kyle, who toils by day as a commercial artist.

Aquaman: A founding member of the Justice League, Aquaman is called upon once again to lend his strength and abilities to the cause. Ruler of a kingdom that covers over two-thirds of the Earth's surface, he is completely at home beneath the waves. Able to survive the immense pressures of the ocean depths and communicate with all its inhabitants, he is the greatest protector of Earth's oceans

Martian Manhunter: The most dedicated member of the Justice League, J'onn J'onzz has been present for every one of the team's many incarnations. His strength rivals that of Earth's mightiest heroes, and his shape-shifting abilities allow him to pass anonymously among our planet's populace.

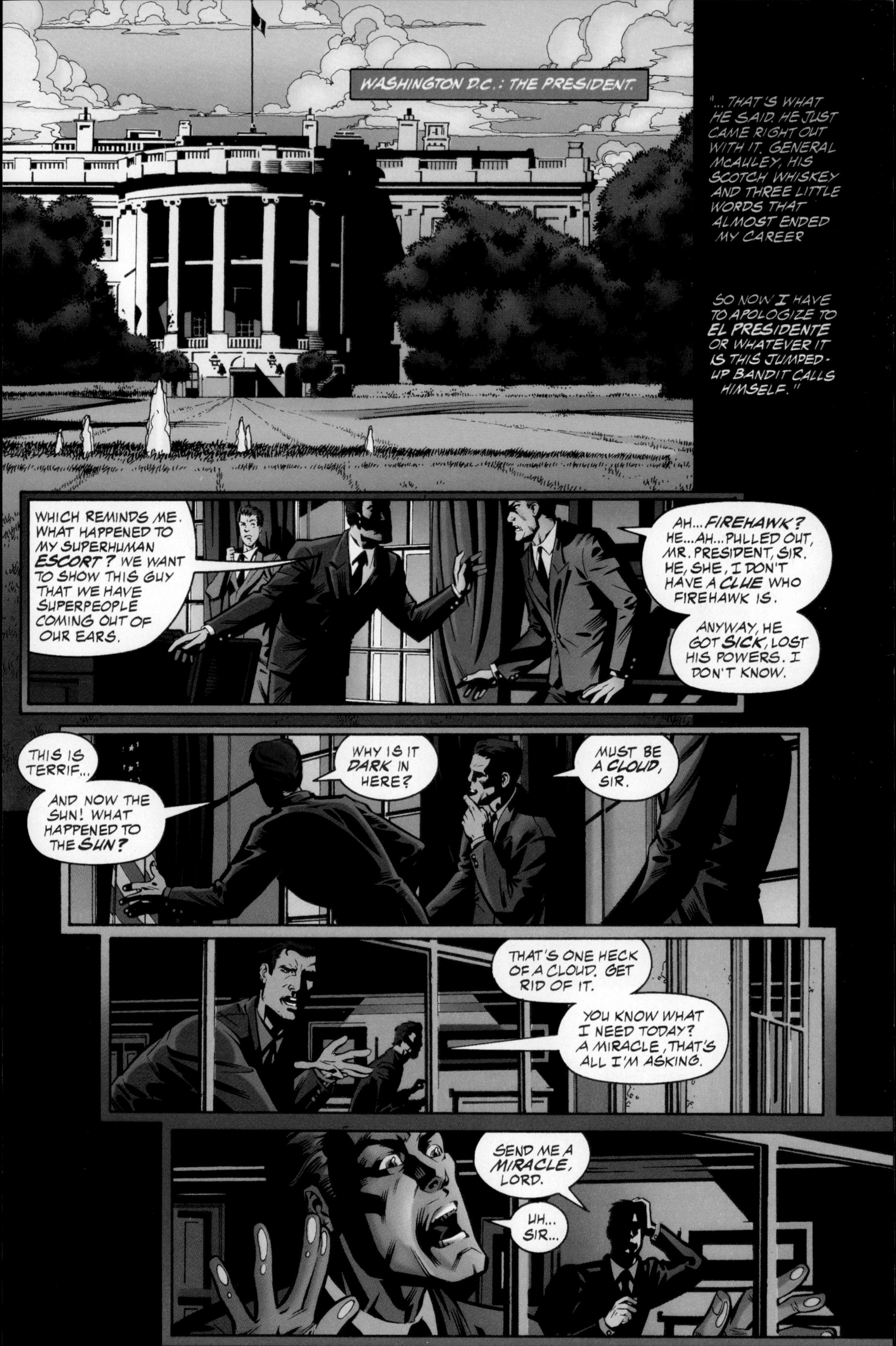
WASHINGTON D.C.: THE PRESIDENT.
"...THAT'S WHAT HE SAID. HE JUST CAME RIGHT OUT WITH IT. GENERAL McAULEY, HIS SCOTCH WHISKEY AND THREE LITTLE WORDS THAT ALMOST ENDED MY CAREER
SO NOW I HAVE TO APOLOGIZE TO EL PRESIDENTE OR WHATEVER IT IS THIS JUMPED-UP BANDIT CALLS HIMSELF."
WHICH REMINDS ME. WHAT HAPPENED TO MY SUPERHUMAN ESCORT? WE WANT TO SHOW THIS GUY THAT WE HAVE SUPERPEOPLE COMING OUT OF OUR EARS.
AH... FIREHAWK? HE...AH...PULLED OUT, MR. PRESIDENT, SIR. HE, SHE, I DON'T HAVE A CLUE WHO FIREHAWK IS.
ANYWAY, HE GOT SICK, LOST HIS POWERS. I DON'T KNOW.
THIS IS TERRIF...
AND NOW THE SUN! WHAT HAPPENED TO THE SUN?
WHY IS IT DARK IN HERE?
MUST BE A CLOUD, SIR.
THAT'S ONE HECK OF A CLOUD. GET RID OF IT.
YOU KNOW WHAT I NEED TODAY? A MIRACLE, THAT'S ALL I'M ASKING.
SEND ME A MIRACLE, LORD.
UH... SIR...

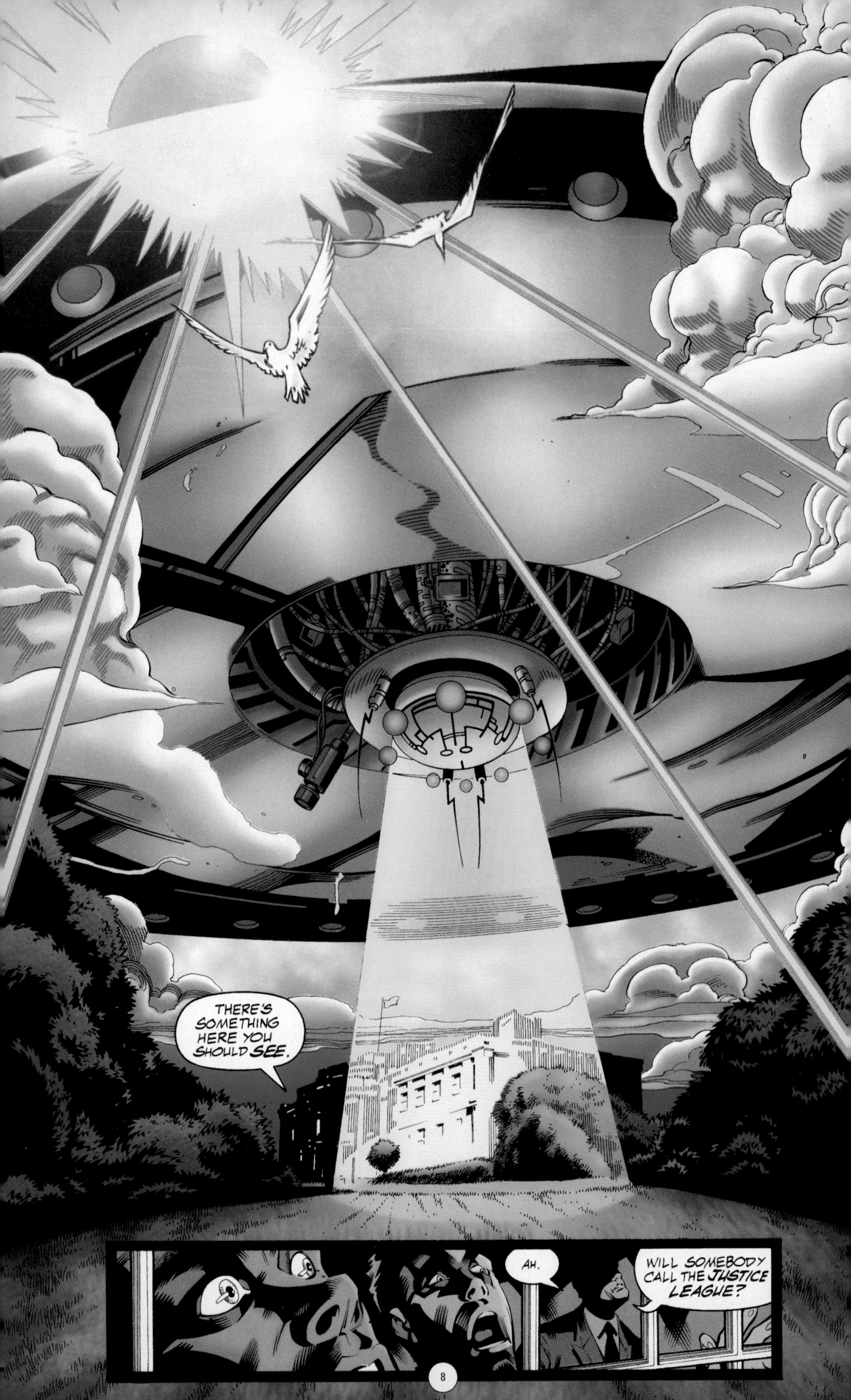
THERE'S SOMETHING HERE YOU SHOULD SEE.
AH.
WILL SOMEBODY CALL THE JUSTICE LEAGUE?

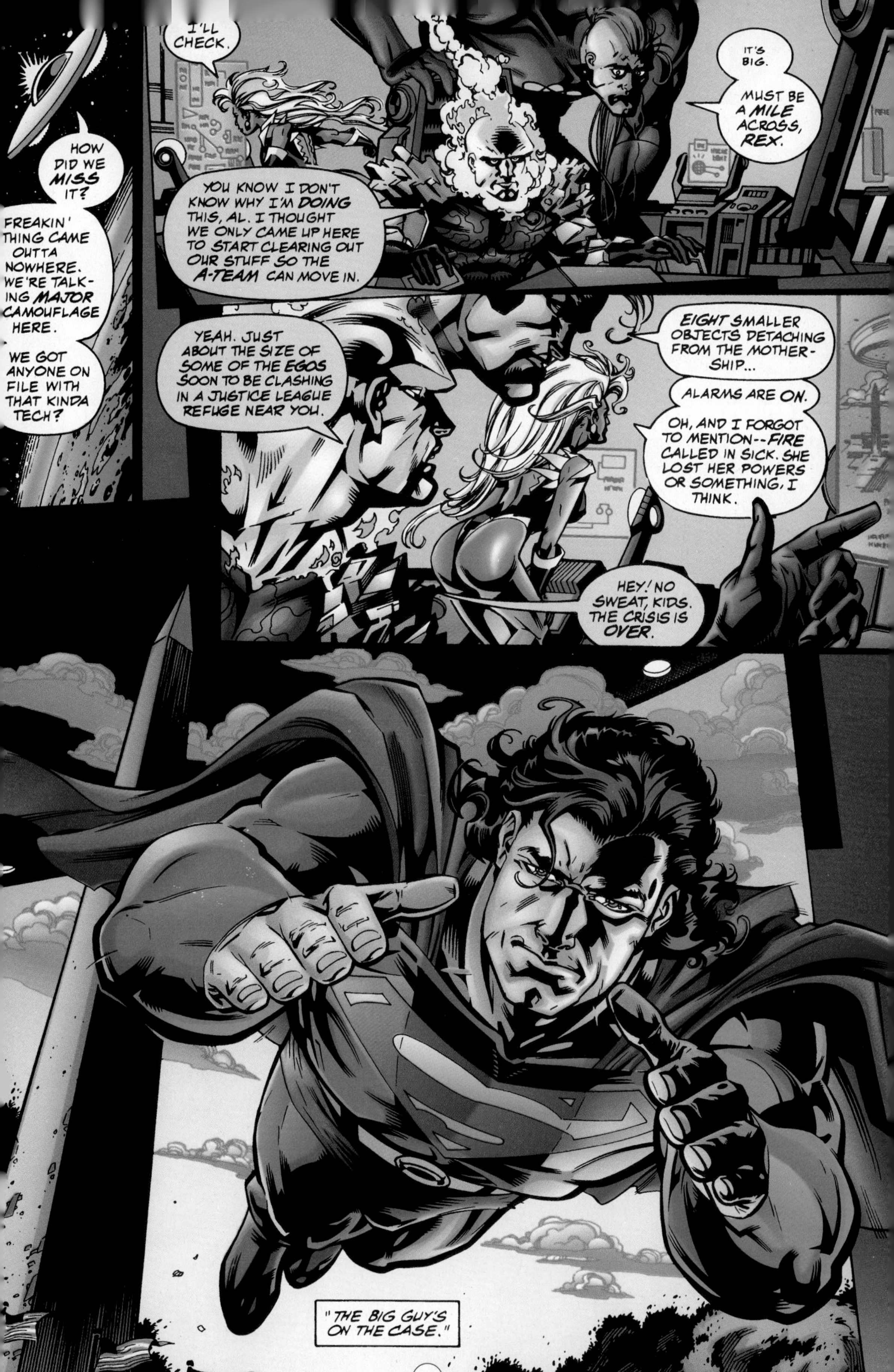

HOW DID WE MISS IT?
FREAKIN' THING CAME OUTTA NOWHERE. WE'RE TALKING MAJOR CAMOUFLAGE HERE.
WE GOT ANYONE ON FILE WITH THAT KINDA TECH?
I'LL CHECK.
IT'S BIG.
MUST BE A MILE ACROSS, REX.
YOU KNOW I DON'T KNOW WHY I'M DOING THIS, AL. I THOUGHT WE ONLY CAME UP HERE TO START CLEARING OUT OUR STUFF SO THE A-TEAM CAN MOVE IN.
YEAH. JUST ABOUT THE SIZE OF SOME OF THE EGOS SOON TO BE CLASHING IN A JUSTICE LEAGUE REFUGE NEAR YOU.
EIGHT SMALLER OBJECTS DETACHING FROM THE MOTHER-SHIP...
ALARMS ARE ON.
OH, AND I FORGOT TO MENTION--FIRE CALLED IN SICK. SHE LOST HER POWERS OR SOMETHING, I THINK.
HEY! NO SWEAT, KIDS. THE CRISIS IS OVER.
"THE BIG GUY'S ON THE CASE."

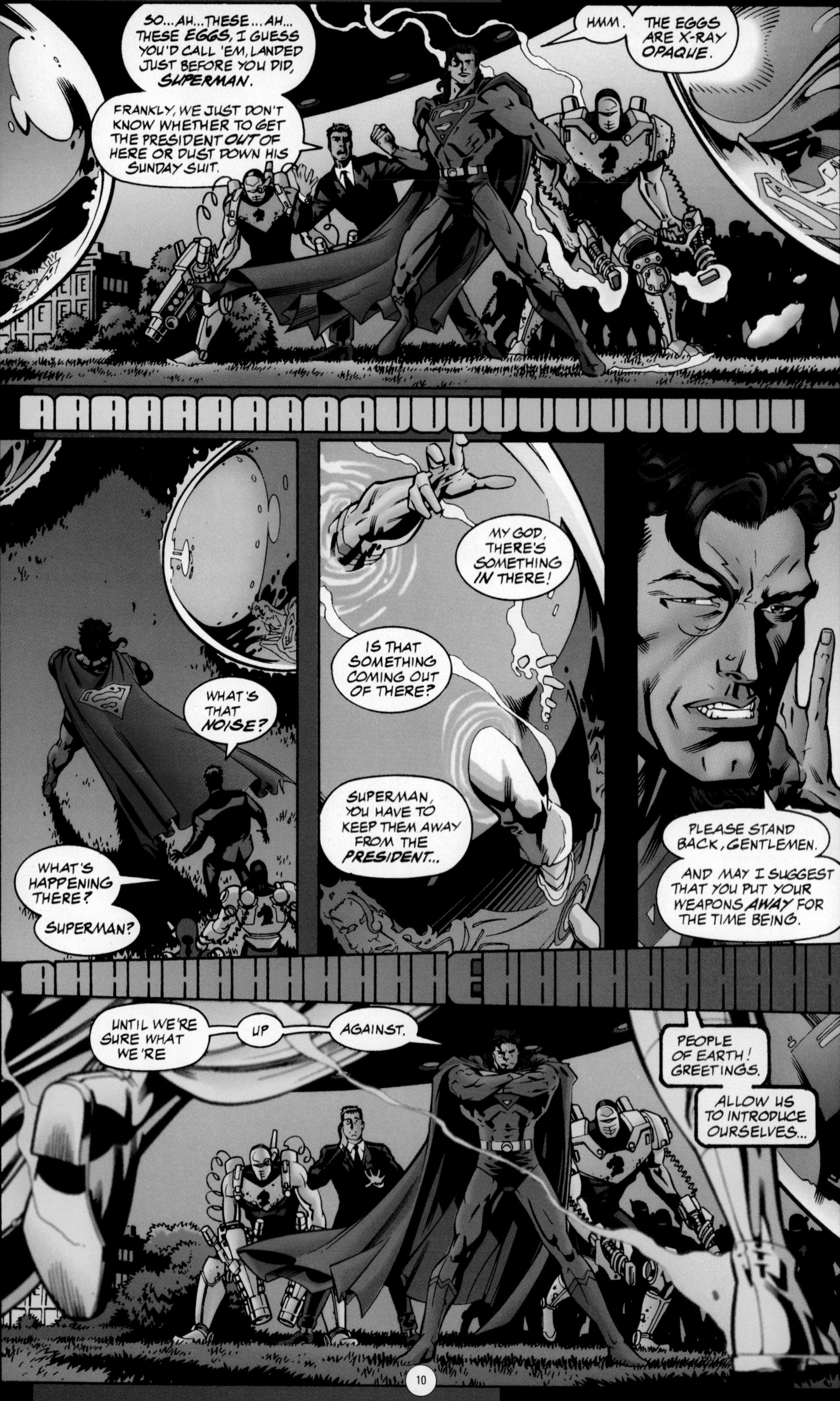
SO...AH...THESE...AH... THESE EGGS, I GUESS YOU'D CALL 'EM, LANDED JUST BEFORE YOU DID, SUPERMAN.
FRANKLY, WE JUST DON'T KNOW WHETHER TO GET THE PRESIDENT OUT OF HERE OR DUST DOWN HIS SUNDAY SUIT.
HMM.
THE EGGS ARE X-RAY OPAQUE.
AAAAAAAAAAAVVVVVVVVVVVVVV
WHAT'S THAT NOISE?
WHAT'S HAPPENING THERE?
SUPERMAN?
MY GOD, THERE'S SOMETHING IN THERE!
IS THAT SOMETHING COMING OUT OF THERE?
SUPERMAN, YOU HAVE TO KEEP THEM AWAY FROM THE PRESIDENT...
PLEASE STAND BACK, GENTLEMEN.
AND MAY I SUGGEST THAT YOU PUT YOUR WEAPONS AWAY FOR THE TIME BEING.
AHHHHHHHHHHHHEHHHHHHHHHHHHH
UNTIL WE'RE SURE WHAT WE'RE
UP
AGAINST.
PEOPLE OF EARTH! GREETINGS.
ALLOW US TO INTRODUCE OURSELVES...

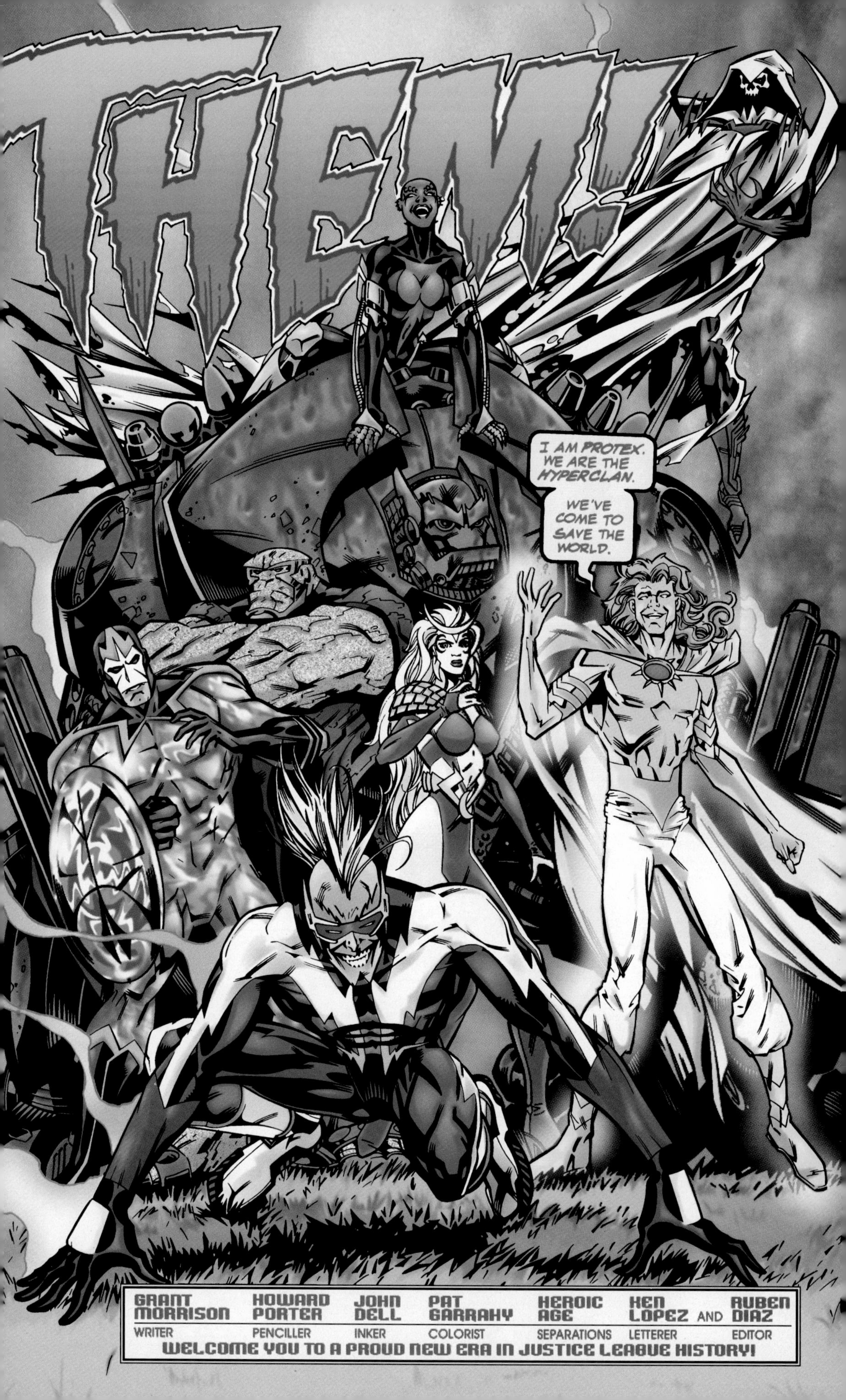
THEM!
I AM PROTEX. WE ARE THE HYPERCLAN.
WE'VE COME TO SAVE THE WORLD.
GRANT MORRISON WRITER
HOWARD PORTER PENCILLER
JOHN DELL INKER
PAT GARRAHY COLORIST
HEROIC AGE SEPARATIONS
KEN LOPEZ LETTERER
AND RUBEN DIAZ EDITOR
WELCOME YOU TO A PROUD NEW ERA IN JUSTICE LEAGUE HISTORY!

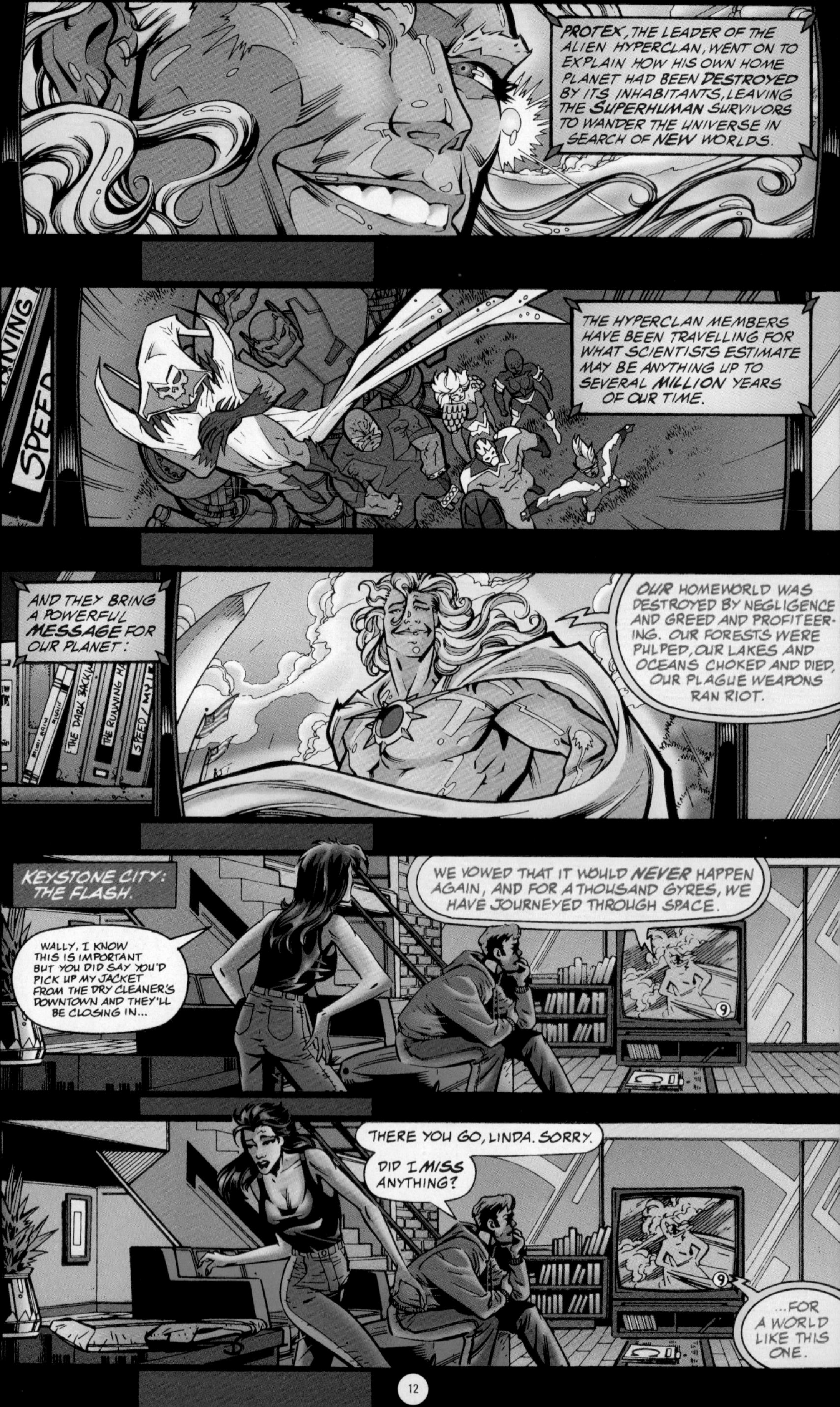
PROTEX, THE LEADER OF THE ALIEN HYPERCLAN, WENT ON TO EXPLAIN HOW HIS OWN HOME PLANET HAD BEEN DESTROYED BY ITS INHABITANTS, LEAVING THE SUPERHUMAN SURVIVORS TO WANDER THE UNIVERSE IN SEARCH OF NEW WORLDS.
SPEED
THE HYPERCLAN MEMBERS HAVE BEEN TRAVELLING FOR WHAT SCIENTISTS ESTIMATE MAY BE ANYTHING UP TO SEVERAL MILLION YEARS OF OUR TIME.
AND THEY BRING A POWERFUL MESSAGE FOR OUR PLANET:
OUR HOMEWORLD WAS DESTROYED BY NEGLIGENCE AND GREED AND PROFITEERING. OUR FORESTS WERE PULPED, OUR LAKES AND OCEANS CHOKED AND DIED, OUR PLAGUE WEAPONS RAN RIOT.
KEYSTONE CITY: THE FLASH.
WE VOWED THAT IT WOULD NEVER HAPPEN AGAIN, AND FOR A THOUSAND GYRES, WE HAVE JOURNEYED THROUGH SPACE.
WALLY, I KNOW THIS IS IMPORTANT BUT YOU DID SAY YOU'D PICK UP MY JACKET FROM THE DRY CLEANER'S DOWNTOWN AND THEY'LL BE CLOSING IN...
THERE YOU GO, LINDA. SORRY.
DID I MISS ANYTHING?
...FOR A WORLD LIKE THIS ONE.

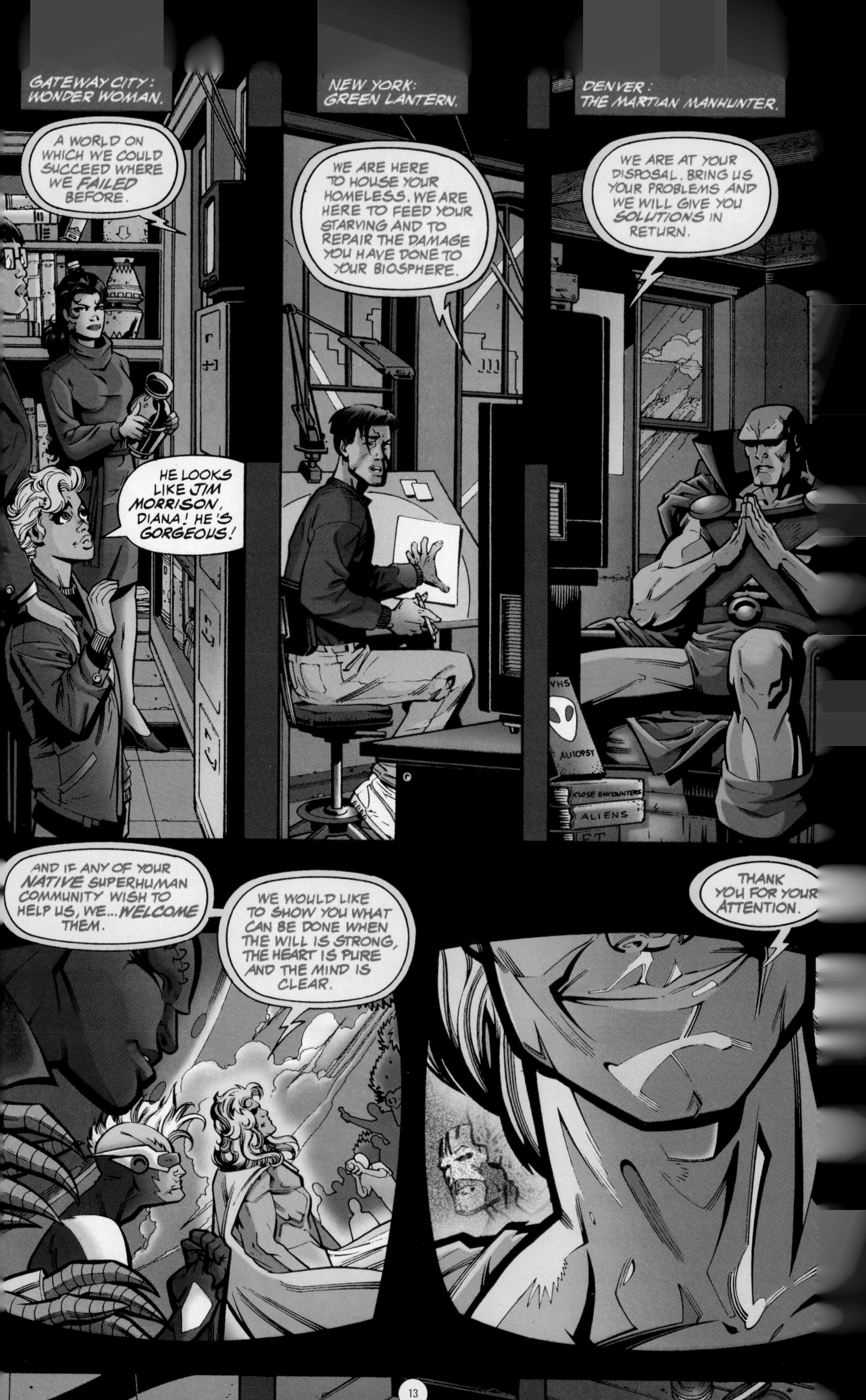
GATEWAY CITY: WONDER WOMAN.
A WORLD ON WHICH WE COULD SUCCEED WHERE WE FAILED BEFORE.
HE LOOKS LIKE JIM MORRISON, DIANA! HE'S GORGEOUS!
NEW YORK: GREEN LANTERN.
WE ARE HERE TO HOUSE YOUR HOMELESS. WE ARE HERE TO FEED YOUR STARVING AND TO REPAIR THE DAMAGE YOU HAVE DONE TO YOUR BIOSPHERE.
DENVER: THE MARTIAN MANHUNTER.
WE ARE AT YOUR DISPOSAL. BRING US YOUR PROBLEMS AND WE WILL GIVE YOU SOLUTIONS IN RETURN.
VHS
AUTOPSY
CLOSE ENCOUNTERS
ALIENS
AND IF ANY OF YOUR NATIVE SUPERHUMAN COMMUNITY WISH TO HELP US, WE...WELCOME THEM.
WE WOULD LIKE TO SHOW YOU WHAT CAN BE DONE WHEN THE WILL IS STRONG, THE HEART IS PURE AND THE MIND IS CLEAR.
THANK YOU FOR YOUR ATTENTION.

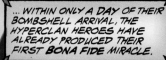

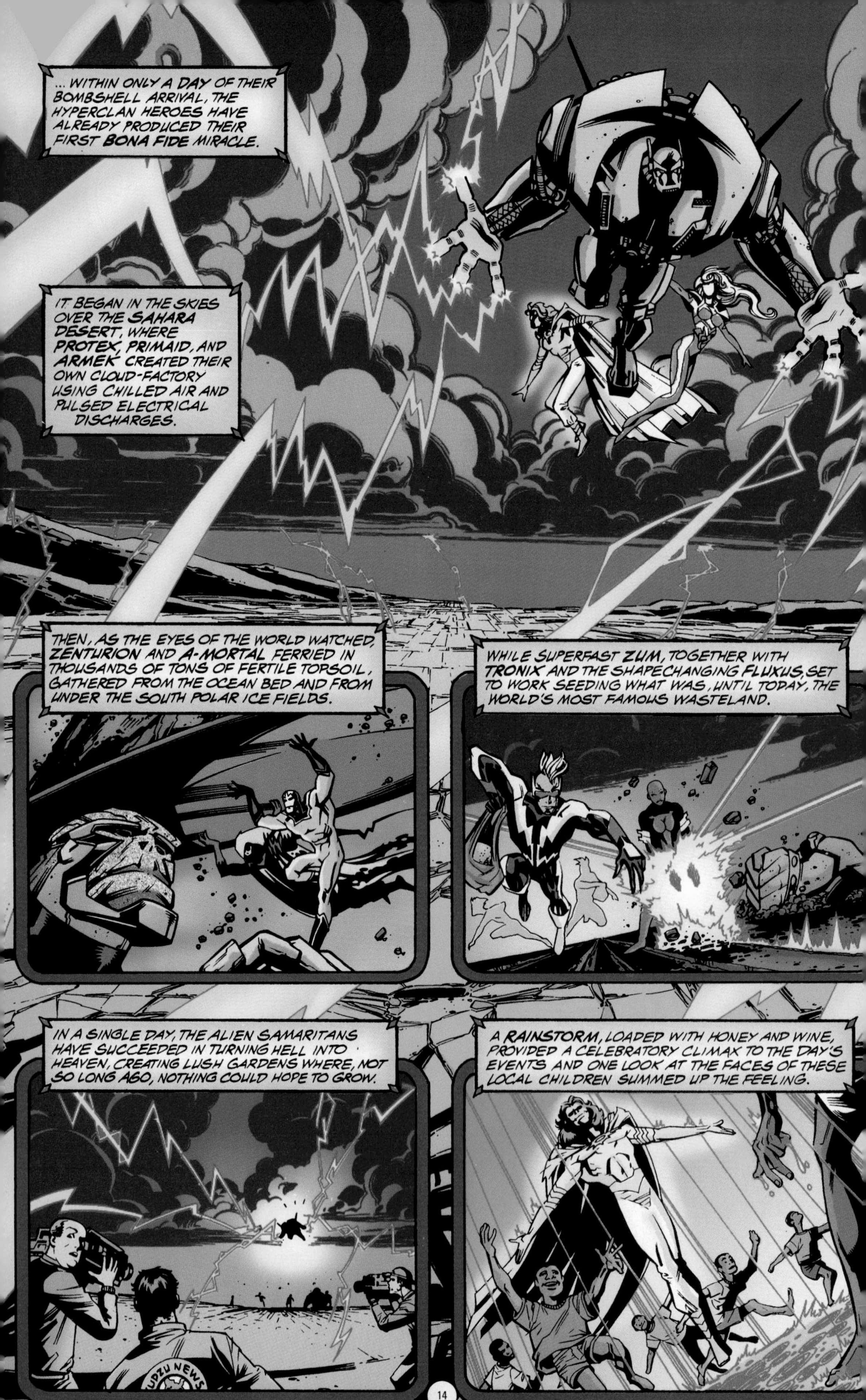

...WITHIN ONLY A DAY OF THEIR BOMBSHELL ARRIVAL, THE HYPERCLAN HEROES HAVE ALREADY PRODUCED THEIR FIRST *BONA FIDE* MIRACLE.

IT BEGAN IN THE SKIES OVER THE *SAHARA DESERT*, WHERE *PROTEX, PRIMAID,* AND *ARMEK* CREATED THEIR OWN *CLOUD-FACTORY* USING CHILLED AIR AND PULSED ELECTRICAL DISCHARGES.

THEN, AS THE EYES OF THE WORLD WATCHED, *ZENTURION* AND *A-MORTAL* FERRIED IN THOUSANDS OF TONS OF FERTILE TOPSOIL, GATHERED FROM THE OCEAN BED AND FROM UNDER THE SOUTH POLAR ICE FIELDS.

WHILE SUPERFAST *ZUM*, TOGETHER WITH *TRONIX* AND THE SHAPECHANGING *FLUXUS*, SET TO WORK SEEDING WHAT WAS, UNTIL TODAY, THE WORLD'S MOST FAMOUS WASTELAND.

IN A SINGLE DAY, THE ALIEN SAMARITANS HAVE SUCCEEDED IN TURNING HELL INTO HEAVEN, CREATING LUSH GARDENS WHERE, NOT SO LONG AGO, NOTHING COULD HOPE TO GROW.

A RAINSTORM, LOADED WITH HONEY AND WINE, PROVIDED A CELEBRATORY CLIMAX TO THE DAY'S EVENTS AND ONE LOOK AT THE FACES OF THESE LOCAL CHILDREN SUMMED UP THE FEELING.

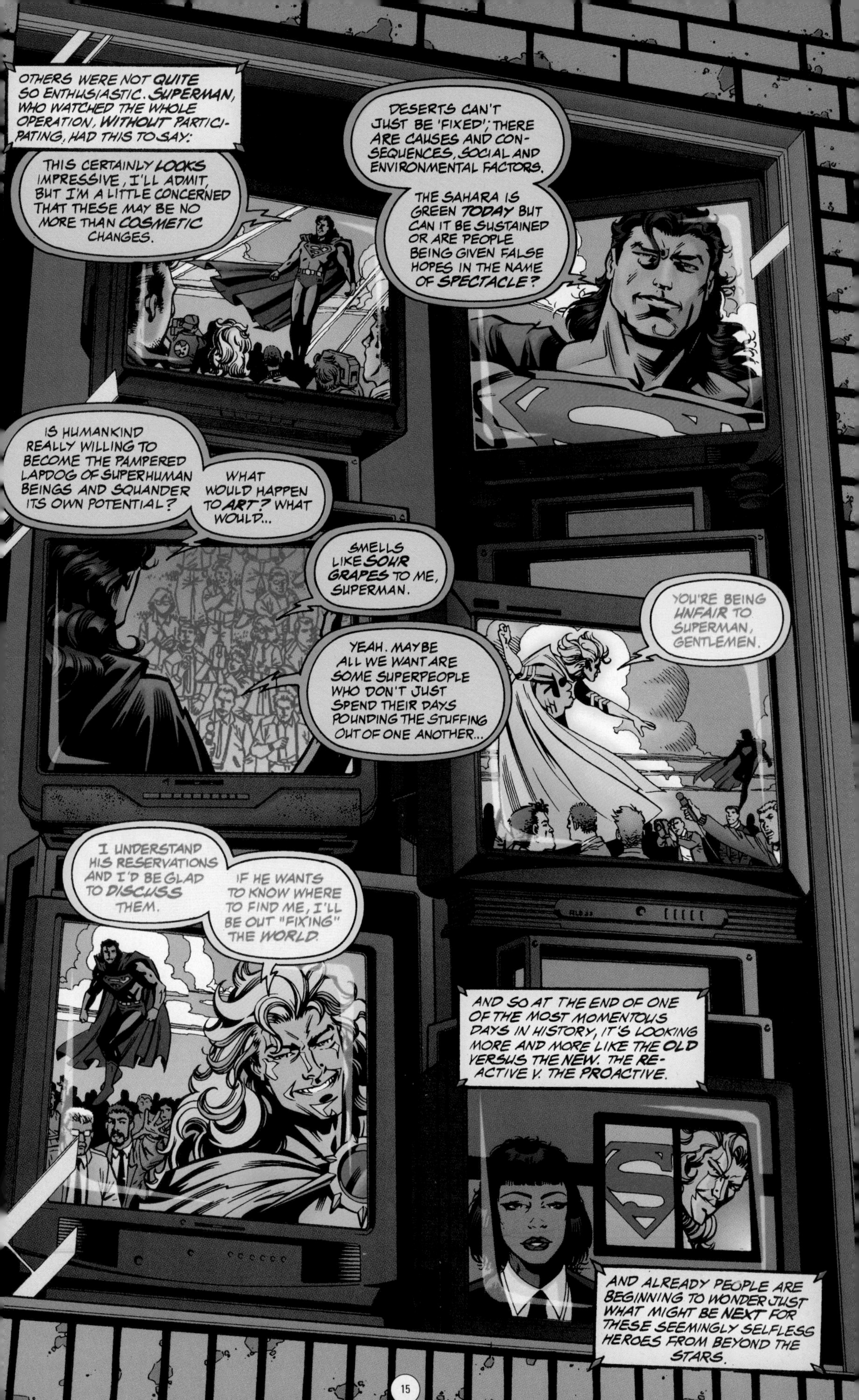
OTHERS WERE NOT QUITE SO ENTHUSIASTIC. SUPERMAN, WHO WATCHED THE WHOLE OPERATION, WITHOUT PARTICIPATING, HAD THIS TO SAY:
THIS CERTAINLY LOOKS IMPRESSIVE, I'LL ADMIT, BUT I'M A LITTLE CONCERNED THAT THESE MAY BE NO MORE THAN COSMETIC CHANGES.
DESERTS CAN'T JUST BE 'FIXED'; THERE ARE CAUSES AND CONSEQUENCES, SOCIAL AND ENVIRONMENTAL FACTORS.
THE SAHARA IS GREEN TODAY BUT CAN IT BE SUSTAINED OR ARE PEOPLE BEING GIVEN FALSE HOPES IN THE NAME OF SPECTACLE?
IS HUMANKIND REALLY WILLING TO BECOME THE PAMPERED LAPDOG OF SUPERHUMAN BEINGS AND SQUANDER ITS OWN POTENTIAL?
WHAT WOULD HAPPEN TO ART? WHAT WOULD...
SMELLS LIKE SOUR GRAPES TO ME, SUPERMAN.
YEAH. MAYBE ALL WE WANT ARE SOME SUPERPEOPLE WHO DON'T JUST SPEND THEIR DAYS POUNDING THE STUFFING OUT OF ONE ANOTHER...
YOU'RE BEING UNFAIR TO SUPERMAN, GENTLEMEN.
I UNDERSTAND HIS RESERVATIONS AND I'D BE GLAD TO DISCUSS THEM.
IF HE WANTS TO KNOW WHERE TO FIND ME, I'LL BE OUT "FIXING" THE WORLD.
AND SO AT THE END OF ONE OF THE MOST MOMENTOUS DAYS IN HISTORY, IT'S LOOKING MORE AND MORE LIKE THE OLD VERSUS THE NEW. THE REACTIVE V. THE PROACTIVE.
AND ALREADY PEOPLE ARE BEGINNING TO WONDER JUST WHAT MIGHT BE NEXT FOR THESE SEEMINGLY SELFLESS HEROES FROM BEYOND THE STARS.

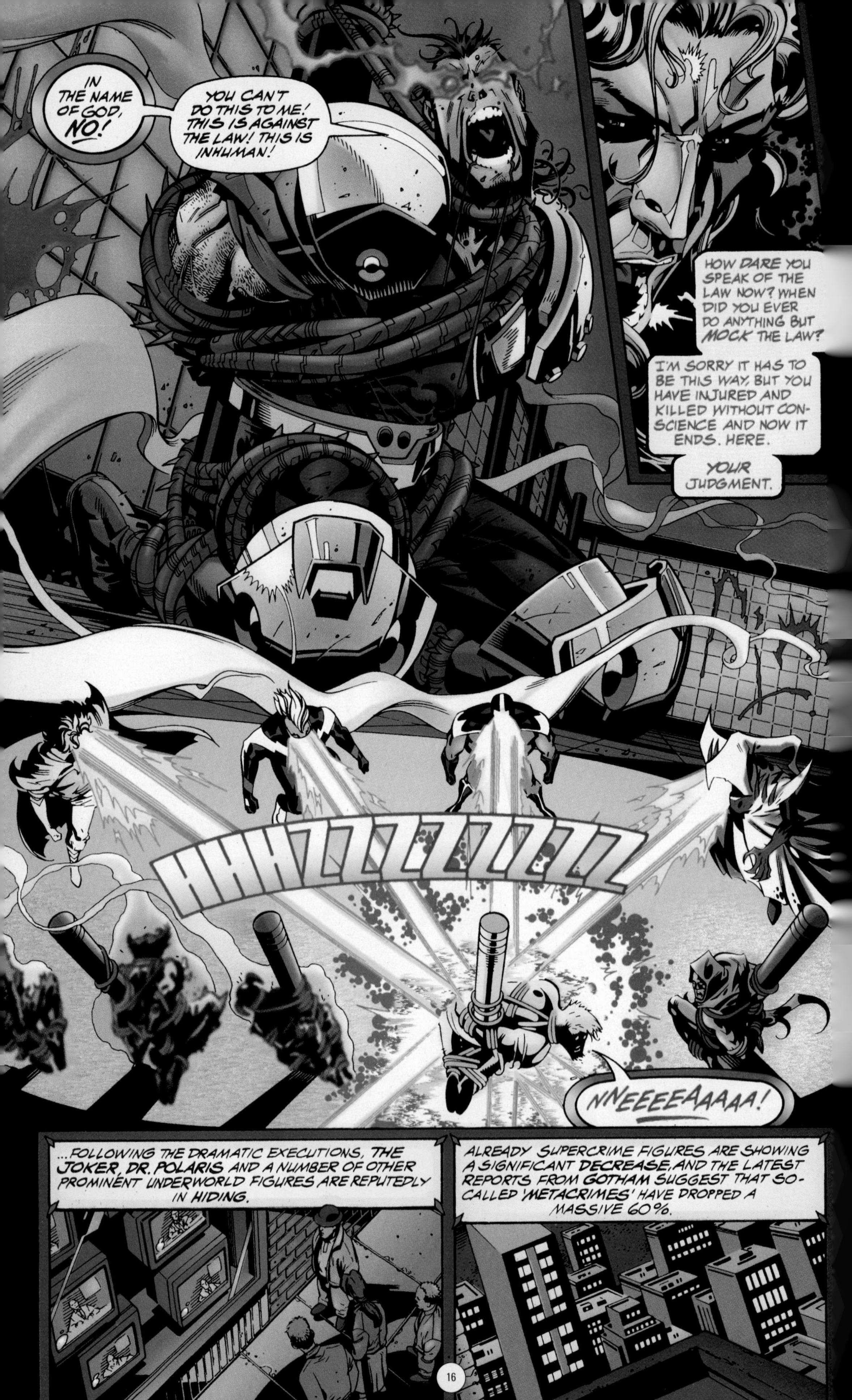

IN THE NAME OF GOD, NO!
YOU CAN'T DO THIS TO ME! THIS IS AGAINST THE LAW! THIS IS INHUMAN!
HOW DARE YOU SPEAK OF THE LAW NOW? WHEN DID YOU EVER DO ANYTHING BUT MOCK THE LAW?
I'M SORRY IT HAS TO BE THIS WAY, BUT YOU HAVE INJURED AND KILLED WITHOUT CONSCIENCE AND NOW IT ENDS. HERE.
YOUR JUDGMENT.
HHHZZZZZZZZZZ
NNEEEEEAAAAA!
...FOLLOWING THE DRAMATIC EXECUTIONS, THE JOKER, DR. POLARIS AND A NUMBER OF OTHER PROMINENT UNDERWORLD FIGURES ARE REPUTEDLY IN HIDING.
ALREADY SUPERCRIME FIGURES ARE SHOWING A SIGNIFICANT DECREASE, AND THE LATEST REPORTS FROM GOTHAM SUGGEST THAT SO-CALLED 'METACRIMES' HAVE DROPPED A MASSIVE 60%.

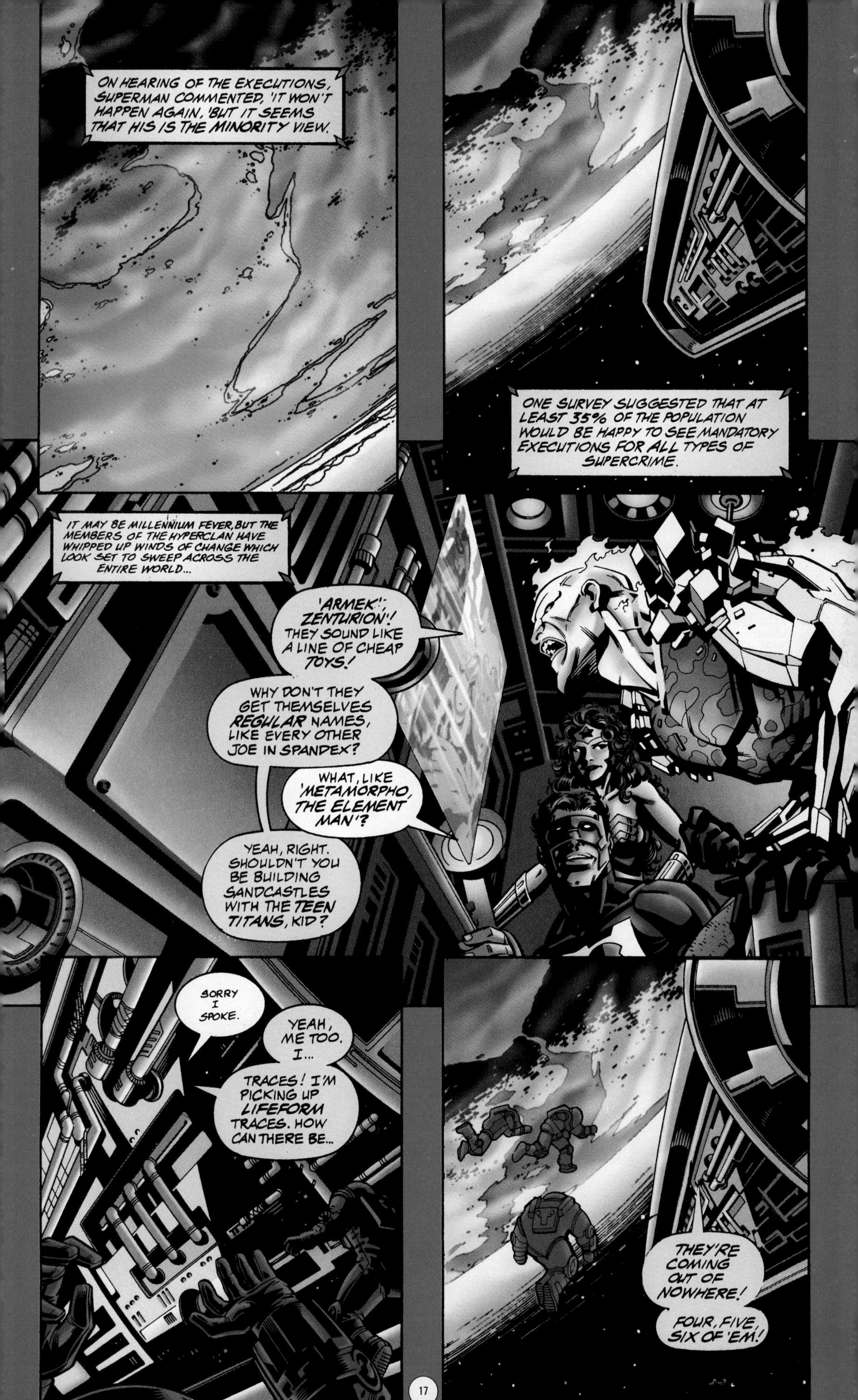
ON HEARING OF THE EXECUTIONS, SUPERMAN COMMENTED, 'IT WON'T HAPPEN AGAIN,' BUT IT SEEMS THAT HIS IS THE MINORITY VIEW.
ONE SURVEY SUGGESTED THAT AT LEAST 35% OF THE POPULATION WOULD BE HAPPY TO SEE MANDATORY EXECUTIONS FOR ALL TYPES OF SUPERCRIME.
IT MAY BE MILLENNIUM FEVER, BUT THE MEMBERS OF THE HYPERCLAN HAVE WHIPPED UP WINDS OF CHANGE WHICH LOOK SET TO SWEEP ACROSS THE ENTIRE WORLD...
'ARMEK'! 'ZENTURION'! THEY SOUND LIKE A LINE OF CHEAP TOYS!
WHY DON'T THEY GET THEMSELVES REGULAR NAMES, LIKE EVERY OTHER JOE IN SPANDEX?
WHAT, LIKE 'METAMORPHO, THE ELEMENT MAN'?
YEAH, RIGHT. SHOULDN'T YOU BE BUILDING SANDCASTLES WITH THE TEEN TITANS, KID?
SORRY I SPOKE.
YEAH, ME TOO. I...
TRACES! I'M PICKING UP LIFEFORM TRACES. HOW CAN THERE BE...
THEY'RE COMING OUT OF NOWHERE!
FOUR, FIVE, SIX OF 'EM!

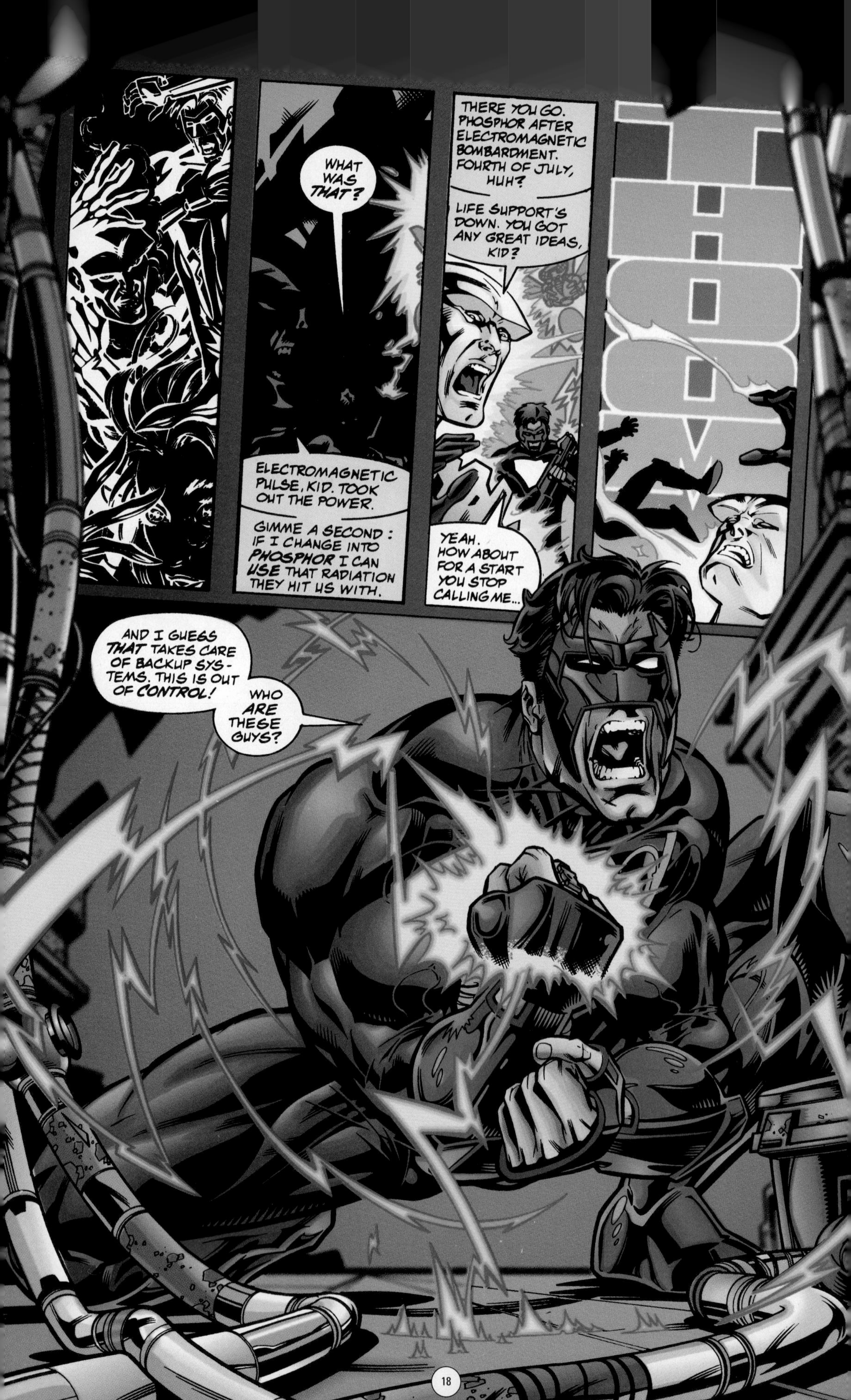
WHAT WAS THAT?
ELECTROMAGNETIC PULSE, KID. TOOK OUT THE POWER.
GIMME A SECOND: IF I CHANGE INTO PHOSPHOR I CAN USE THAT RADIATION THEY HIT US WITH.
THERE YOU GO. PHOSPHOR AFTER ELECTROMAGNETIC BOMBARDMENT. FOURTH OF JULY, HUH?
LIFE SUPPORT'S DOWN. YOU GOT ANY GREAT IDEAS, KID?
YEAH. HOW ABOUT FOR A START YOU STOP CALLING ME...
AND I GUESS THAT TAKES CARE OF BACKUP SYS-TEMS. THIS IS OUT OF CONTROL!
WHO ARE THESE GUYS?

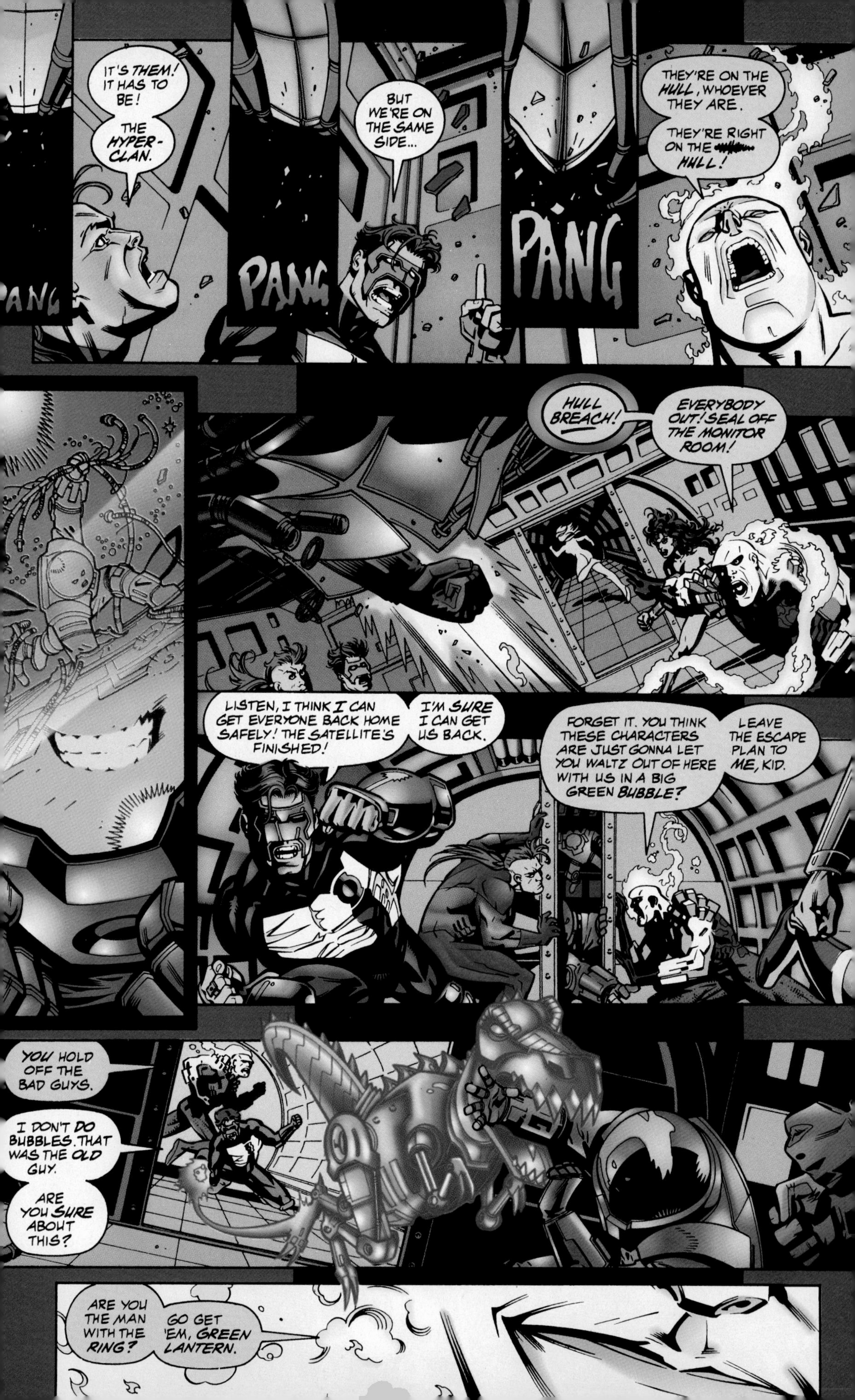
PANG
IT'S THEM! IT HAS TO BE!
THE HYPER-CLAN.
PANG
BUT WE'RE ON THE SAME SIDE...
PANG
THEY'RE ON THE HULL, WHOEVER THEY ARE.
THEY'RE RIGHT ON THE [redacted] HULL!
HULL BREACH!
EVERYBODY OUT! SEAL OFF THE MONITOR ROOM!
LISTEN, I THINK I CAN GET EVERYONE BACK HOME SAFELY! THE SATELLITE'S FINISHED!
I'M SURE I CAN GET US BACK.
FORGET IT. YOU THINK THESE CHARACTERS ARE JUST GONNA LET YOU WALTZ OUT OF HERE WITH US IN A BIG GREEN BUBBLE?
LEAVE THE ESCAPE PLAN TO ME, KID.
YOU HOLD OFF THE BAD GUYS.
I DON'T DO BUBBLES. THAT WAS THE OLD GUY.
ARE YOU SURE ABOUT THIS?
ARE YOU THE MAN WITH THE RING?
GO GET 'EM, GREEN LANTERN.

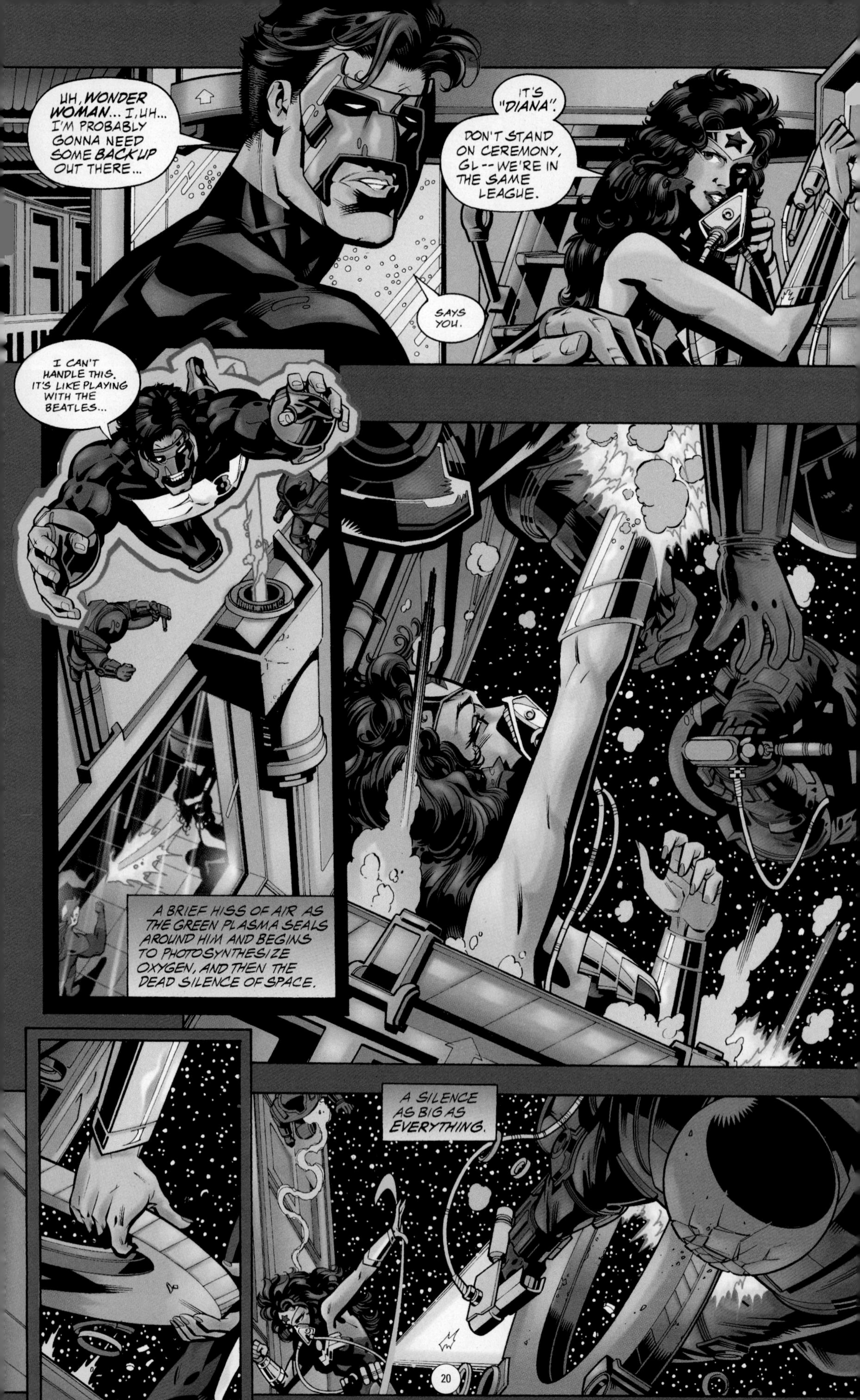
UH, WONDER WOMAN... I, UH... I'M PROBABLY GONNA NEED SOME BACKUP OUT THERE...
IT'S "DIANA".
DON'T STAND ON CEREMONY, GL--WE'RE IN THE SAME LEAGUE.
SAYS YOU.
I CAN'T HANDLE THIS. IT'S LIKE PLAYING WITH THE BEATLES...
A BRIEF HISS OF AIR AS THE GREEN PLASMA SEALS AROUND HIM AND BEGINS TO PHOTOSYNTHESIZE OXYGEN, AND THEN THE DEAD SILENCE OF SPACE.
A SILENCE AS BIG AS EVERYTHING.

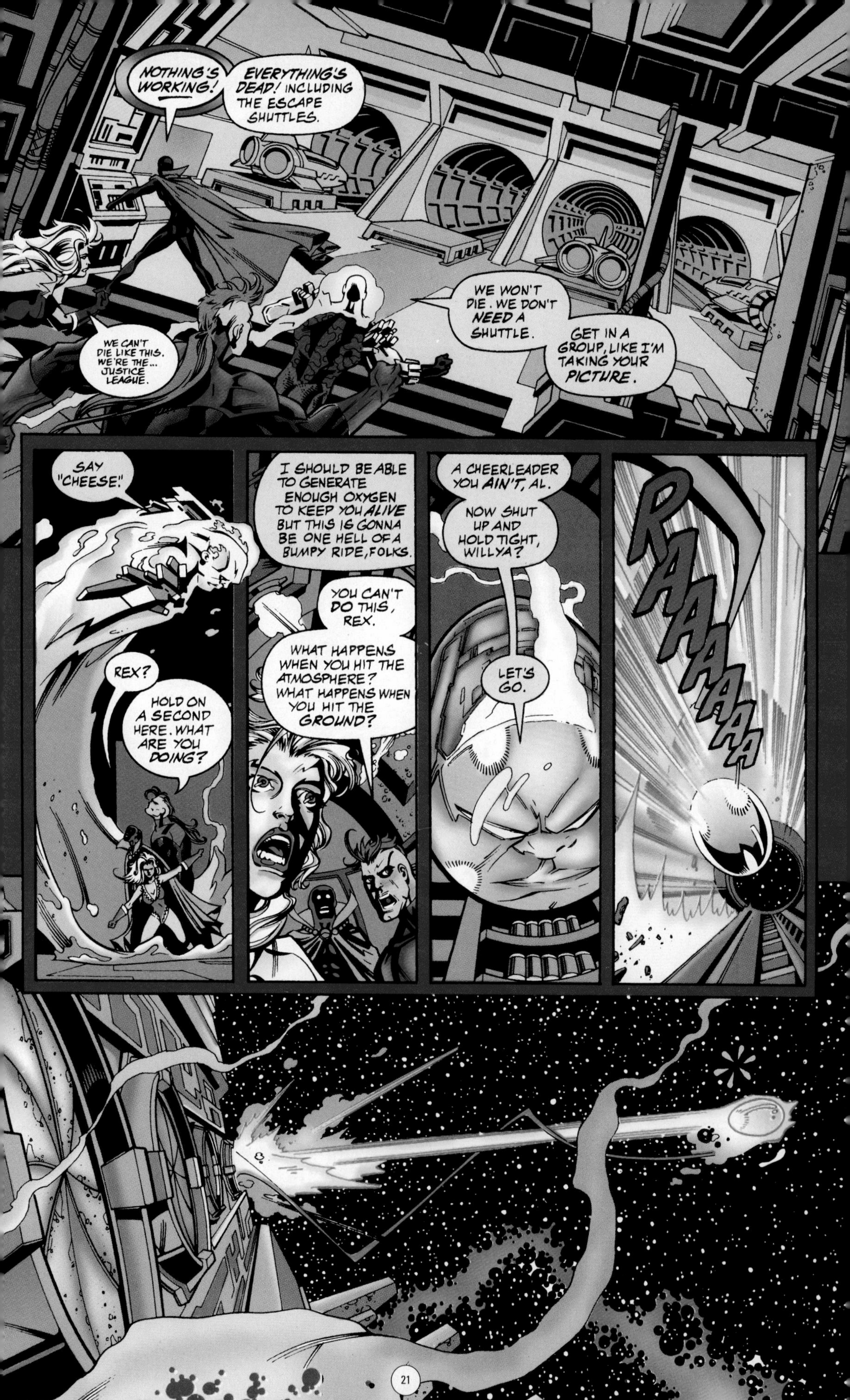

NOTHING'S WORKING!
EVERYTHING'S DEAD! INCLUDING THE ESCAPE SHUTTLES.
WE CAN'T DIE LIKE THIS. WE'RE THE... JUSTICE LEAGUE.
WE WON'T DIE. WE DON'T NEED A SHUTTLE.
GET IN A GROUP, LIKE I'M TAKING YOUR PICTURE.
SAY "CHEESE."
REX?
HOLD ON A SECOND HERE. WHAT ARE YOU DOING?
I SHOULD BE ABLE TO GENERATE ENOUGH OXYGEN TO KEEP YOU ALIVE BUT THIS IS GONNA BE ONE HELL OF A BUMPY RIDE, FOLKS.
YOU CAN'T DO THIS, REX.
WHAT HAPPENS WHEN YOU HIT THE ATMOSPHERE? WHAT HAPPENS WHEN YOU HIT THE GROUND?
A CHEERLEADER YOU AIN'T, AL.
NOW SHUT UP AND HOLD TIGHT, WILLYA?
LET'S GO.
RAAAAAA

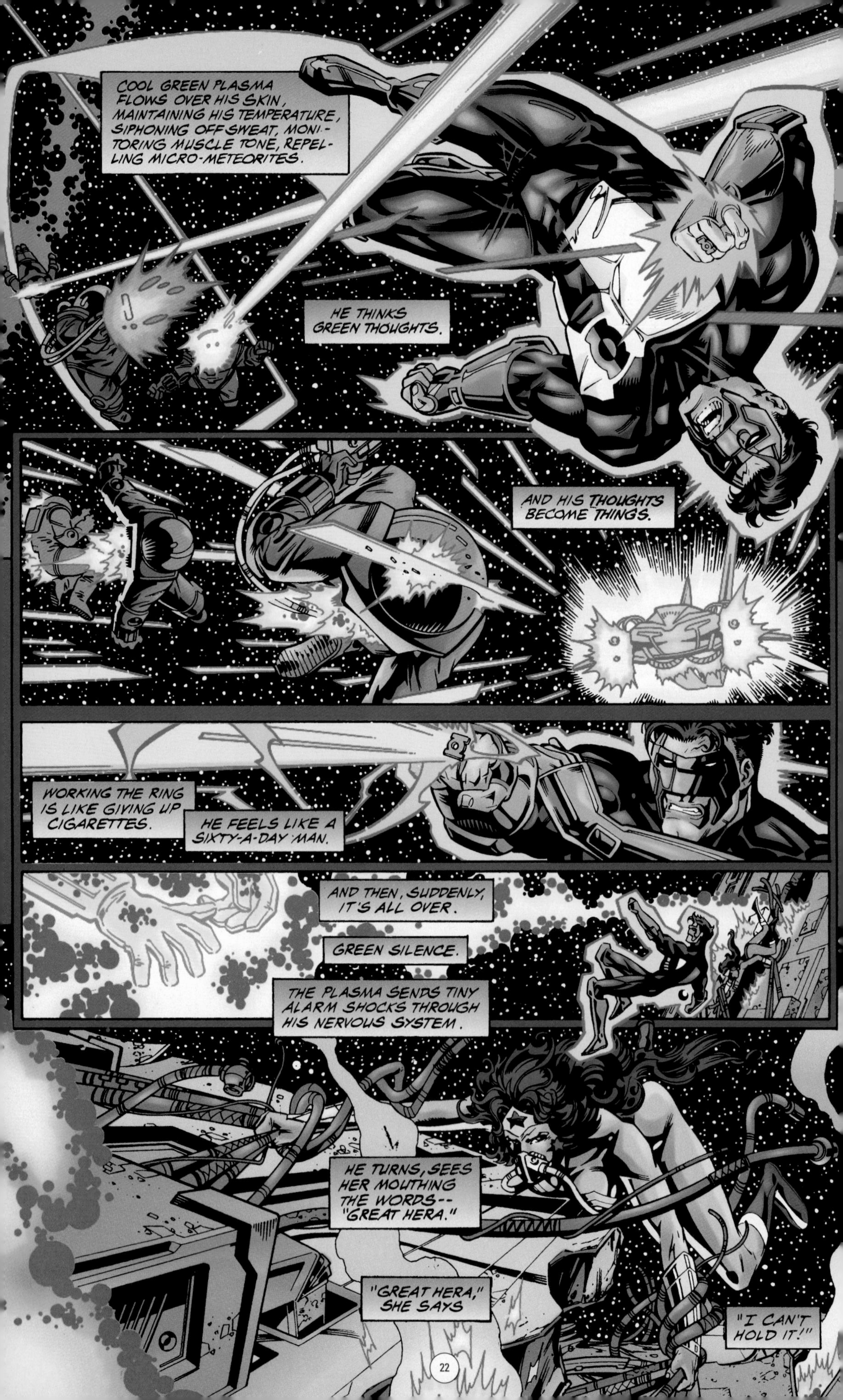
COOL GREEN PLASMA FLOWS OVER HIS SKIN, MAINTAINING HIS TEMPERATURE, SIPHONING OFF SWEAT, MONITORING MUSCLE TONE, REPELLING MICRO-METEORITES.
HE THINKS GREEN THOUGHTS.
AND HIS THOUGHTS BECOME THINGS.
WORKING THE RING IS LIKE GIVING UP CIGARETTES.
HE FEELS LIKE A SIXTY-A-DAY MAN.
AND THEN, SUDDENLY, IT'S ALL OVER.
GREEN SILENCE.
THE PLASMA SENDS TINY ALARM SHOCKS THROUGH HIS NERVOUS SYSTEM.
HE TURNS, SEES HER MOUTHING THE WORDS-- "GREAT HERA."
"GREAT HERA," SHE SAYS
"I CAN'T HOLD IT!"

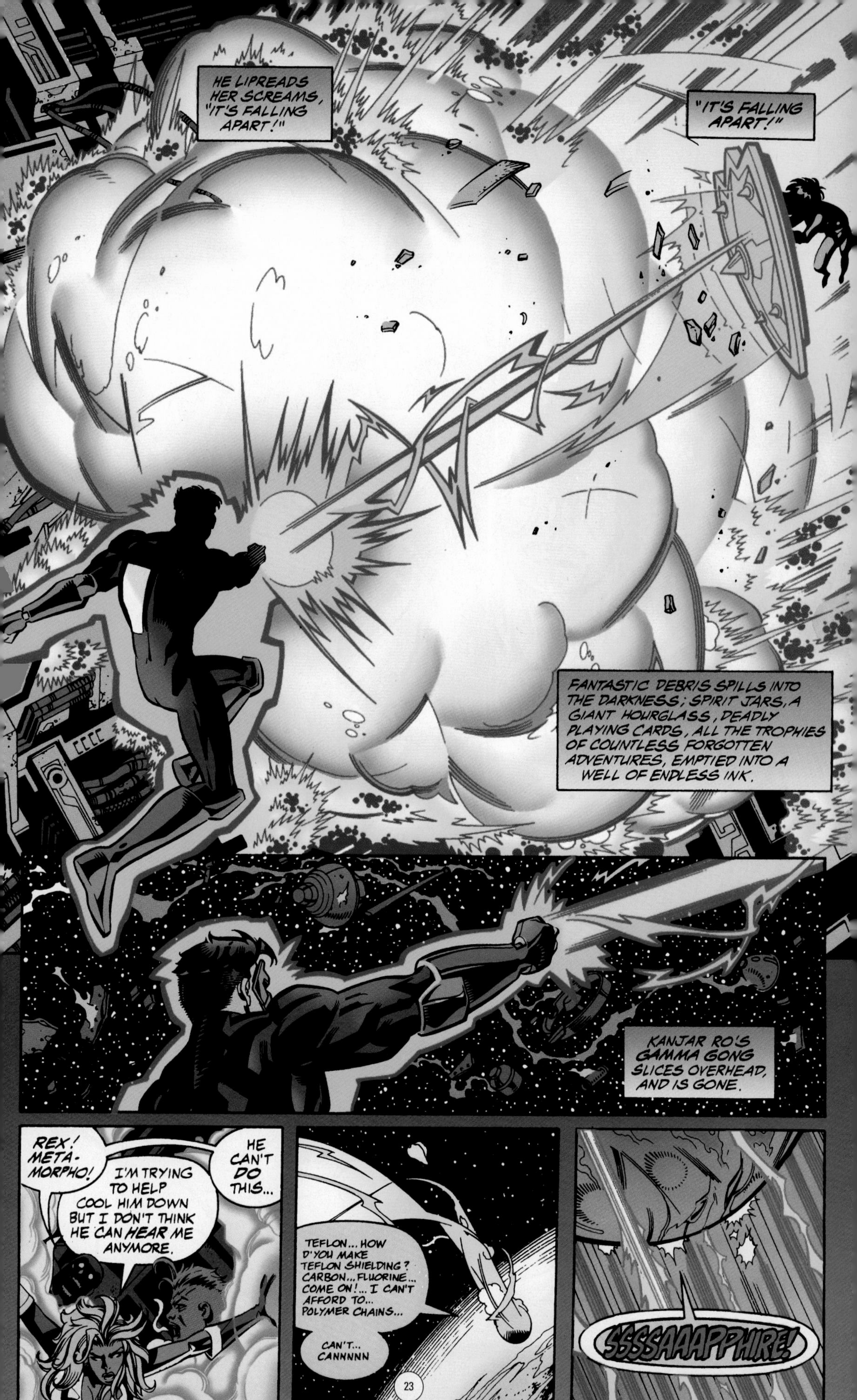
HE LIPREADS HER SCREAMS, "IT'S FALLING APART!"
"IT'S FALLING APART!"
FANTASTIC DEBRIS SPILLS INTO THE DARKNESS; SPIRIT JARS, A GIANT HOURGLASS, DEADLY PLAYING CARDS, ALL THE TROPHIES OF COUNTLESS FORGOTTEN ADVENTURES, EMPTIED INTO A WELL OF ENDLESS INK.
KANJAR RO'S GAMMA GONG SLICES OVERHEAD, AND IS GONE.
REX! METAMORPHO!
I'M TRYING TO HELP COOL HIM DOWN BUT I DON'T THINK HE CAN HEAR ME ANYMORE.
HE CAN'T DO THIS...
TEFLON... HOW D'YOU MAKE TEFLON SHIELDING? CARBON... FLUORINE... COME ON!... I CAN'T AFFORD TO... POLYMER CHAINS...
CAN'T... CANNNNN
SSSSAAAAPPHIRE!

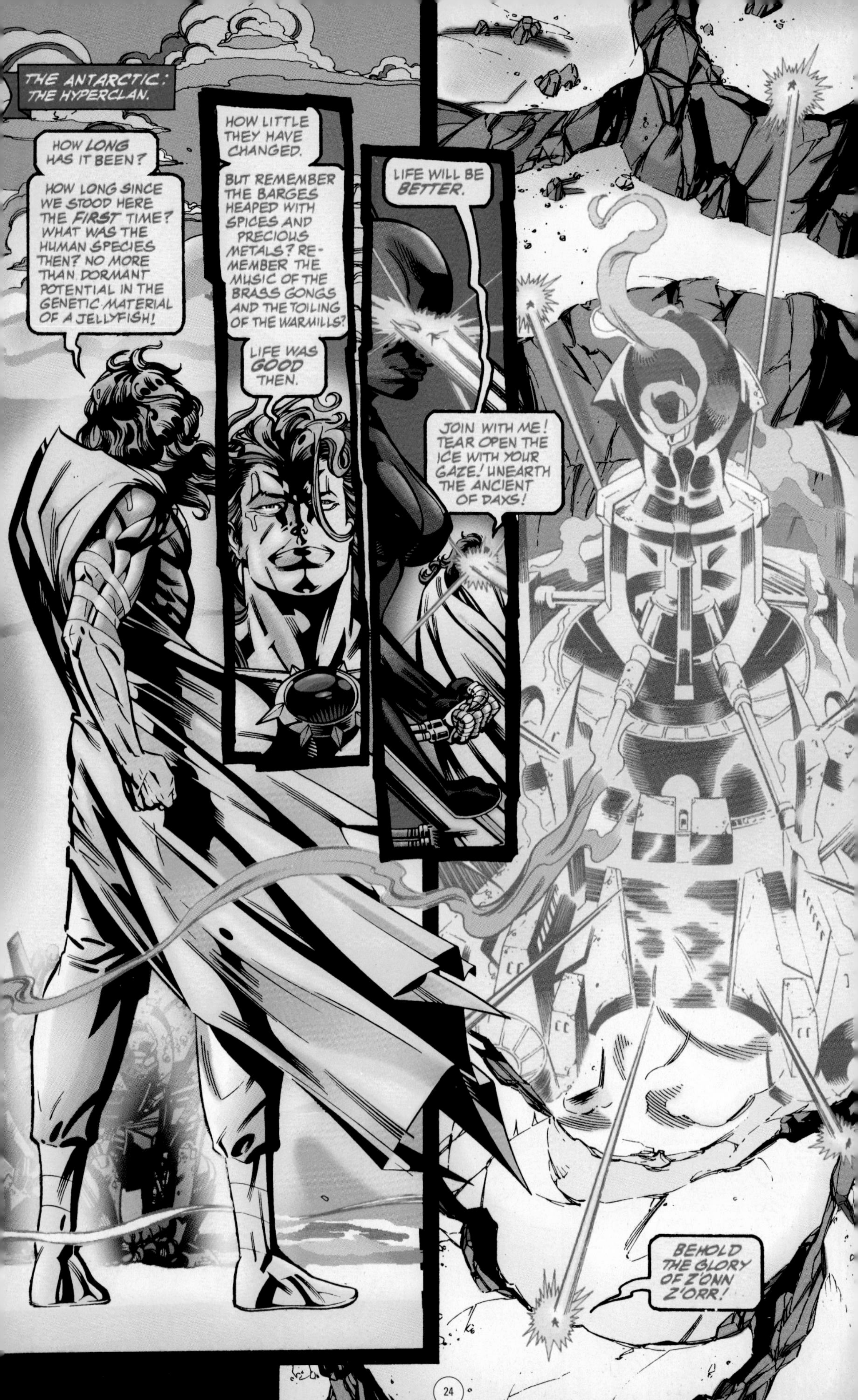
THE ANTARCTIC: THE HYPERCLAN.
HOW LONG HAS IT BEEN?
HOW LONG SINCE WE STOOD HERE THE FIRST TIME? WHAT WAS THE HUMAN SPECIES THEN? NO MORE THAN DORMANT POTENTIAL IN THE GENETIC MATERIAL OF A JELLYFISH!
HOW LITTLE THEY HAVE CHANGED.
BUT REMEMBER THE BARGES HEAPED WITH SPICES AND PRECIOUS METALS? REMEMBER THE MUSIC OF THE BRASS GONGS AND THE TOILING OF THE WARMILLS?
LIFE WAS GOOD THEN.
LIFE WILL BE BETTER.
JOIN WITH ME! TEAR OPEN THE ICE WITH YOUR GAZE! UNEARTH THE ANCIENT OF DAXS!
BEHOLD THE GLORY OF Z'ONN Z'ORR!

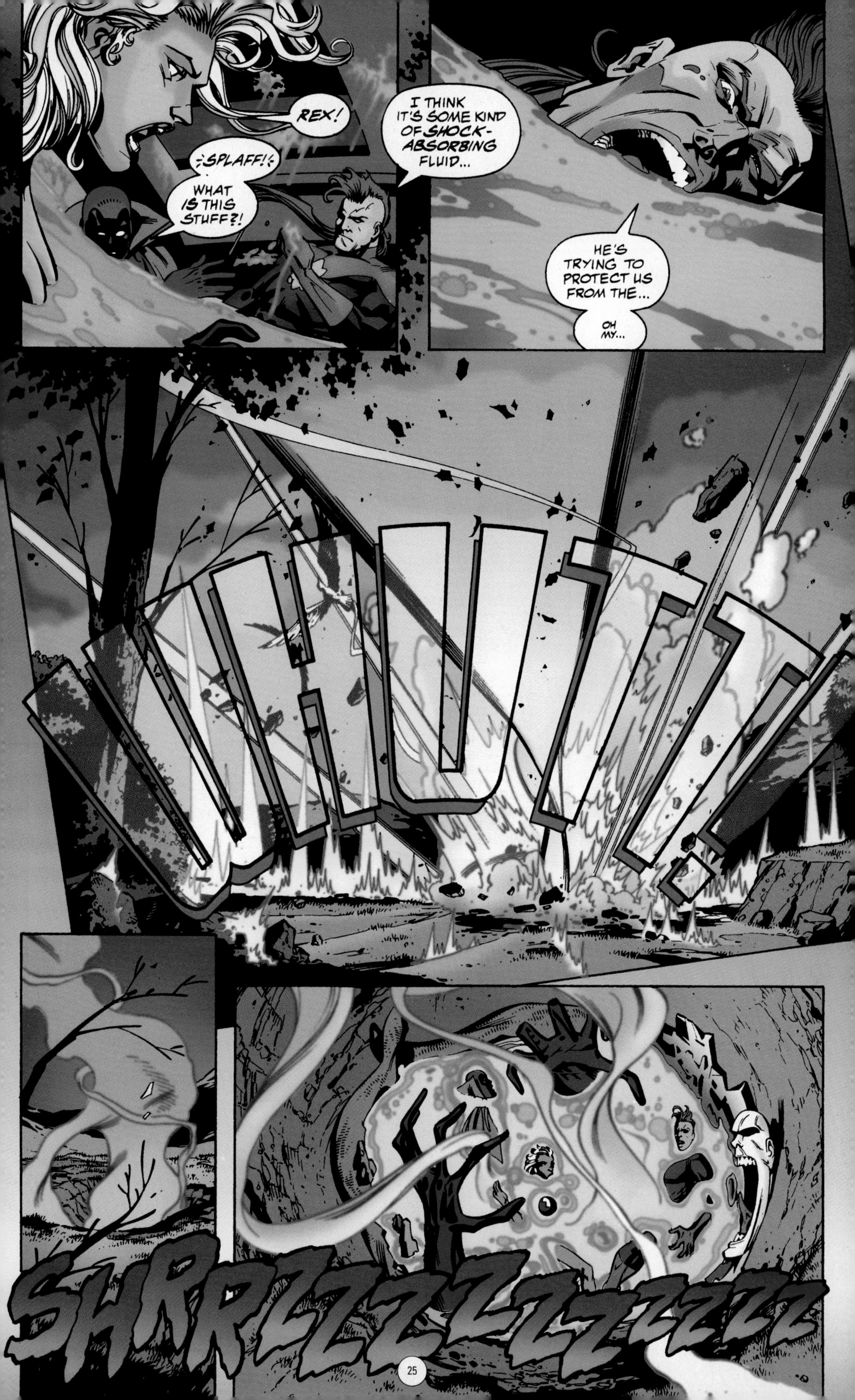
REX!
:SPLAFF!:
WHAT IS THIS STUFF?!
I THINK IT'S SOME KIND OF SHOCK-ABSORBING FLUID...
HE'S TRYING TO PROTECT US FROM THE...
OH MY...

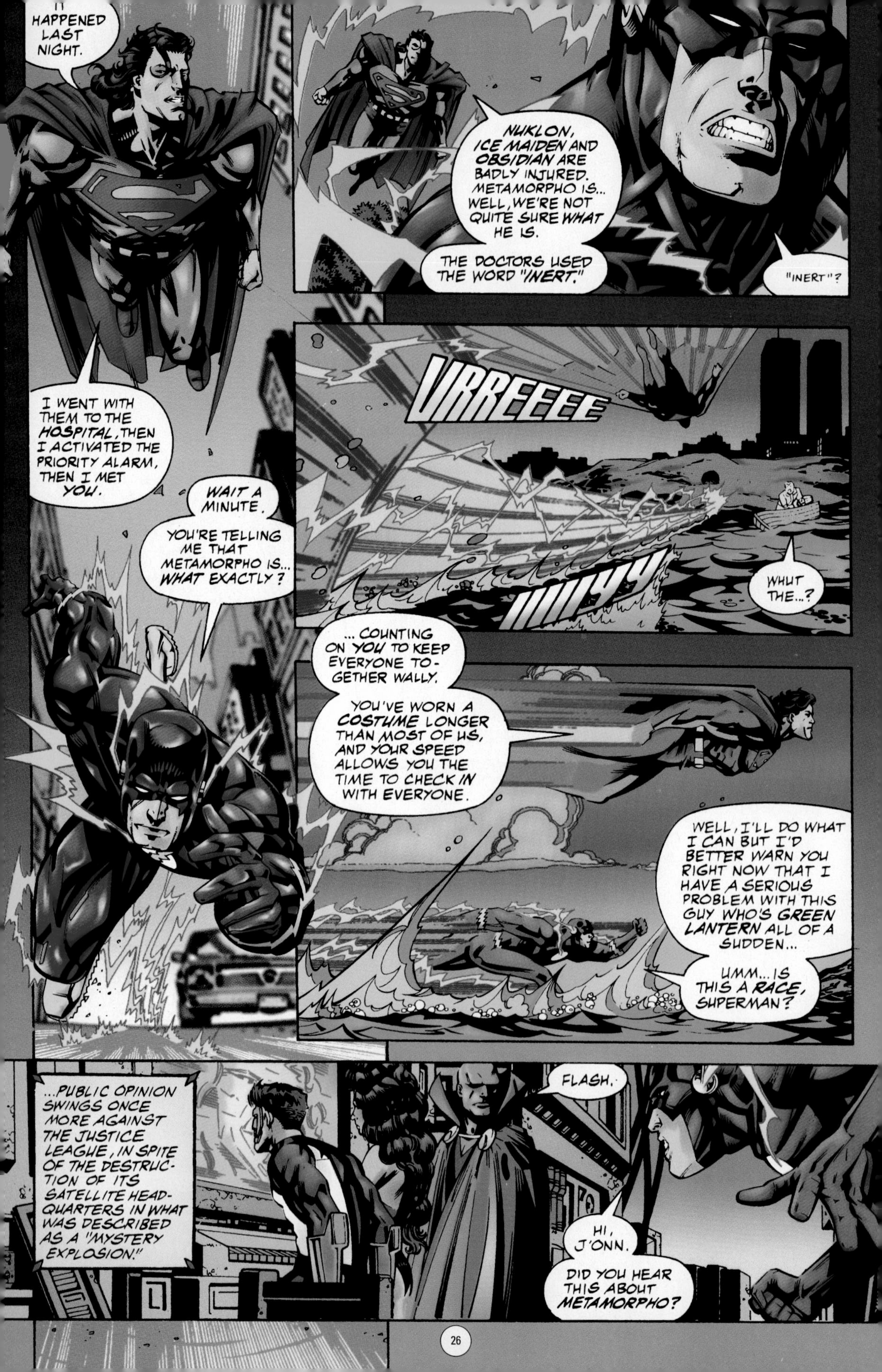
IT HAPPENED LAST NIGHT.
NUKLON, ICE MAIDEN AND OBSIDIAN ARE BADLY INJURED. METAMORPHO IS... WELL, WE'RE NOT QUITE SURE WHAT HE IS.
THE DOCTORS USED THE WORD "INERT."
"INERT"?
I WENT WITH THEM TO THE HOSPITAL, THEN I ACTIVATED THE PRIORITY ALARM, THEN I MET YOU.
WAIT A MINUTE.
YOU'RE TELLING ME THAT METAMORPHO IS... WHAT EXACTLY?
URREEEEE
IIIIIIYY
WHUT THE...?
... COUNTING ON YOU TO KEEP EVERYONE TO-GETHER WALLY.
YOU'VE WORN A COSTUME LONGER THAN MOST OF US, AND YOUR SPEED ALLOWS YOU THE TIME TO CHECK IN WITH EVERYONE.
WELL, I'LL DO WHAT I CAN BUT I'D BETTER WARN YOU RIGHT NOW THAT I HAVE A SERIOUS PROBLEM WITH THIS GUY WHO'S GREEN LANTERN ALL OF A SUDDEN...
UMM... IS THIS A RACE, SUPERMAN?
...PUBLIC OPINION SWINGS ONCE MORE AGAINST THE JUSTICE LEAGUE, IN SPITE OF THE DESTRUCTION OF ITS SATELLITE HEAD-QUARTERS IN WHAT WAS DESCRIBED AS A "MYSTERY EXPLOSION."
FLASH.
HI, J'ONN.
DID YOU HEAR THIS ABOUT METAMORPHO?

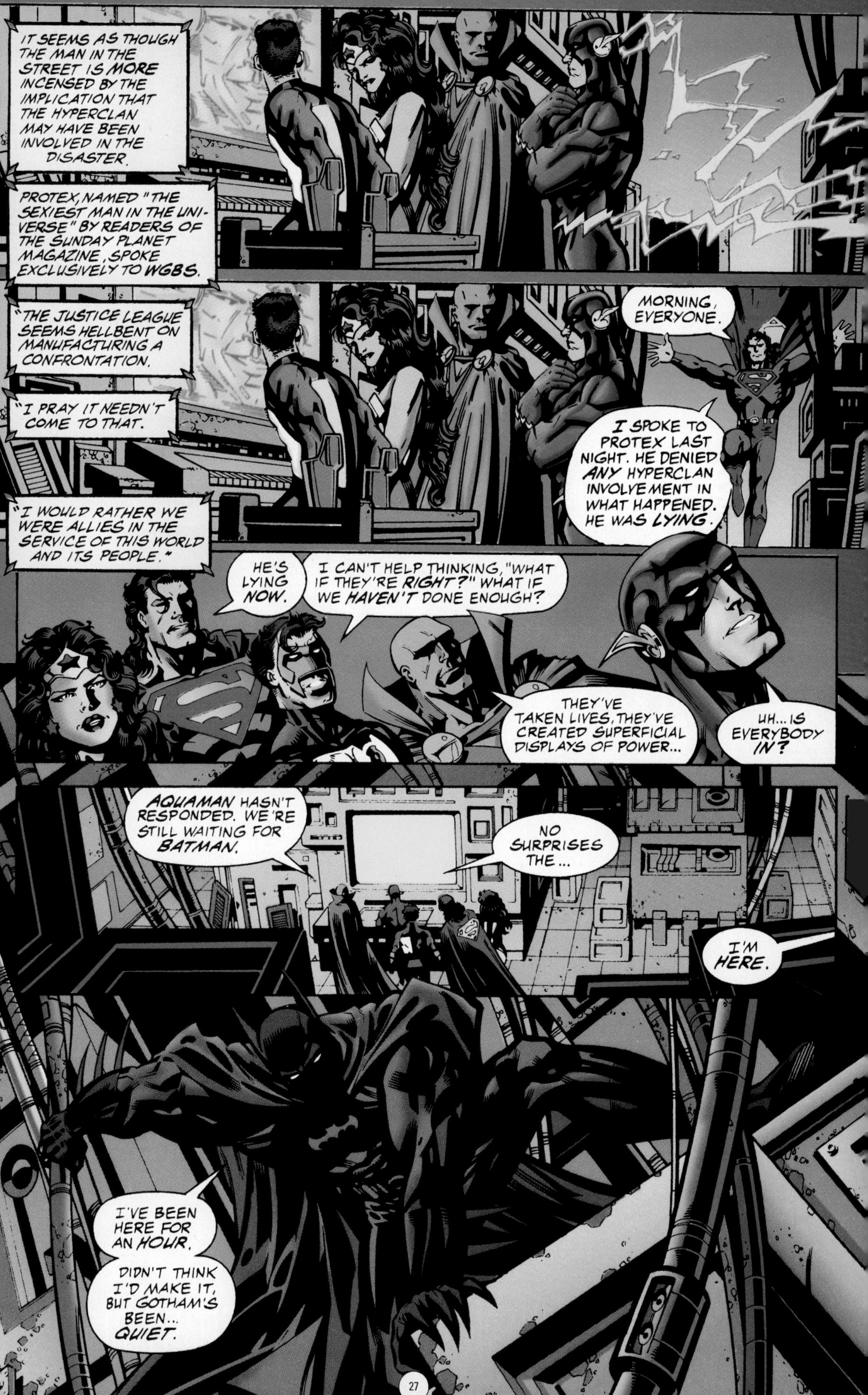

IT SEEMS AS THOUGH THE MAN IN THE STREET IS MORE INCENSED BY THE IMPLICATION THAT THE HYPERCLAN MAY HAVE BEEN INVOLVED IN THE DISASTER.
PROTEX, NAMED "THE SEXIEST MAN IN THE UNIVERSE" BY READERS OF THE SUNDAY PLANET MAGAZINE, SPOKE EXCLUSIVELY TO WGBS.
"THE JUSTICE LEAGUE SEEMS HELLBENT ON MANUFACTURING A CONFRONTATION.
"I PRAY IT NEEDN'T COME TO THAT.
"I WOULD RATHER WE WERE ALLIES IN THE SERVICE OF THIS WORLD AND ITS PEOPLE."
MORNING, EVERYONE.
I SPOKE TO PROTEX LAST NIGHT. HE DENIED ANY HYPERCLAN INVOLVEMENT IN WHAT HAPPENED. HE WAS LYING.
HE'S LYING NOW.
I CAN'T HELP THINKING, "WHAT IF THEY'RE RIGHT?" WHAT IF WE HAVEN'T DONE ENOUGH?
THEY'VE TAKEN LIVES, THEY'VE CREATED SUPERFICIAL DISPLAYS OF POWER...
UH... IS EVERYBODY IN?
AQUAMAN HASN'T RESPONDED. WE'RE STILL WAITING FOR BATMAN.
NO SURPRISES THE...
I'M HERE.
I'VE BEEN HERE FOR AN HOUR.
DIDN'T THINK I'D MAKE IT, BUT GOTHAM'S BEEN... QUIET.

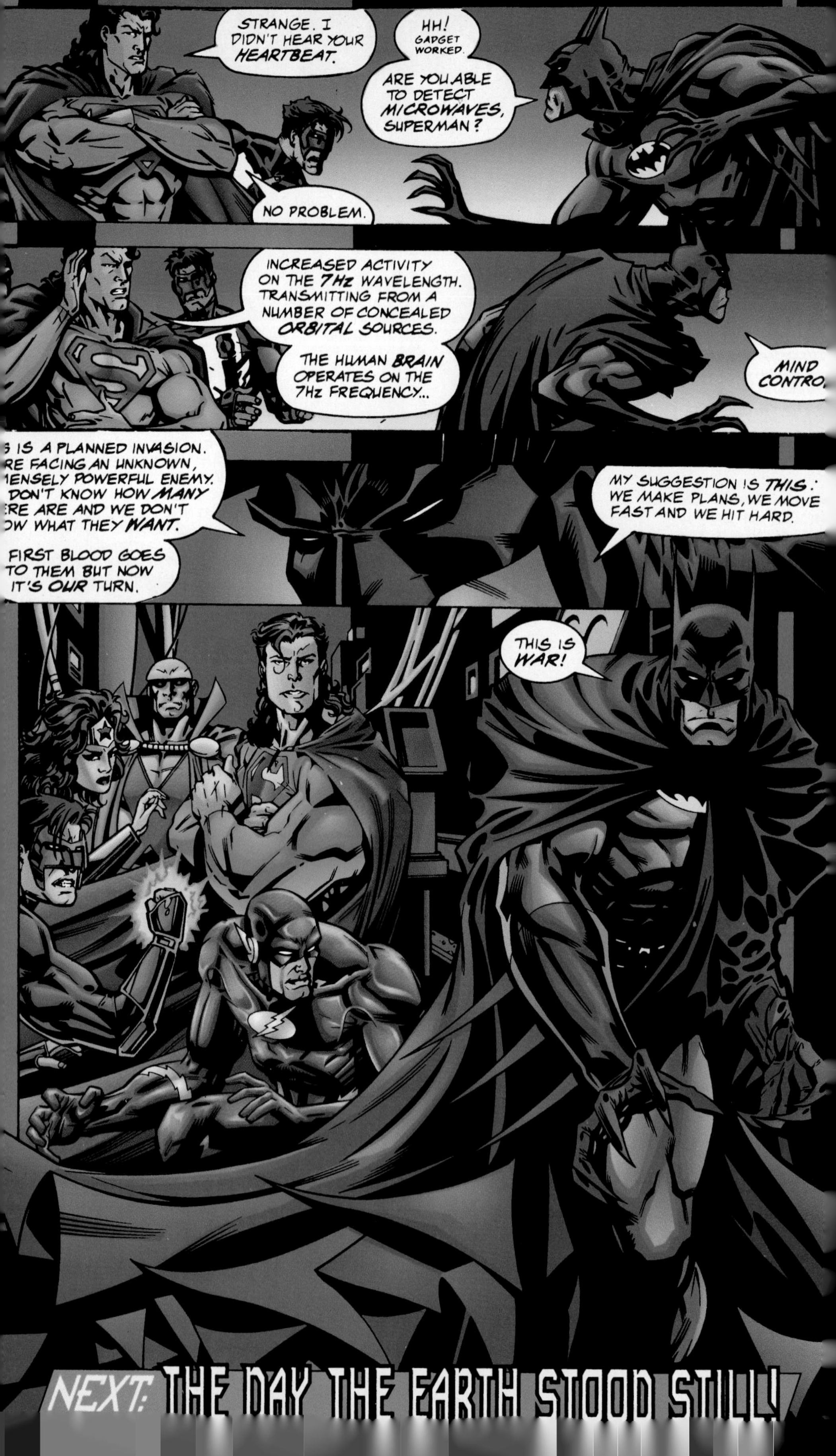

STRANGE. I DIDN'T HEAR YOUR HEARTBEAT.
HH! GADGET WORKED.
ARE YOU ABLE TO DETECT MICROWAVES, SUPERMAN?
NO PROBLEM.
INCREASED ACTIVITY ON THE 7Hz WAVELENGTH. TRANSMITTING FROM A NUMBER OF CONCEALED ORBITAL SOURCES.
THE HUMAN BRAIN OPERATES ON THE 7Hz FREQUENCY...
MIND CONTRO
S IS A PLANNED INVASION. RE FACING AN UNKNOWN, MENSELY POWERFUL ENEMY. DON'T KNOW HOW MANY ERE ARE AND WE DON'T OW WHAT THEY WANT.
FIRST BLOOD GOES TO THEM BUT NOW IT'S OUR TURN.
MY SUGGESTION IS THIS: WE MAKE PLANS, WE MOVE FAST AND WE HIT HARD.
THIS IS WAR!
NEXT: THE DAY THE EARTH STOOD STILL!

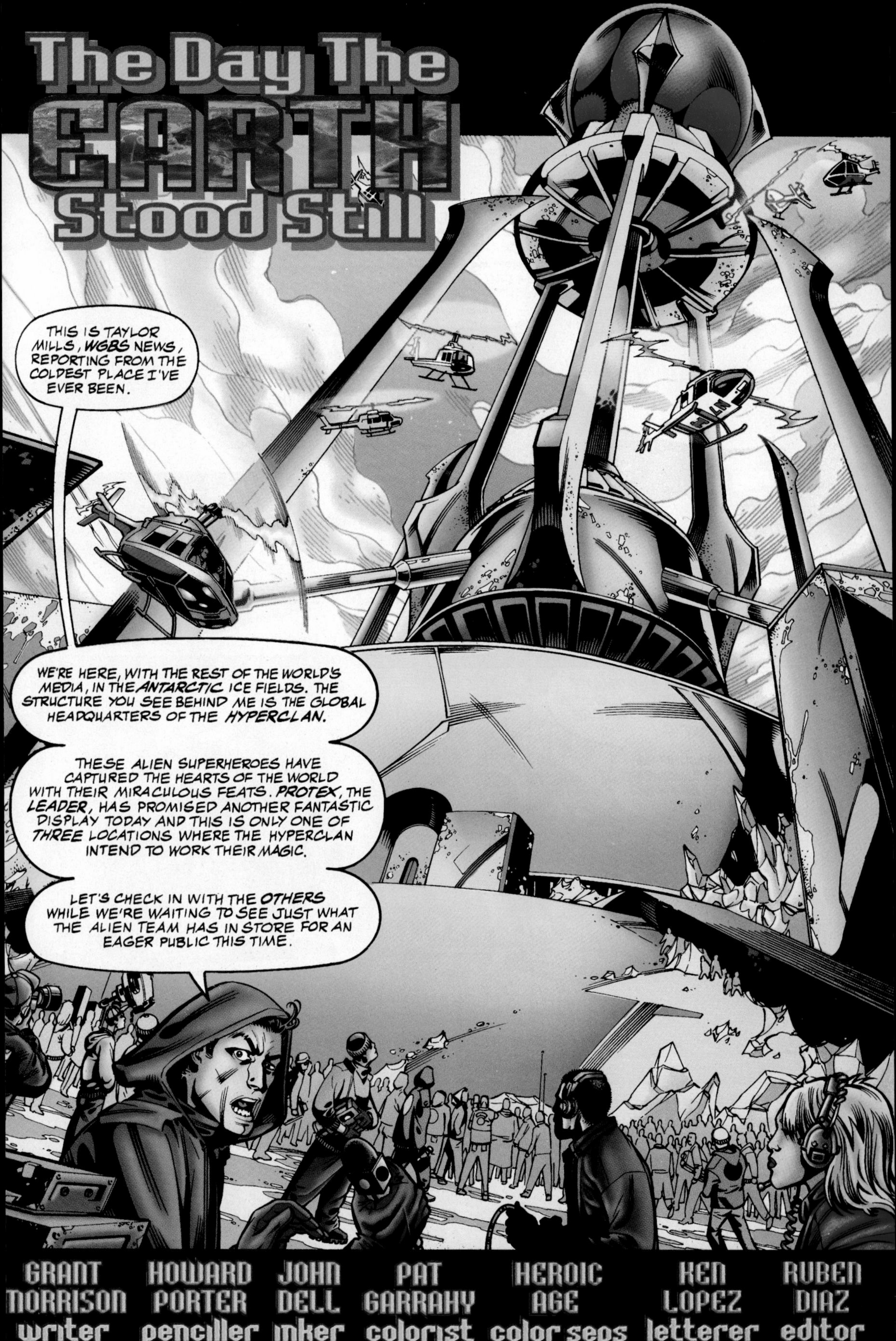
The Day The EARTH Stood Still
THIS IS TAYLOR MILLS, WGBS NEWS, REPORTING FROM THE COLDEST PLACE I'VE EVER BEEN.
WE'RE HERE, WITH THE REST OF THE WORLD'S MEDIA, IN THE ANTARCTIC ICE FIELDS. THE STRUCTURE YOU SEE BEHIND ME IS THE GLOBAL HEADQUARTERS OF THE HYPERCLAN.
THESE ALIEN SUPERHEROES HAVE CAPTURED THE HEARTS OF THE WORLD WITH THEIR MIRACULOUS FEATS. PROTEX, THE LEADER, HAS PROMISED ANOTHER FANTASTIC DISPLAY TODAY AND THIS IS ONLY ONE OF THREE LOCATIONS WHERE THE HYPERCLAN INTEND TO WORK THEIR MAGIC.
LET'S CHECK IN WITH THE OTHERS WHILE WE'RE WAITING TO SEE JUST WHAT THE ALIEN TEAM HAS IN STORE FOR AN EAGER PUBLIC THIS TIME.
GRANT MORRISON writer
HOWARD PORTER penciller
JOHN DELL inker
PAT GARRAHY colorist
HEROIC AGE color seps
KEN LOPEZ letterer
RUBEN DIAZ editor

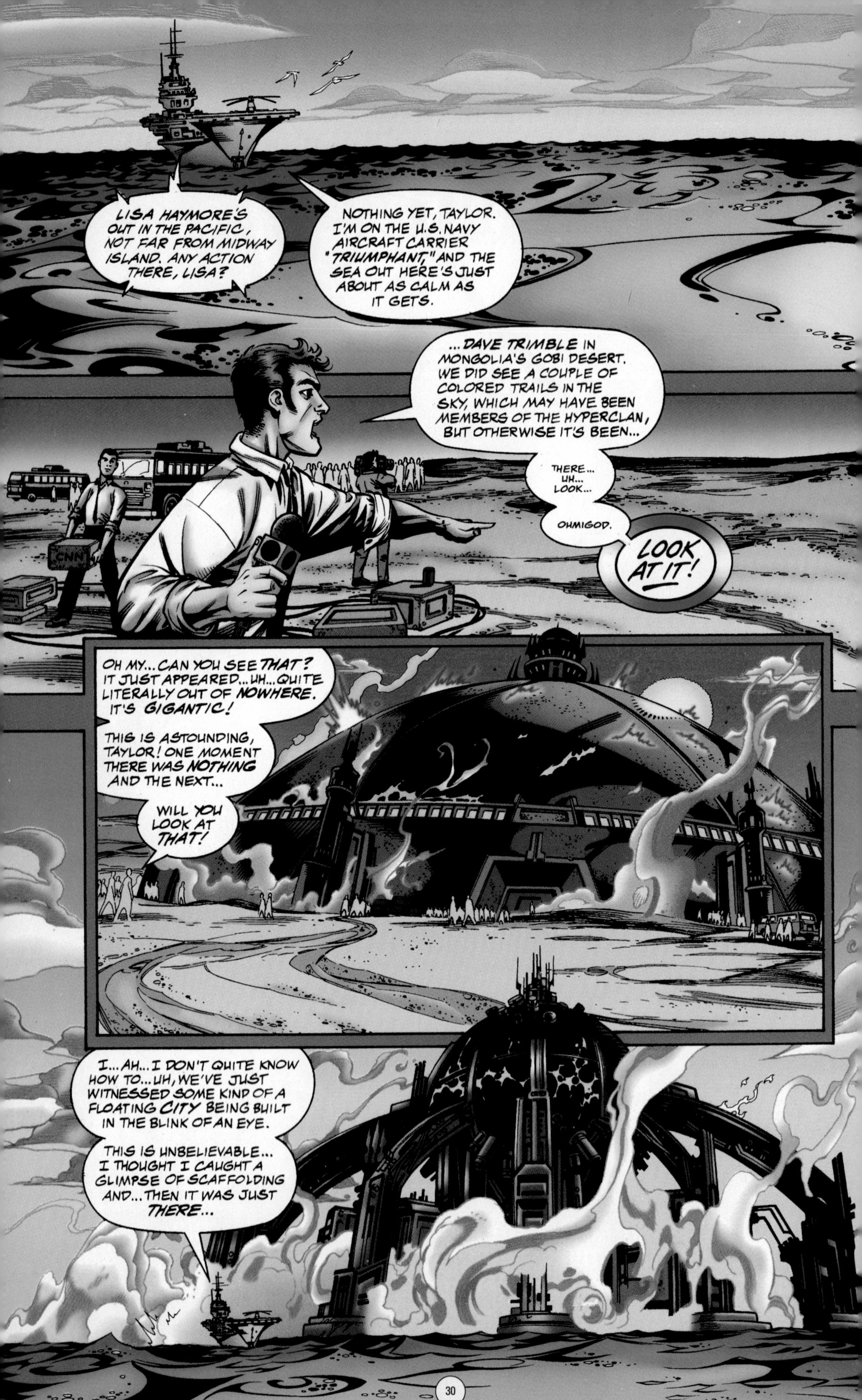
LISA HAYMORE'S OUT IN THE PACIFIC, NOT FAR FROM MIDWAY ISLAND. ANY ACTION THERE, LISA?
NOTHING YET, TAYLOR. I'M ON THE U.S. NAVY AIRCRAFT CARRIER "TRIUMPHANT," AND THE SEA OUT HERE'S JUST ABOUT AS CALM AS IT GETS.
...DAVE TRIMBLE IN MONGOLIA'S GOBI DESERT. WE DID SEE A COUPLE OF COLORED TRAILS IN THE SKY, WHICH MAY HAVE BEEN MEMBERS OF THE HYPERCLAN, BUT OTHERWISE IT'S BEEN...
THERE... UH... LOOK...
OHMIGOD.
LOOK AT IT!
CNN
OH MY...CAN YOU SEE THAT? IT JUST APPEARED...UH...QUITE LITERALLY OUT OF NOWHERE. IT'S GIGANTIC!
THIS IS ASTOUNDING, TAYLOR! ONE MOMENT THERE WAS NOTHING AND THE NEXT...
WILL YOU LOOK AT THAT!
I...AH...I DON'T QUITE KNOW HOW TO...UH, WE'VE JUST WITNESSED SOME KIND OF A FLOATING CITY BEING BUILT IN THE BLINK OF AN EYE.
THIS IS UNBELIEVABLE... I THOUGHT I CAUGHT A GLIMPSE OF SCAFFOLDING AND...THEN IT WAS JUST THERE...

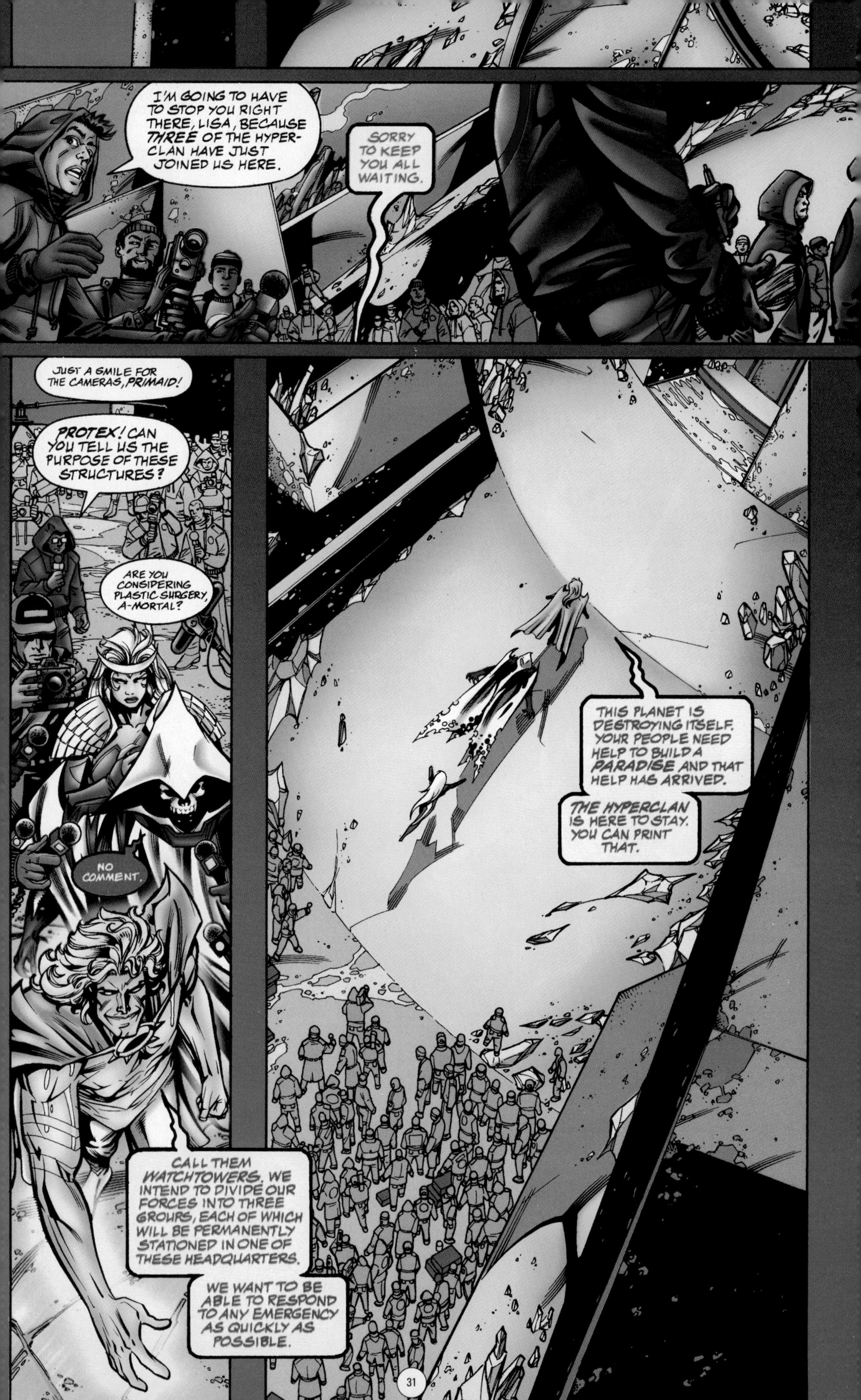
I'M GOING TO HAVE TO STOP YOU RIGHT THERE, LISA, BECAUSE THREE OF THE HYPER-CLAN HAVE JUST JOINED US HERE.
SORRY TO KEEP YOU ALL WAITING.
JUST A SMILE FOR THE CAMERAS, PRIMAID!
PROTEX! CAN YOU TELL US THE PURPOSE OF THESE STRUCTURES?
ARE YOU CONSIDERING PLASTIC SURGERY, A-MORTAL?
NO COMMENT.
CALL THEM WATCHTOWERS. WE INTEND TO DIVIDE OUR FORCES INTO THREE GROUPS, EACH OF WHICH WILL BE PERMANENTLY STATIONED IN ONE OF THESE HEADQUARTERS.
WE WANT TO BE ABLE TO RESPOND TO ANY EMERGENCY AS QUICKLY AS POSSIBLE.
THIS PLANET IS DESTROYING ITSELF. YOUR PEOPLE NEED HELP TO BUILD A PARADISE AND THAT HELP HAS ARRIVED.
THE HYPERCLAN IS HERE TO STAY. YOU CAN PRINT THAT.

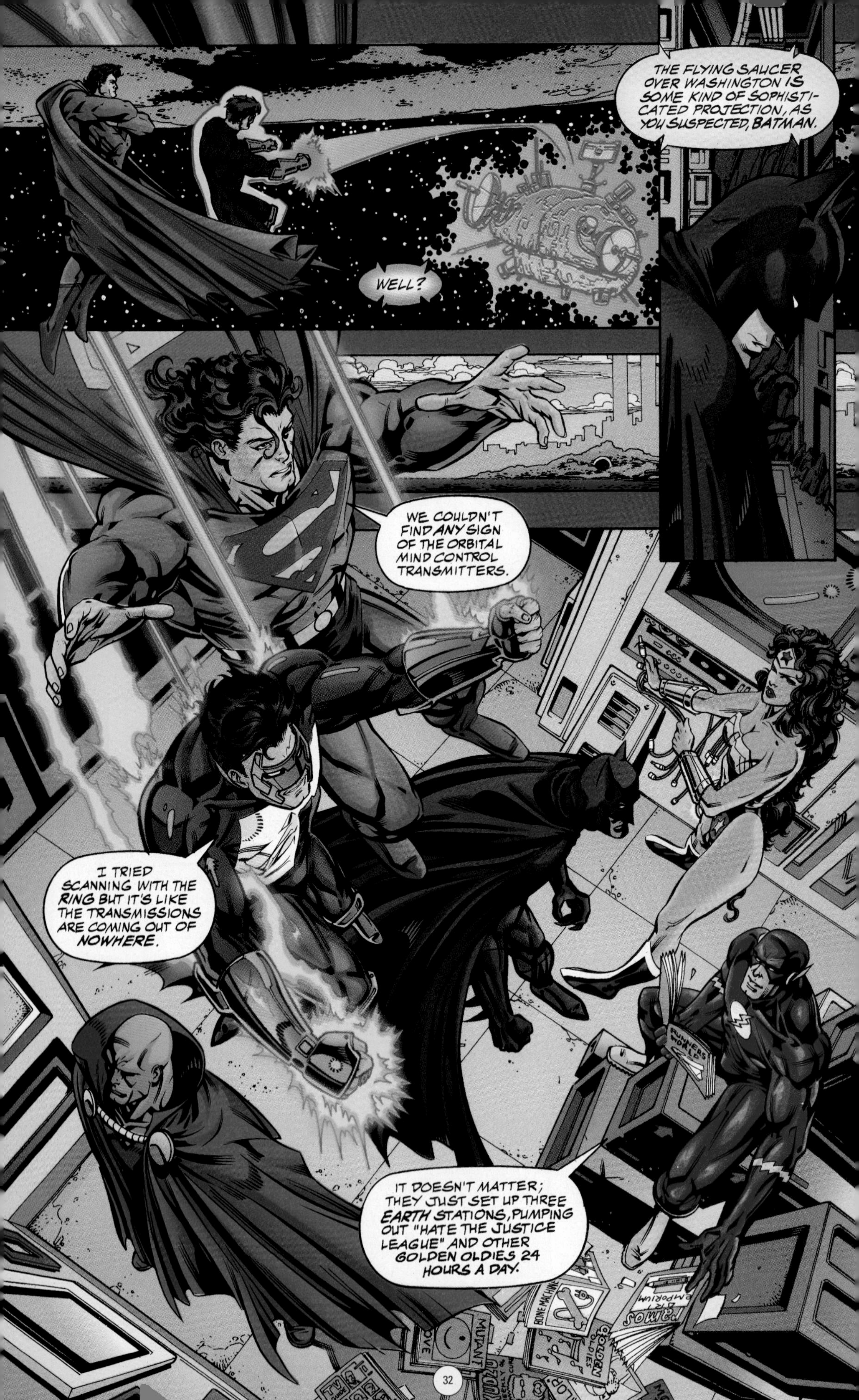
THE FLYING SAUCER OVER WASHINGTON IS SOME KIND OF SOPHISTICATED PROJECTION, AS YOU SUSPECTED, BATMAN.
WELL?
WE COULDN'T FIND ANY SIGN OF THE ORBITAL MIND CONTROL TRANSMITTERS.
I TRIED SCANNING WITH THE RING BUT IT'S LIKE THE TRANSMISSIONS ARE COMING OUT OF NOWHERE.
IT DOESN'T MATTER; THEY JUST SET UP THREE EARTH STATIONS, PUMPING OUT "HATE THE JUSTICE LEAGUE" AND OTHER GOLDEN OLDIES 24 HOURS A DAY.

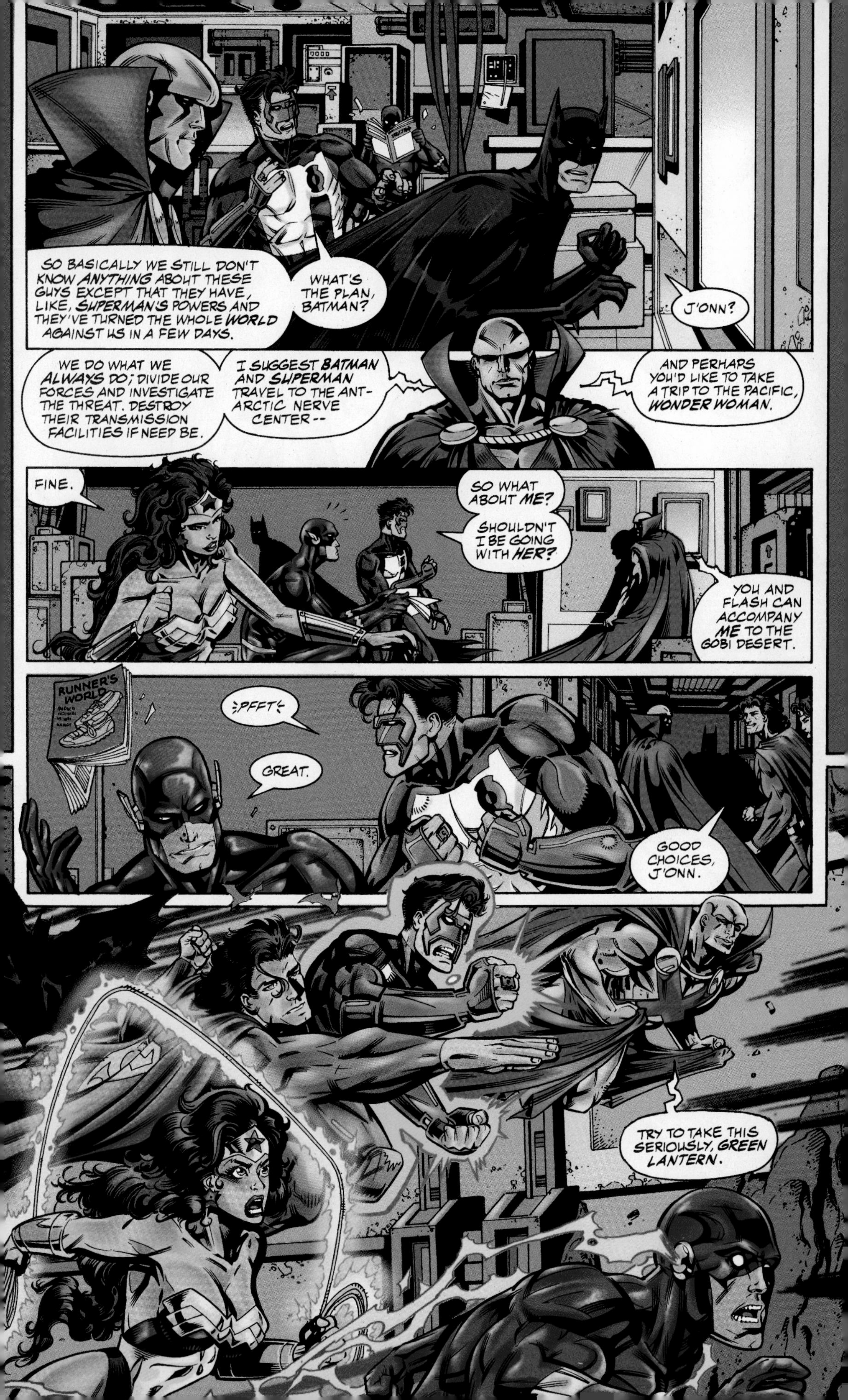

SO BASICALLY WE STILL DON'T KNOW ANYTHING ABOUT THESE GUYS EXCEPT THAT THEY HAVE, LIKE, SUPERMAN'S POWERS AND THEY'VE TURNED THE WHOLE WORLD AGAINST US IN A FEW DAYS.
WHAT'S THE PLAN, BATMAN?
J'ONN?
WE DO WHAT WE ALWAYS DO; DIVIDE OUR FORCES AND INVESTIGATE THE THREAT. DESTROY THEIR TRANSMISSION FACILITIES IF NEED BE.
I SUGGEST BATMAN AND SUPERMAN TRAVEL TO THE ANTARCTIC NERVE CENTER--
AND PERHAPS YOU'D LIKE TO TAKE A TRIP TO THE PACIFIC, WONDER WOMAN.
FINE.
SO WHAT ABOUT ME?
SHOULDN'T I BE GOING WITH HER?
YOU AND FLASH CAN ACCOMPANY ME TO THE GOBI DESERT.
RUNNER'S WORLD
PFFT
GREAT.
GOOD CHOICES, J'ONN.
TRY TO TAKE THIS SERIOUSLY, GREEN LANTERN.

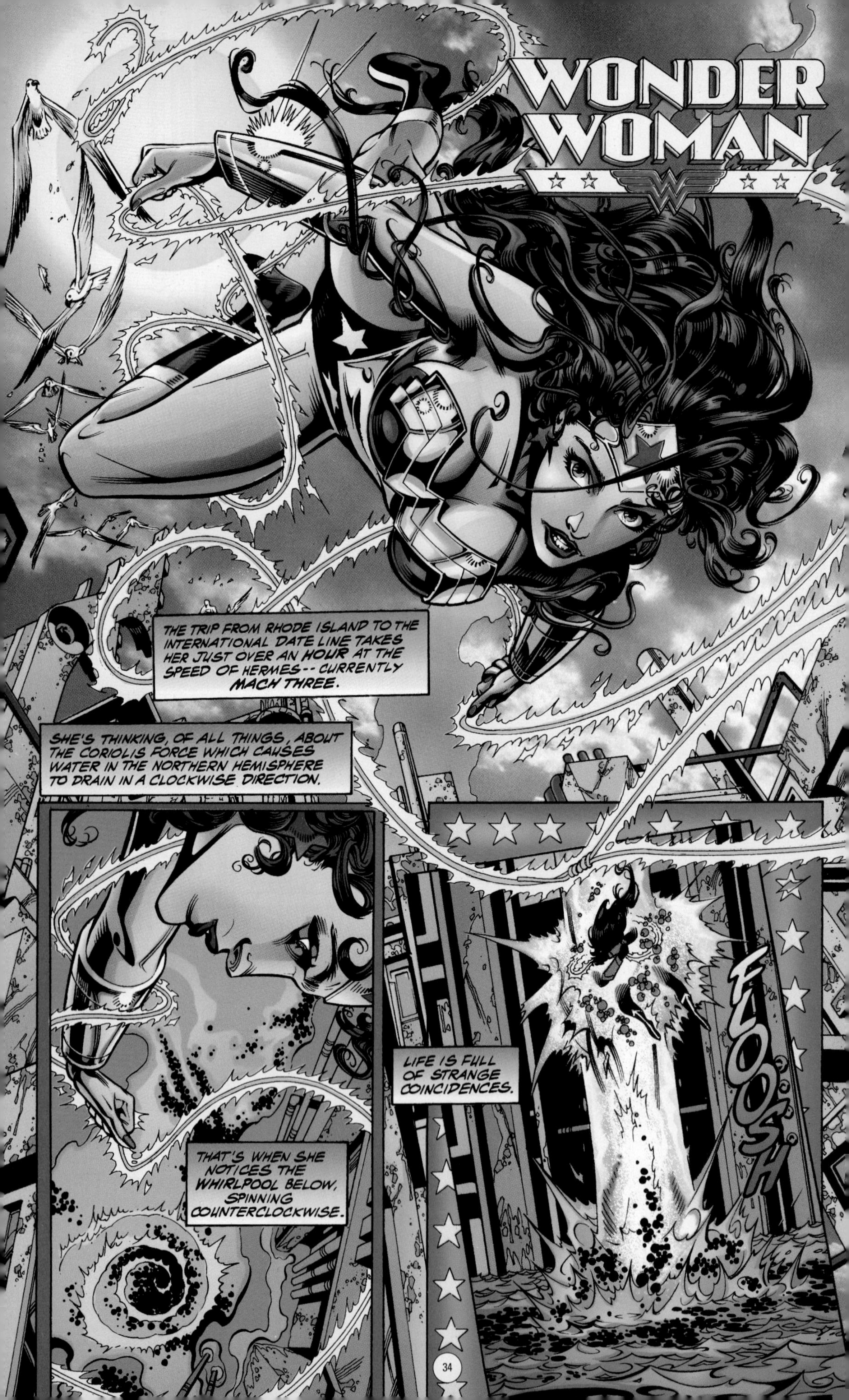
WONDER WOMAN
THE TRIP FROM RHODE ISLAND TO THE INTERNATIONAL DATE LINE TAKES HER JUST OVER AN HOUR AT THE SPEED OF HERMES-- CURRENTLY MACH THREE.
SHE'S THINKING, OF ALL THINGS, ABOUT THE CORIOLIS FORCE WHICH CAUSES WATER IN THE NORTHERN HEMISPHERE TO DRAIN IN A CLOCKWISE DIRECTION.
THAT'S WHEN SHE NOTICES THE WHIRLPOOL BELOW, SPINNING COUNTERCLOCKWISE.
LIFE IS FULL OF STRANGE COINCIDENCES.
FLOOSH

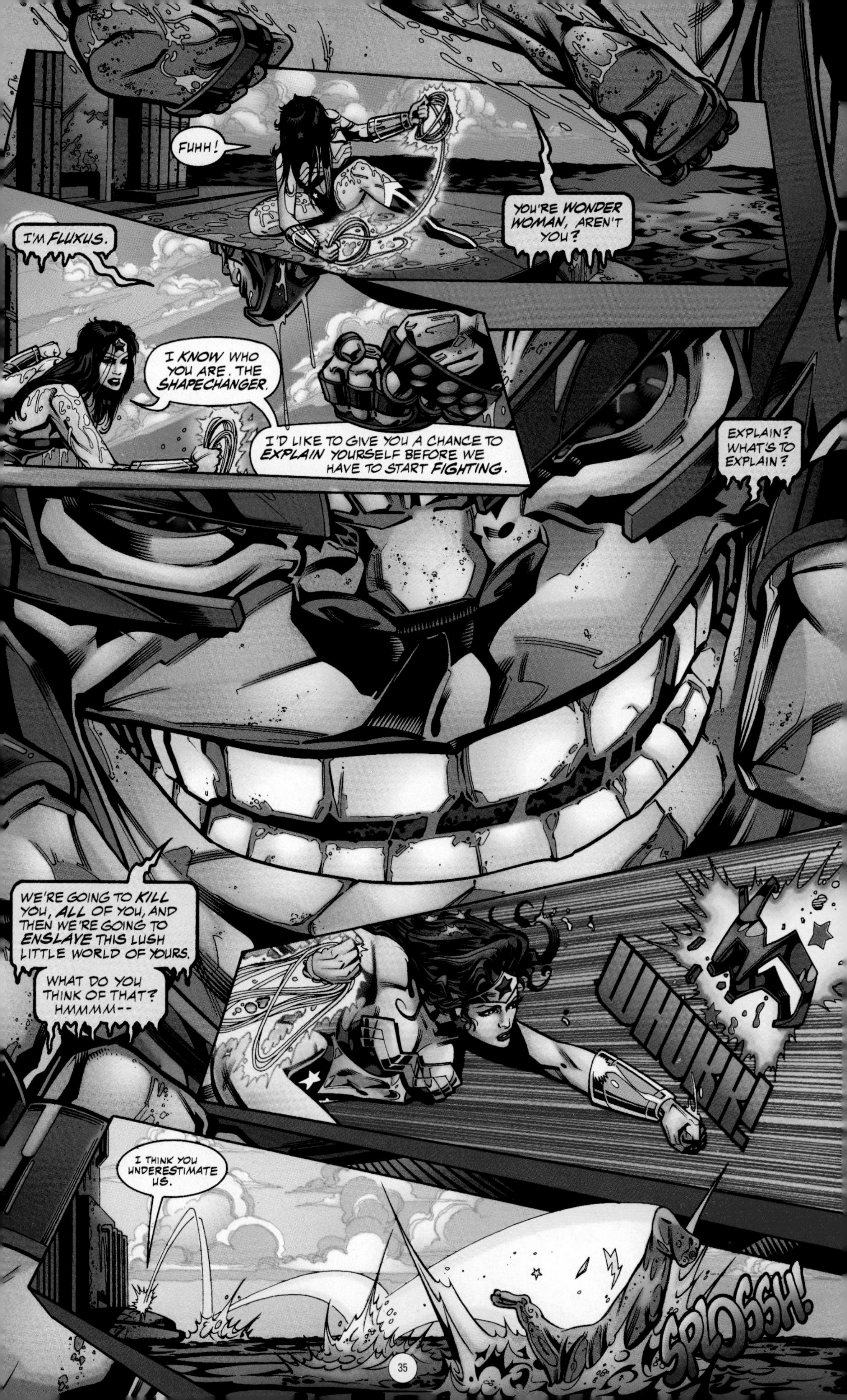
FUHH!
YOU'RE WONDER WOMAN, AREN'T YOU?
I'M FLUXUS.
I KNOW WHO YOU ARE. THE SHAPECHANGER.
I'D LIKE TO GIVE YOU A CHANCE TO EXPLAIN YOURSELF BEFORE WE HAVE TO START FIGHTING.
EXPLAIN? WHAT'S TO EXPLAIN?
WE'RE GOING TO KILL YOU, ALL OF YOU, AND THEN WE'RE GOING TO ENSLAVE THIS LUSH LITTLE WORLD OF YOURS.
WHAT DO YOU THINK OF THAT? HMMMM--
WHUHKK!
I THINK YOU UNDERESTIMATE US.
SPLOSSH!

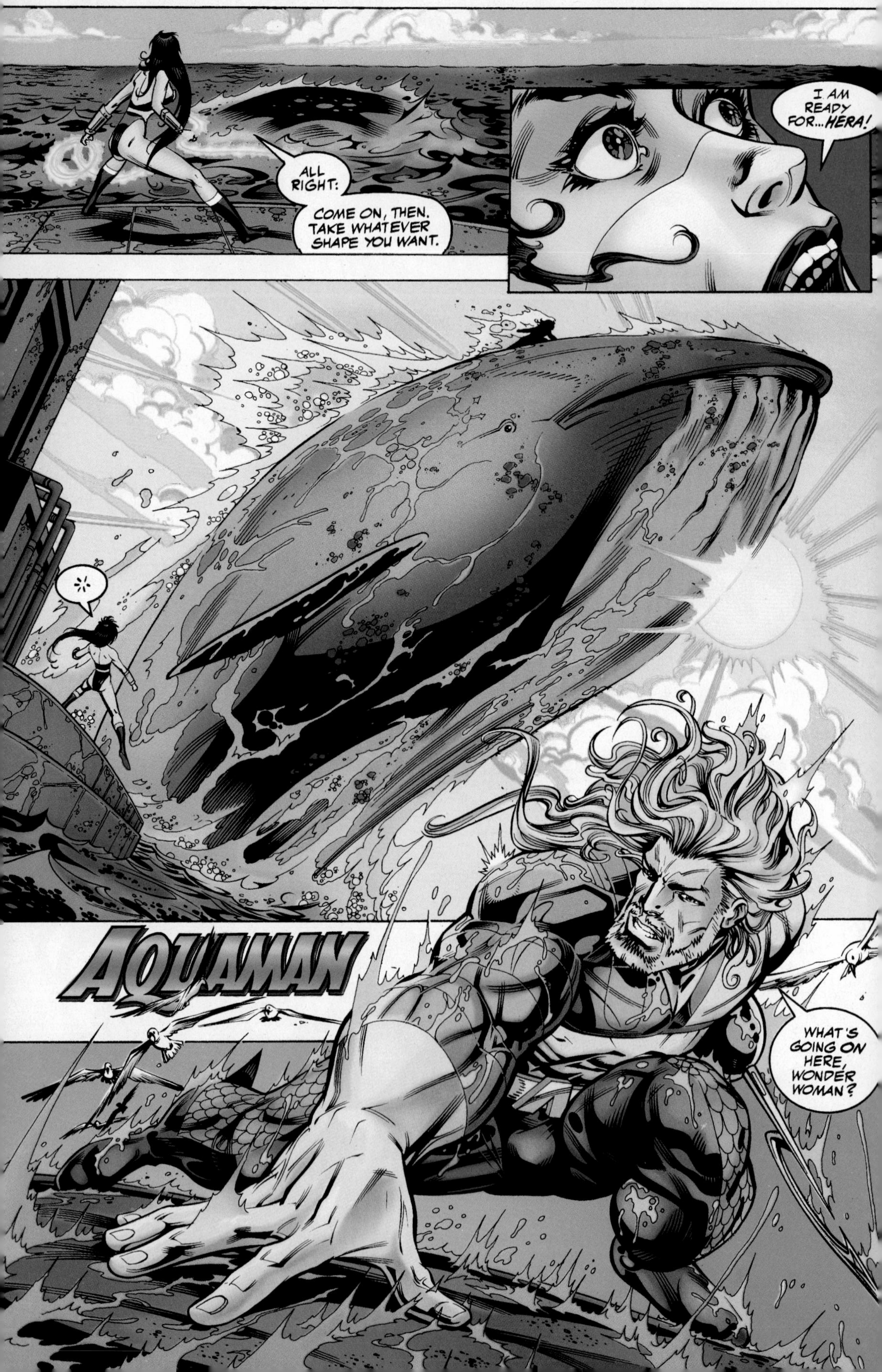
ALL RIGHT:
COME ON, THEN. TAKE WHATEVER SHAPE YOU WANT.
I AM READY FOR...HERA!
AQUAMAN
WHAT'S GOING ON HERE, WONDER WOMAN?

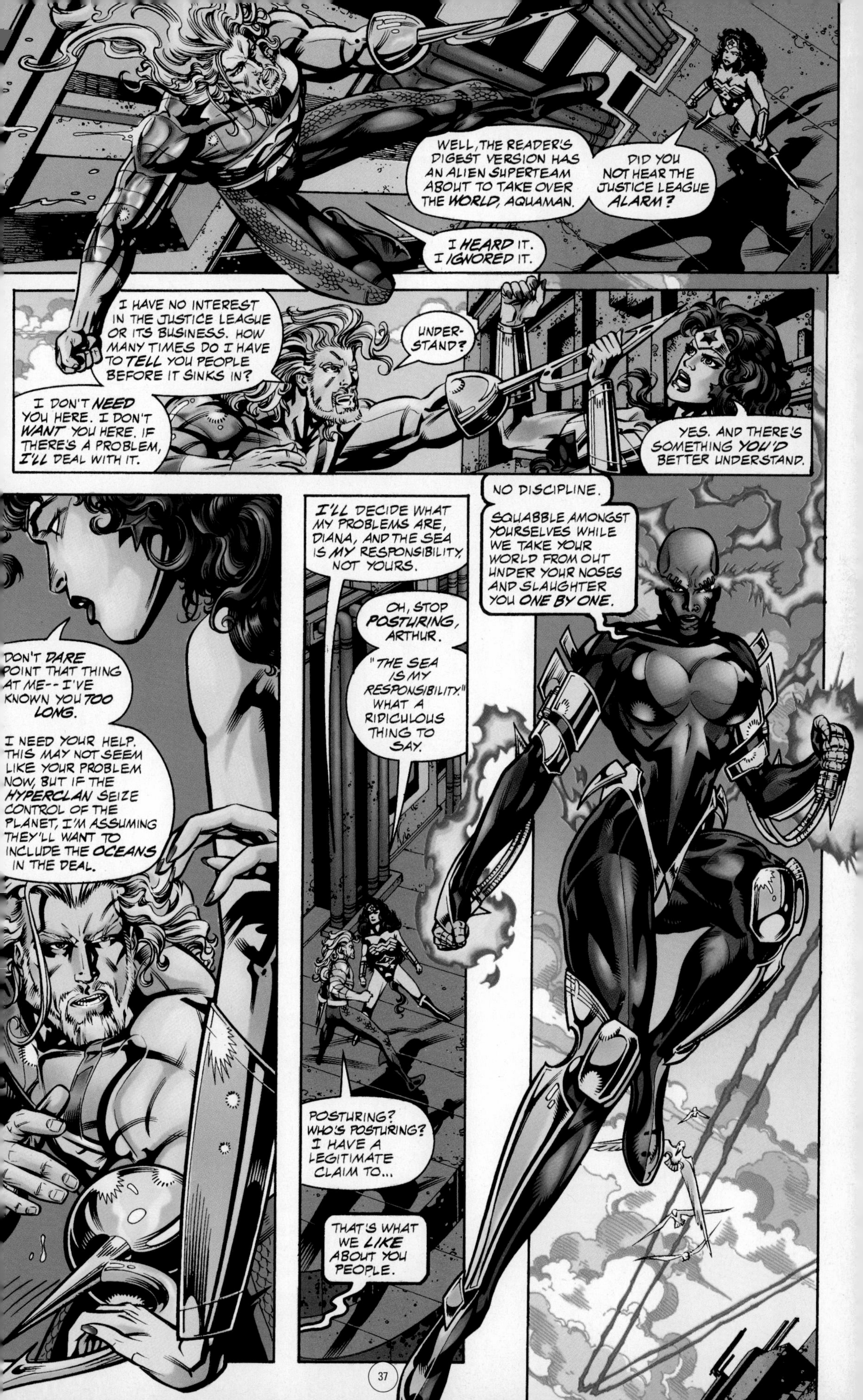
WELL, THE READER'S DIGEST VERSION HAS AN ALIEN SUPERTEAM ABOUT TO TAKE OVER THE WORLD, AQUAMAN.
DID YOU NOT HEAR THE JUSTICE LEAGUE ALARM?
I HEARD IT. I IGNORED IT.
I HAVE NO INTEREST IN THE JUSTICE LEAGUE OR ITS BUSINESS. HOW MANY TIMES DO I HAVE TO TELL YOU PEOPLE BEFORE IT SINKS IN?
I DON'T NEED YOU HERE. I DON'T WANT YOU HERE. IF THERE'S A PROBLEM, I'LL DEAL WITH IT.
UNDER-STAND?
YES. AND THERE'S SOMETHING YOU'D BETTER UNDERSTAND.
DON'T DARE POINT THAT THING AT ME-- I'VE KNOWN YOU TOO LONG.
I NEED YOUR HELP. THIS MAY NOT SEEM LIKE YOUR PROBLEM NOW, BUT IF THE HYPERCLAN SEIZE CONTROL OF THE PLANET, I'M ASSUMING THEY'LL WANT TO INCLUDE THE OCEANS IN THE DEAL.
I'LL DECIDE WHAT MY PROBLEMS ARE, DIANA, AND THE SEA IS MY RESPONSIBILITY, NOT YOURS.
OH, STOP POSTURING, ARTHUR.
"THE SEA IS MY RESPONSIBILITY." WHAT A RIDICULOUS THING TO SAY.
POSTURING? WHO'S POSTURING? I HAVE A LEGITIMATE CLAIM TO...
NO DISCIPLINE.
SQUABBLE AMONGST YOURSELVES WHILE WE TAKE YOUR WORLD FROM OUT UNDER YOUR NOSES AND SLAUGHTER YOU ONE BY ONE.
THAT'S WHAT WE LIKE ABOUT YOU PEOPLE.

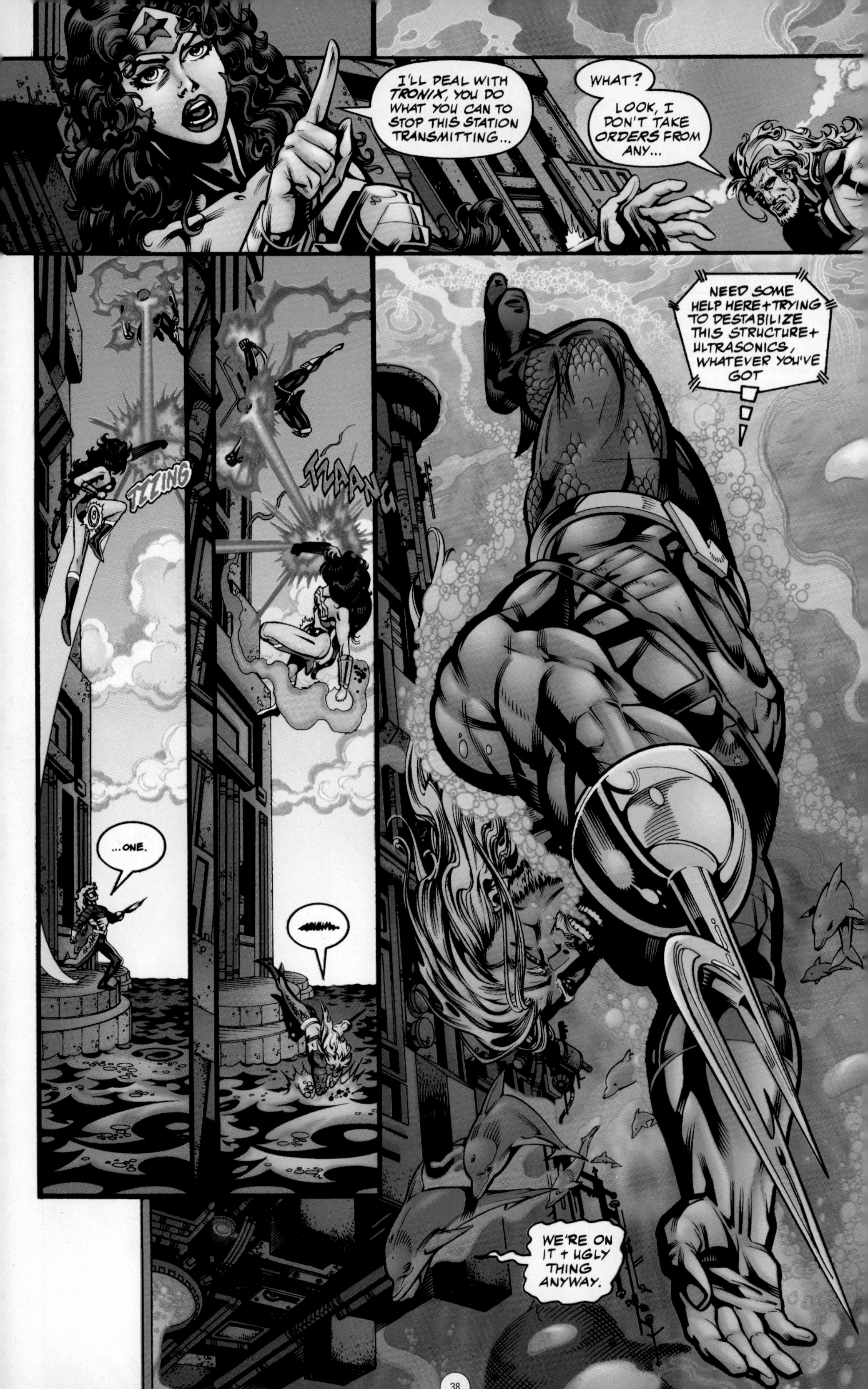
I'LL DEAL WITH TRONIX, YOU DO WHAT YOU CAN TO STOP THIS STATION TRANSMITTING...
WHAT?
LOOK, I DON'T TAKE ORDERS FROM ANY...
TZZING
...ONE.
TZZAANG
NEED SOME HELP HERE+TRYING TO DESTABILIZE THIS STRUCTURE+ ULTRASONICS, WHATEVER YOU'VE GOT
WE'RE ON IT + UGLY THING ANYWAY.

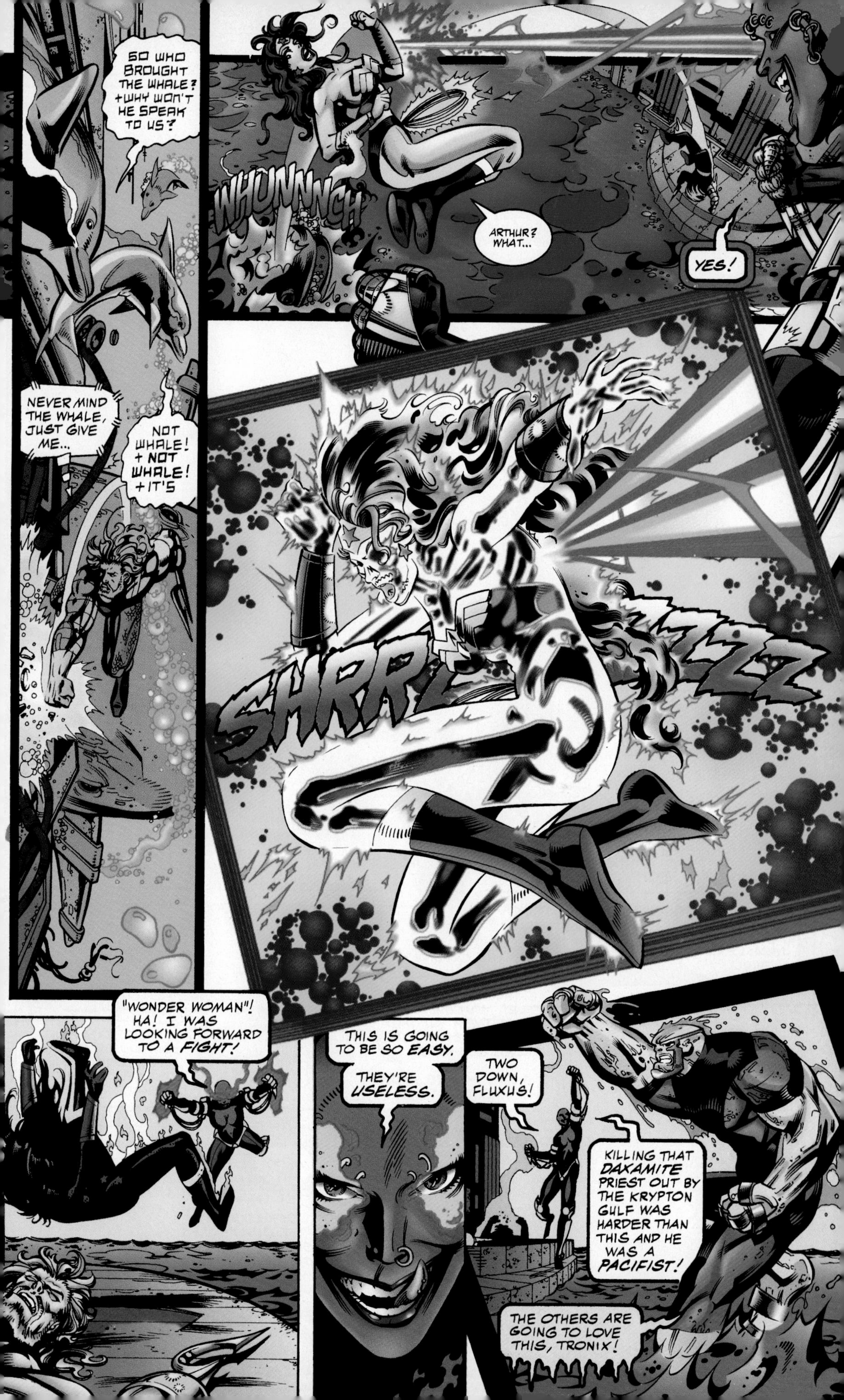
SO WHO BROUGHT THE WHALE? + WHY WON'T HE SPEAK TO US?
WHUNNNCH
ARTHUR? WHAT...
YES!
NEVER MIND THE WHALE, JUST GIVE ME...
NOT WHALE! + NOT WHALE! + IT'S
SHRRZZZ
"WONDER WOMAN"! HA! I WAS LOOKING FORWARD TO A FIGHT!
THIS IS GOING TO BE SO EASY.
THEY'RE USELESS.
TWO DOWN, FLUXUS!
KILLING THAT DAXAMITE PRIEST OUT BY THE KRYPTON GULF WAS HARDER THAN THIS AND HE WAS A PACIFIST!
THE OTHERS ARE GOING TO LOVE THIS, TRONIX!

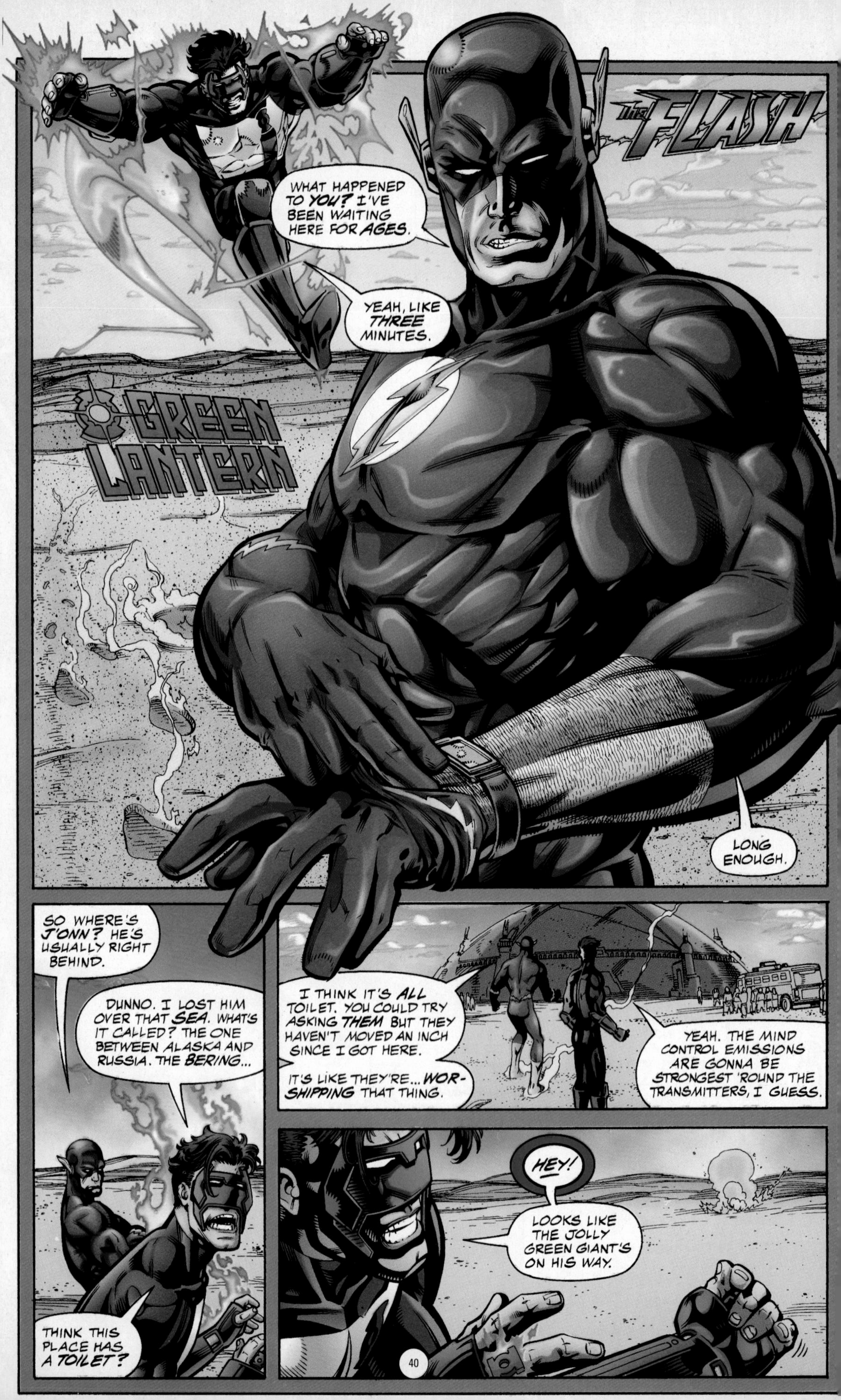
THE FLASH
WHAT HAPPENED TO YOU? I'VE BEEN WAITING HERE FOR AGES.
YEAH, LIKE THREE MINUTES.
GREEN LANTERN
LONG ENOUGH.
SO WHERE'S J'ONN? HE'S USUALLY RIGHT BEHIND.
DUNNO. I LOST HIM OVER THAT SEA. WHAT'S IT CALLED? THE ONE BETWEEN ALASKA AND RUSSIA. THE BERING...
THINK THIS PLACE HAS A TOILET?
I THINK IT'S ALL TOILET. YOU COULD TRY ASKING THEM BUT THEY HAVEN'T MOVED AN INCH SINCE I GOT HERE.
IT'S LIKE THEY'RE... WOR-SHIPPING THAT THING.
YEAH. THE MIND CONTROL EMISSIONS ARE GONNA BE STRONGEST 'ROUND THE TRANSMITTERS, I GUESS.
HEY!
LOOKS LIKE THE JOLLY GREEN GIANT'S ON HIS WAY.

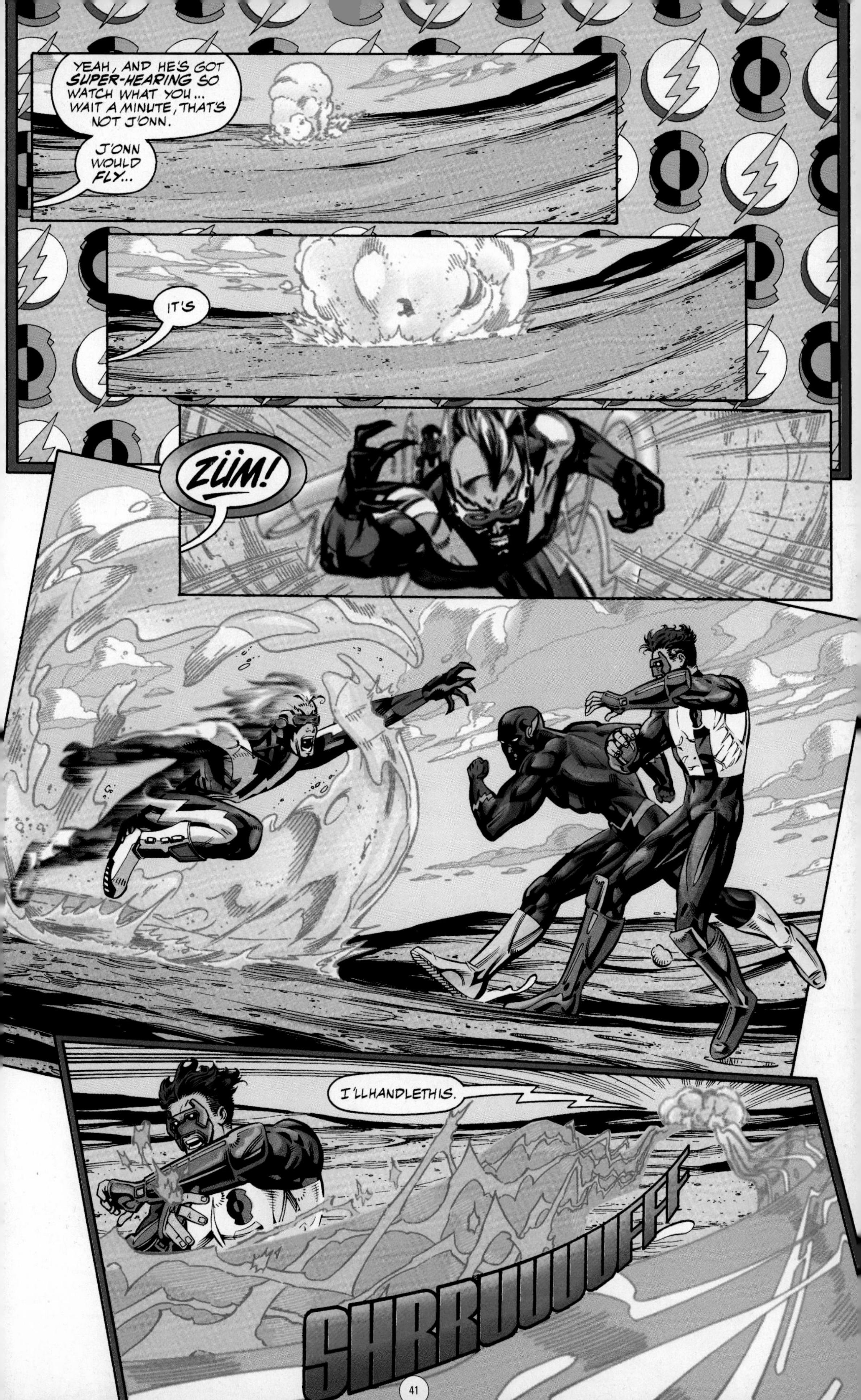

YEAH, AND HE'S GOT SUPER-HEARING SO WATCH WHAT YOU... WAIT A MINUTE, THAT'S NOT J'ONN.
J'ONN WOULD FLY...
IT'S
ZÜM!
I'LLHANDLETHIS.
SHRRUUUUFFT

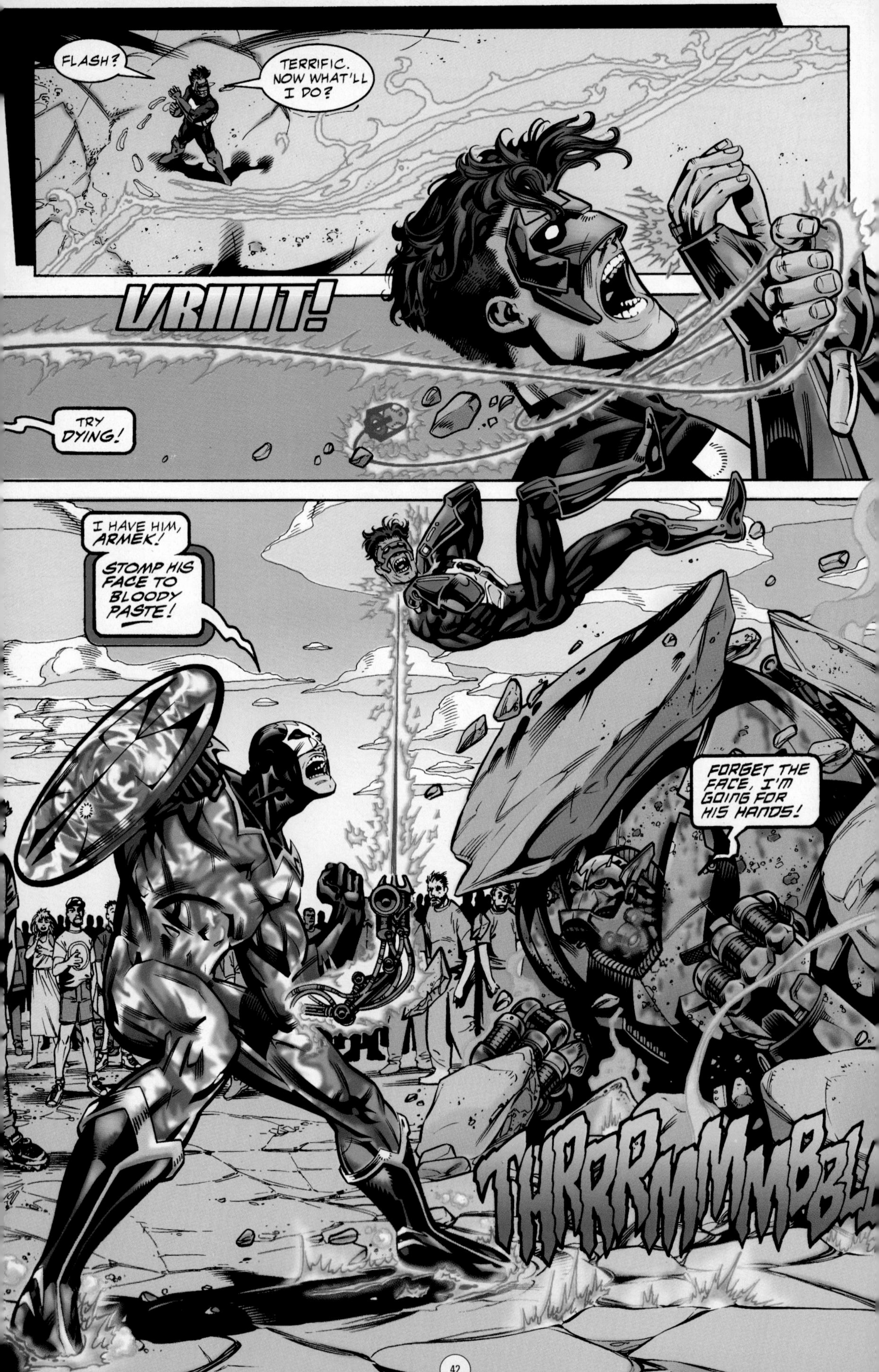
FLASH?
TERRIFIC. NOW WHAT'LL I DO?
VRIIIIT!
TRY DYING!
I HAVE HIM, ARMEK!
STOMP HIS FACE TO BLOODY PASTE!
FORGET THE FACE, I'M GOING FOR HIS HANDS!
THRRMMMBL

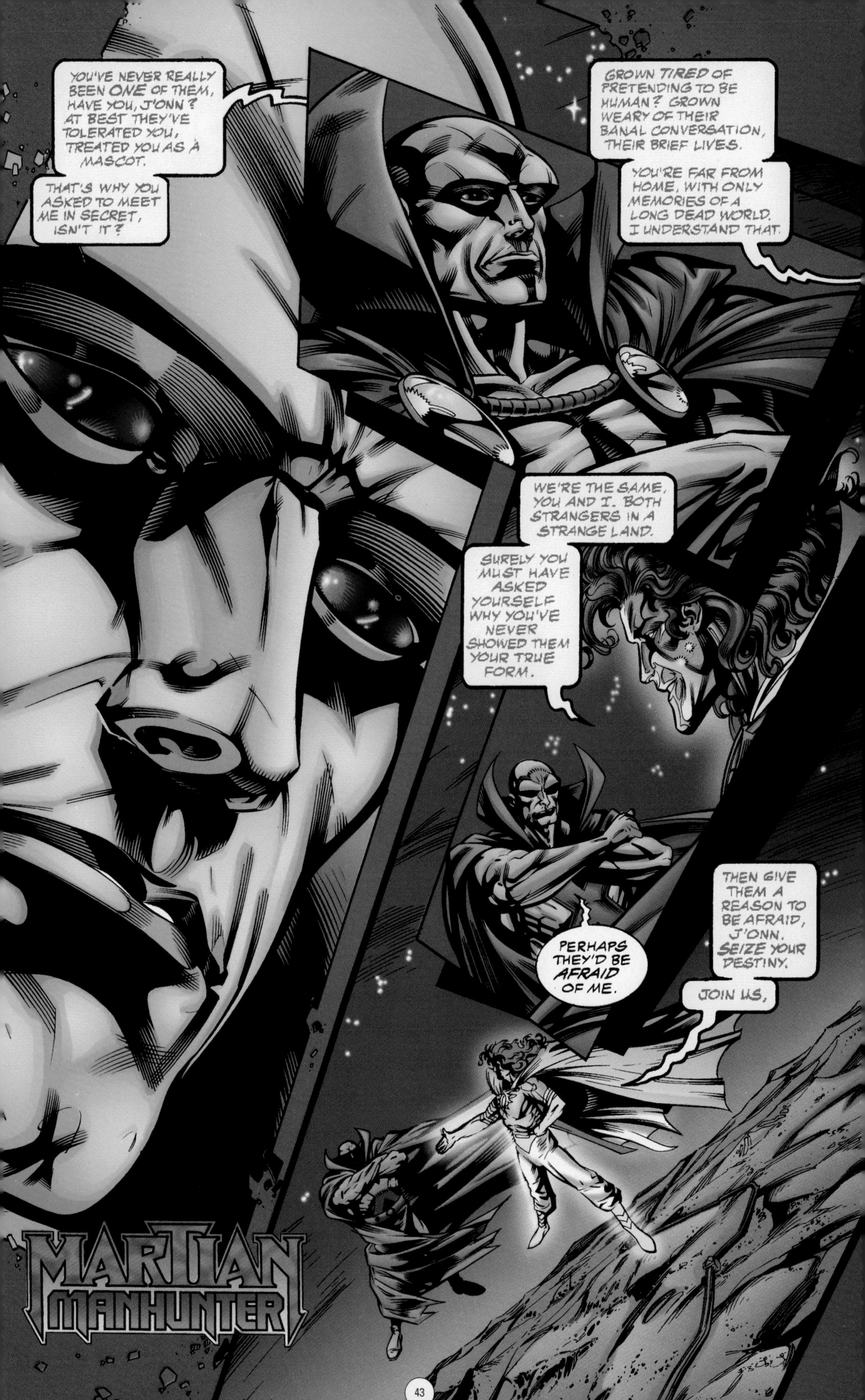
YOU'VE NEVER REALLY BEEN ONE OF THEM, HAVE YOU, J'ONN? AT BEST THEY'VE TOLERATED YOU, TREATED YOU AS A MASCOT.
THAT'S WHY YOU ASKED TO MEET ME IN SECRET, ISN'T IT?
GROWN TIRED OF PRETENDING TO BE HUMAN? GROWN WEARY OF THEIR BANAL CONVERSATION, THEIR BRIEF LIVES.
YOU'RE FAR FROM HOME, WITH ONLY MEMORIES OF A LONG DEAD WORLD. I UNDERSTAND THAT.
WE'RE THE SAME, YOU AND I. BOTH STRANGERS IN A STRANGE LAND.
SURELY YOU MUST HAVE ASKED YOURSELF WHY YOU'VE NEVER SHOWED THEM YOUR TRUE FORM.
PERHAPS THEY'D BE AFRAID OF ME.
THEN GIVE THEM A REASON TO BE AFRAID, J'ONN. SEIZE YOUR DESTINY.
JOIN US,
MARTIAN MANHUNTER

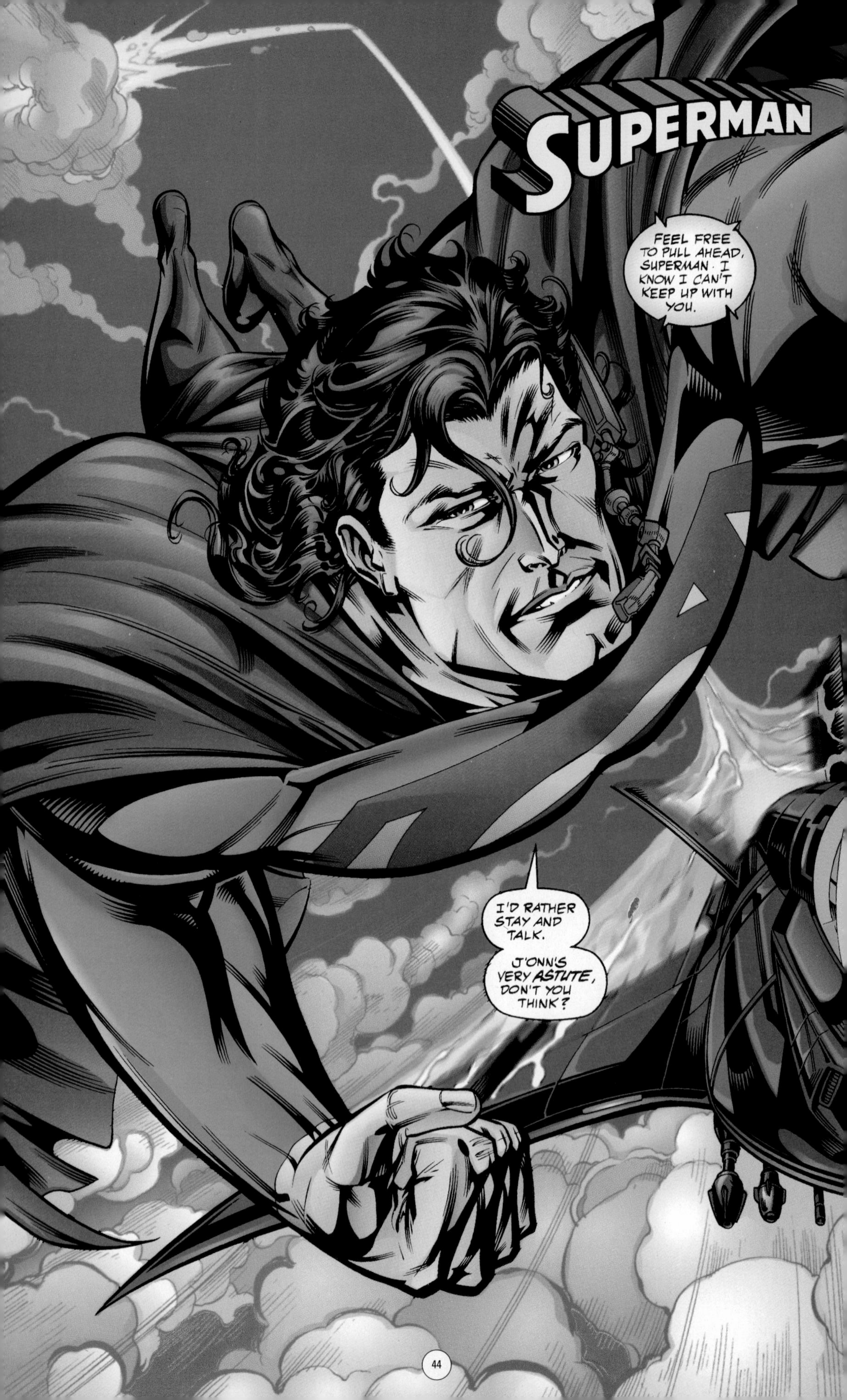
SUPERMAN
FEEL FREE TO PULL AHEAD, SUPERMAN. I KNOW I CAN'T KEEP UP WITH YOU.
I'D RATHER STAY AND TALK.
J'ONN'S VERY ASTUTE, DON'T YOU THINK?

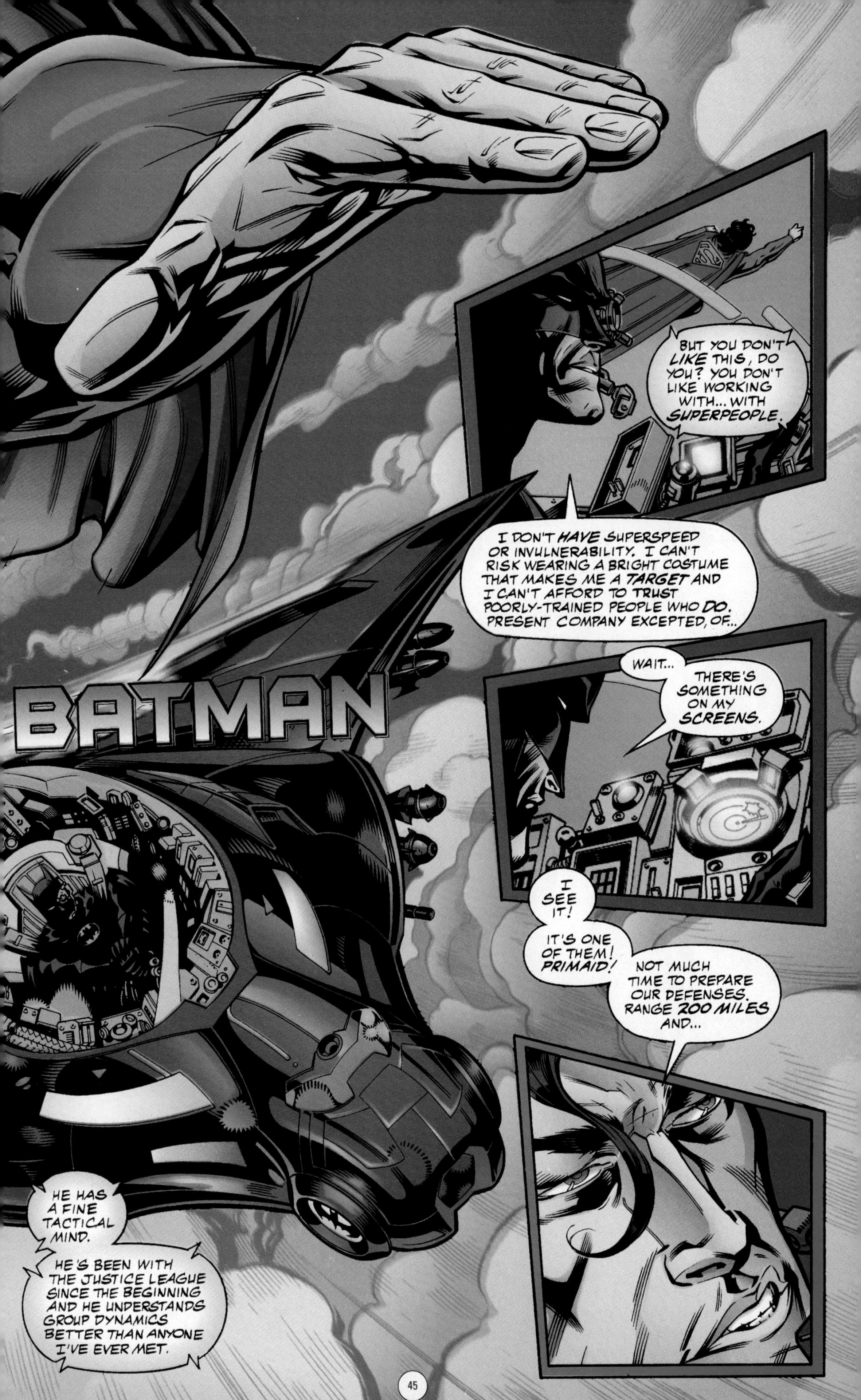

BATMAN
BUT YOU DON'T LIKE THIS, DO YOU? YOU DON'T LIKE WORKING WITH... WITH SUPERPEOPLE.
I DON'T HAVE SUPERSPEED OR INVULNERABILITY. I CAN'T RISK WEARING A BRIGHT COSTUME THAT MAKES ME A TARGET AND I CAN'T AFFORD TO TRUST POORLY-TRAINED PEOPLE WHO DO. PRESENT COMPANY EXCEPTED, OF...
WAIT...
THERE'S SOMETHING ON MY SCREENS.
I SEE IT!
IT'S ONE OF THEM! PRIMAID!
NOT MUCH TIME TO PREPARE OUR DEFENSES. RANGE 200 MILES AND...
HE HAS A FINE TACTICAL MIND.
HE'S BEEN WITH THE JUSTICE LEAGUE SINCE THE BEGINNING AND HE UNDERSTANDS GROUP DYNAMICS BETTER THAN ANYONE I'VE EVER MET.

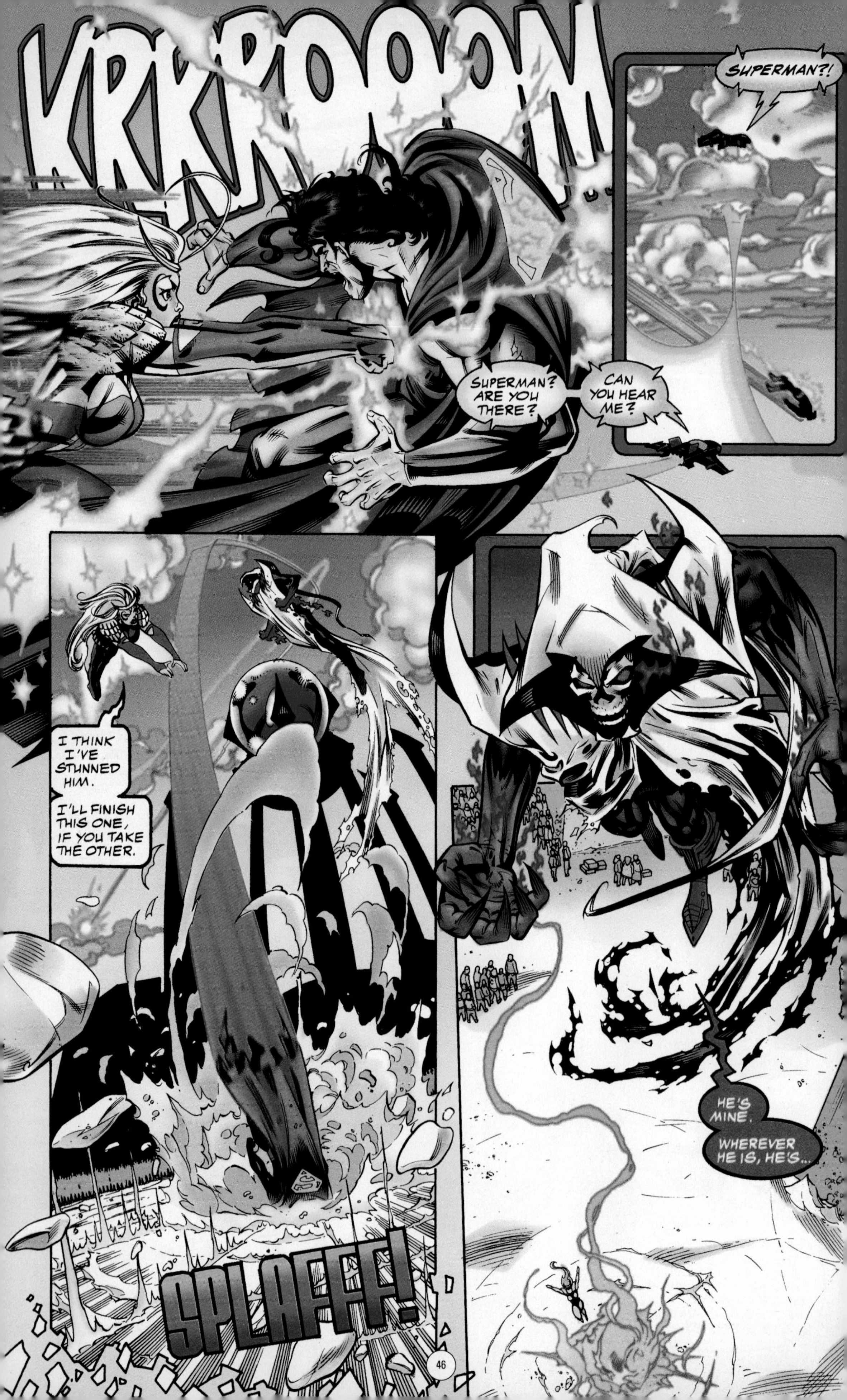
KRKROOOM
SUPERMAN?!
SUPERMAN? ARE YOU THERE?
CAN YOU HEAR ME?
I THINK I'VE STUNNED HIM.
I'LL FINISH THIS ONE, IF YOU TAKE THE OTHER.
SPLAFFF!
HE'S MINE.
WHEREVER HE IS, HE'S...

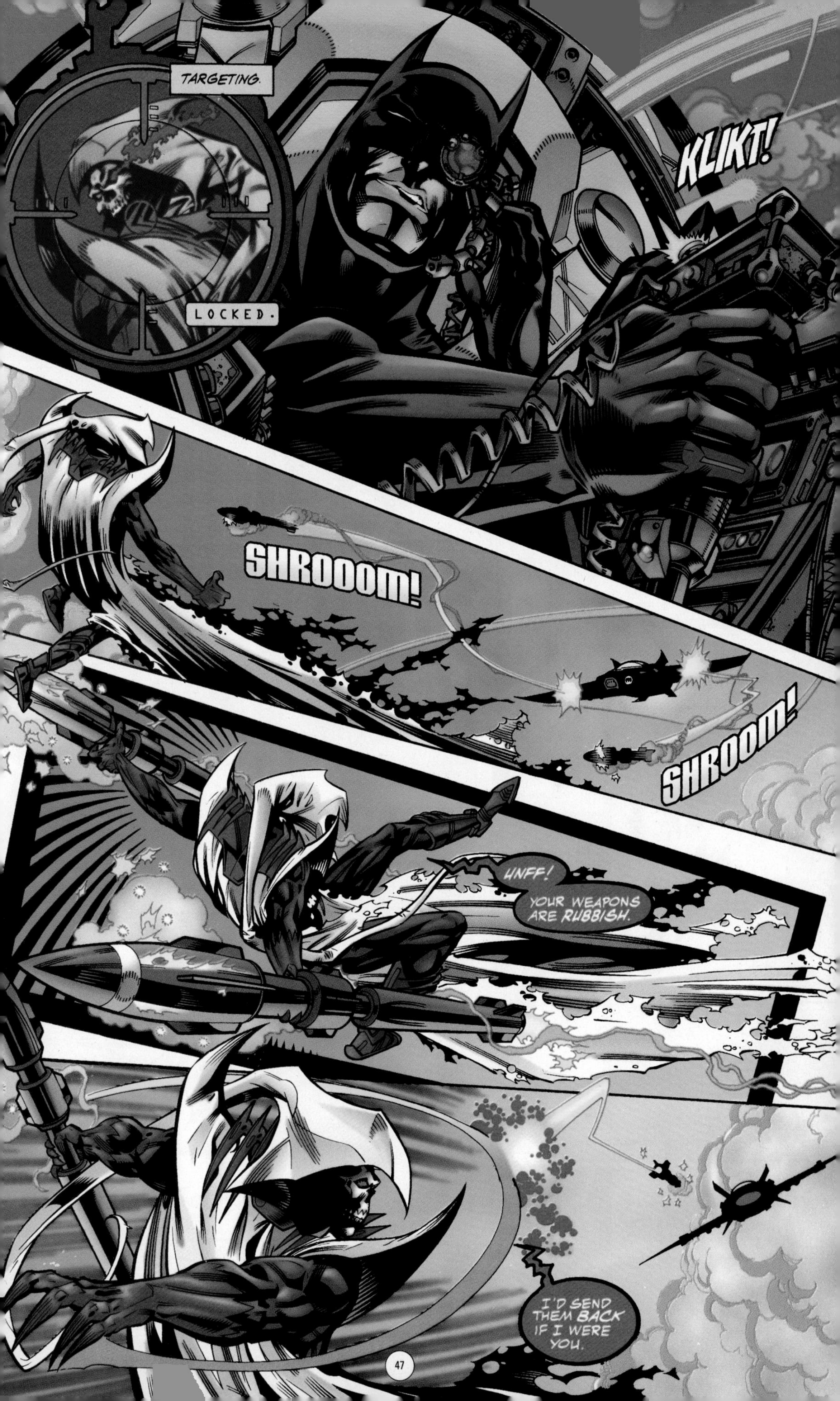
TARGETING.
LOCKED.
KLIKT!
SHROOOM!
SHROOM!
UNFF!
YOUR WEAPONS ARE RUBBISH.
I'D SEND THEM BACK IF I WERE YOU.

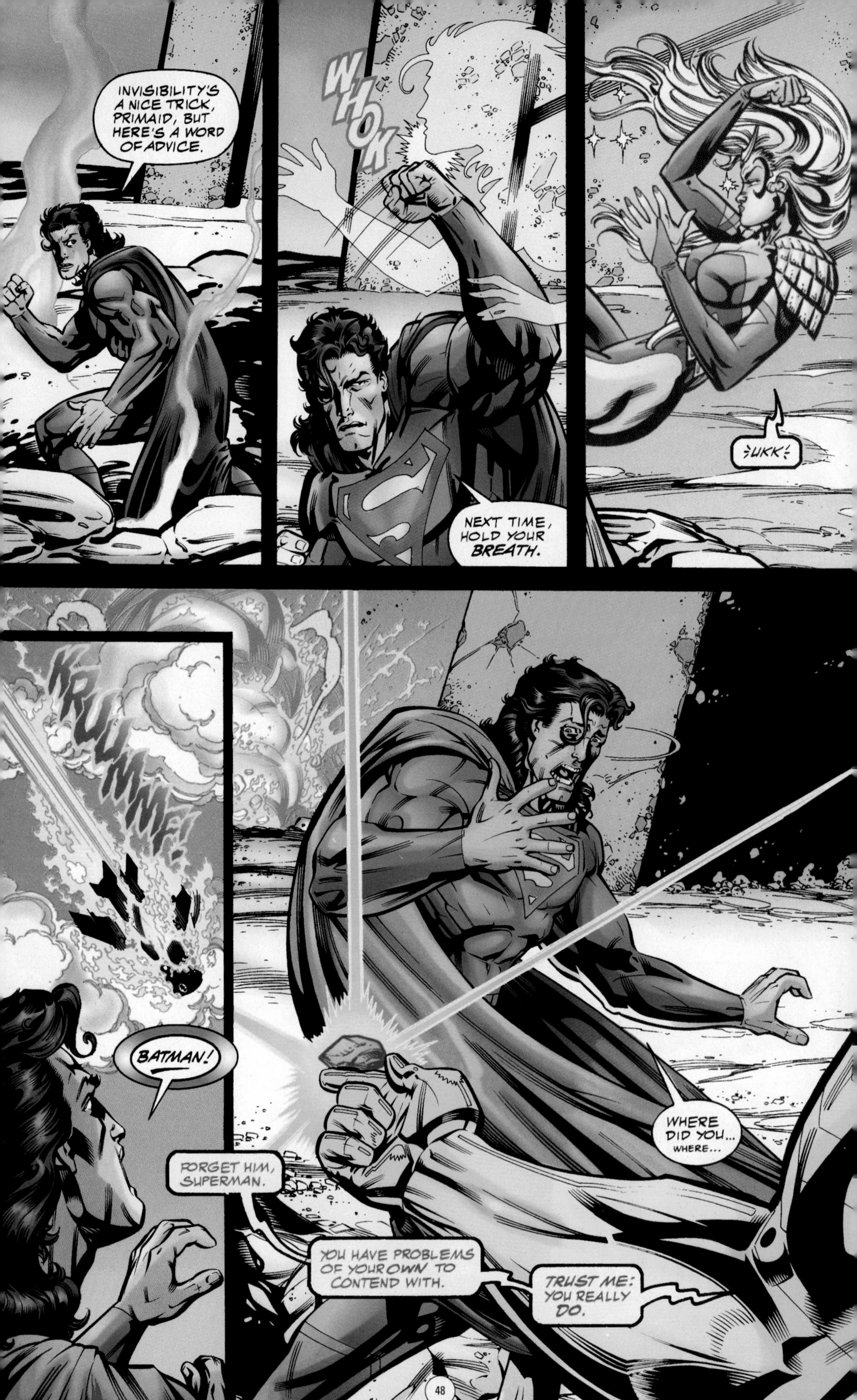
INVISIBILITY'S A NICE TRICK, PRIMAID, BUT HERE'S A WORD OF ADVICE.
WHOK
NEXT TIME, HOLD YOUR BREATH.
UKK
KRUMMF!
BATMAN!
FORGET HIM, SUPERMAN.
WHERE DID YOU... WHERE...
YOU HAVE PROBLEMS OF YOUR OWN TO CONTEND WITH.
TRUST ME: YOU REALLY DO.

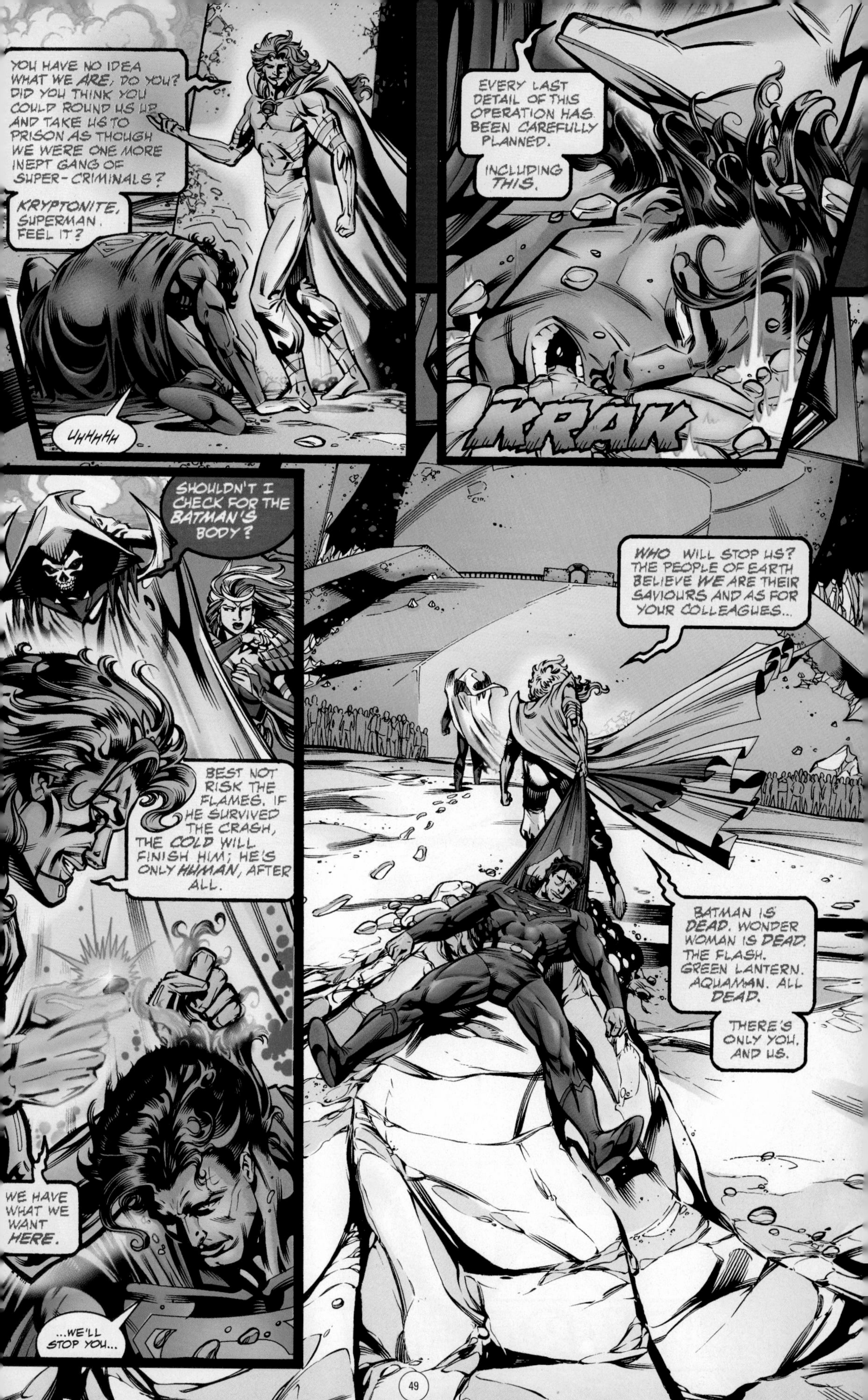

YOU HAVE NO IDEA WHAT WE ARE, DO YOU? DID YOU THINK YOU COULD ROUND US UP AND TAKE US TO PRISON AS THOUGH WE WERE ONE MORE INEPT GANG OF SUPER-CRIMINALS?
KRYPTONITE, SUPERMAN. FEEL IT?
UHHHHH
EVERY LAST DETAIL OF THIS OPERATION HAS BEEN CAREFULLY PLANNED.
INCLUDING THIS.
KRAK
SHOULDN'T I CHECK FOR THE BATMAN'S BODY?
BEST NOT RISK THE FLAMES. IF HE SURVIVED THE CRASH, THE COLD WILL FINISH HIM; HE'S ONLY HUMAN, AFTER ALL.
WE HAVE WHAT WE WANT HERE.
...WE'LL STOP YOU...
WHO WILL STOP US? THE PEOPLE OF EARTH BELIEVE WE ARE THEIR SAVIOURS AND AS FOR YOUR COLLEAGUES...
BATMAN IS DEAD. WONDER WOMAN IS DEAD. THE FLASH. GREEN LANTERN. AQUAMAN. ALL DEAD.
THERE'S ONLY YOU. AND US.

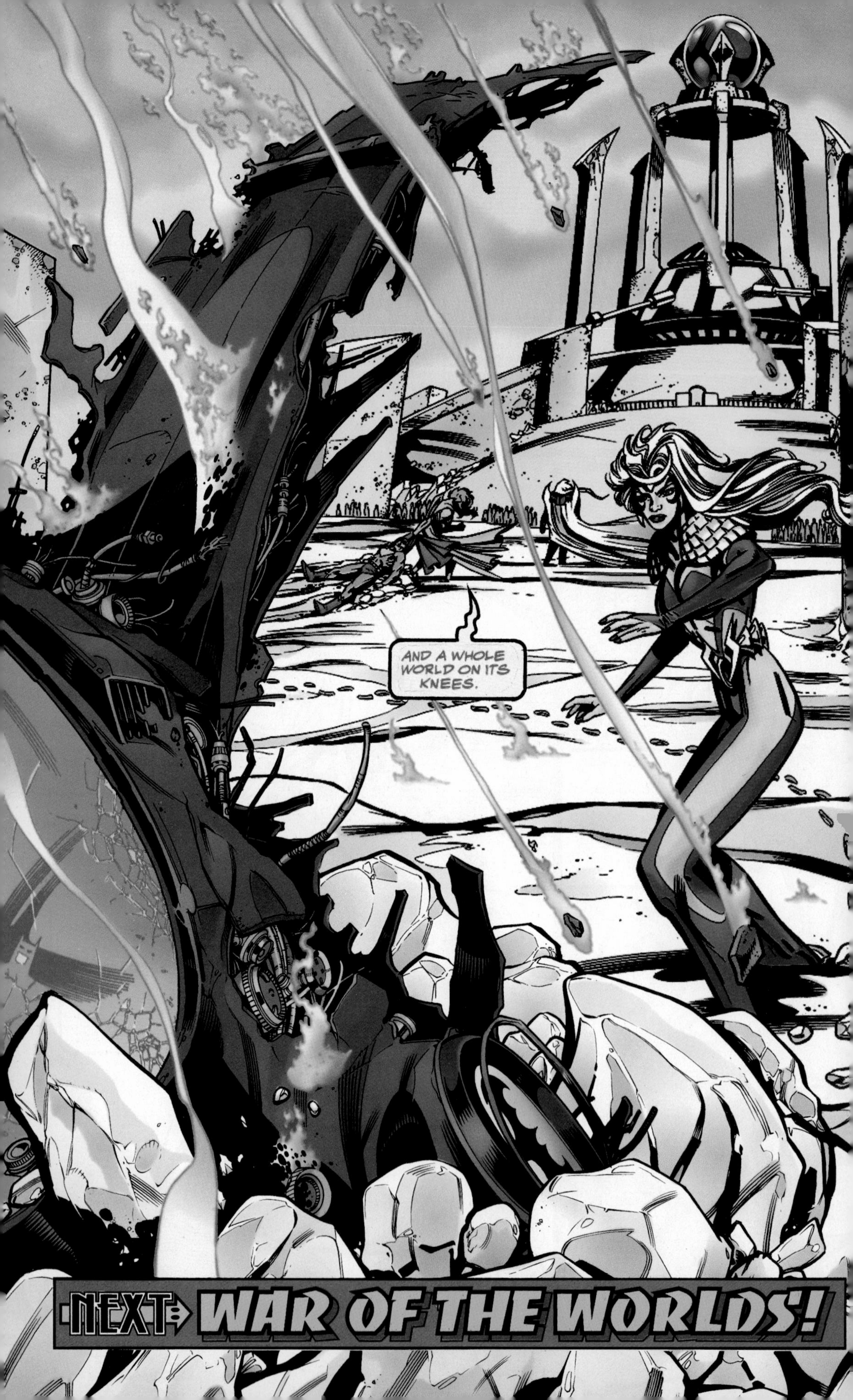
AND A WHOLE WORLD ON ITS KNEES.
NEXT WAR OF THE WORLDS!

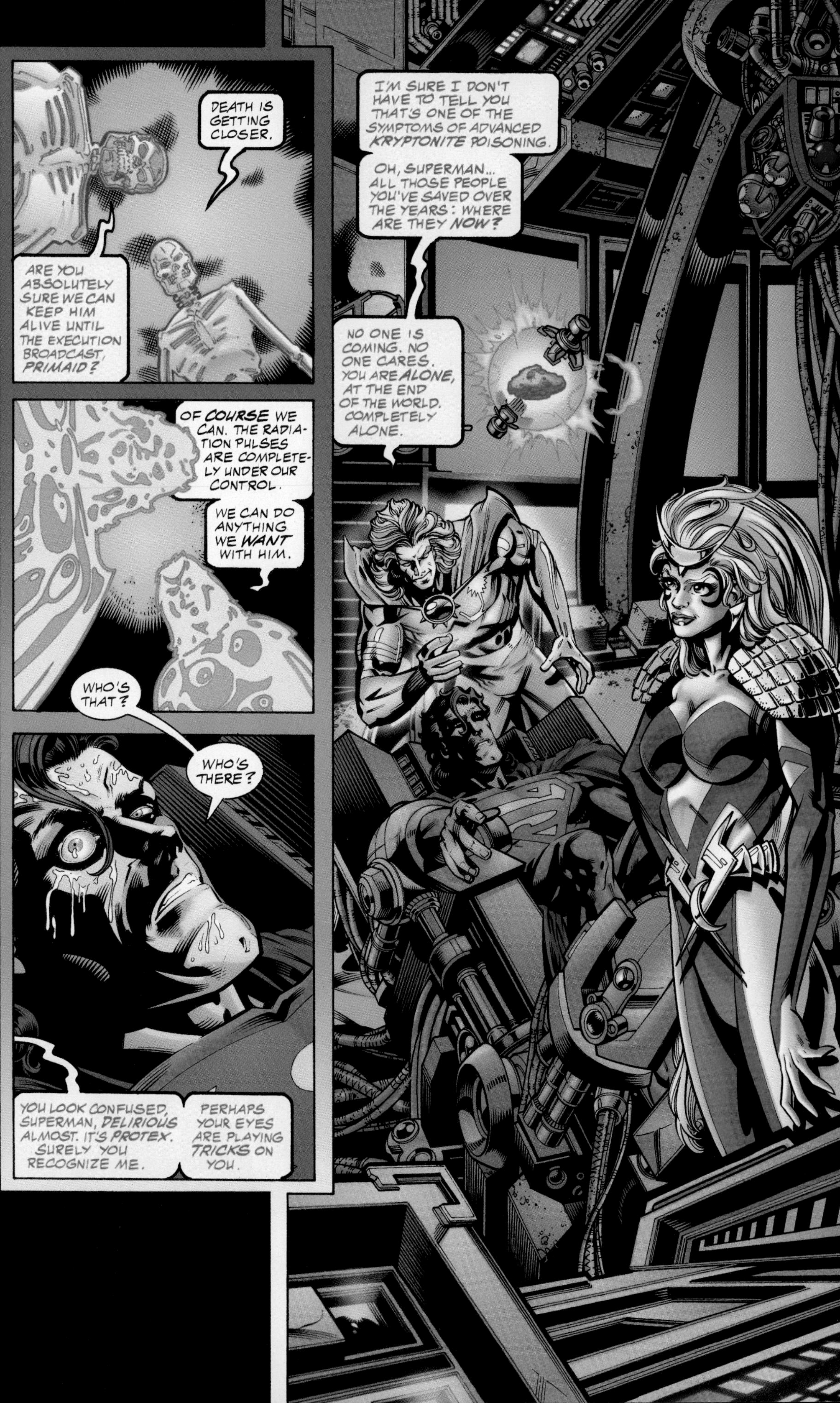

DEATH IS GETTING CLOSER.
ARE YOU ABSOLUTELY SURE WE CAN KEEP HIM ALIVE UNTIL THE EXECUTION BROADCAST, PRIMAID?
OF COURSE WE CAN. THE RADIATION PULSES ARE COMPLETELY UNDER OUR CONTROL.
WE CAN DO ANYTHING WE WANT WITH HIM.
WHO'S THAT?
WHO'S THERE?
YOU LOOK CONFUSED, SUPERMAN, DELIRIOUS ALMOST. IT'S PROTEX. SURELY YOU RECOGNIZE ME.
PERHAPS YOUR EYES ARE PLAYING TRICKS ON YOU.
I'M SURE I DON'T HAVE TO TELL YOU THAT'S ONE OF THE SYMPTOMS OF ADVANCED KRYPTONITE POISONING.
OH, SUPERMAN... ALL THOSE PEOPLE YOU'VE SAVED OVER THE YEARS: WHERE ARE THEY NOW?
NO ONE IS COMING. NO ONE CARES. YOU ARE ALONE, AT THE END OF THE WORLD. COMPLETELY ALONE.

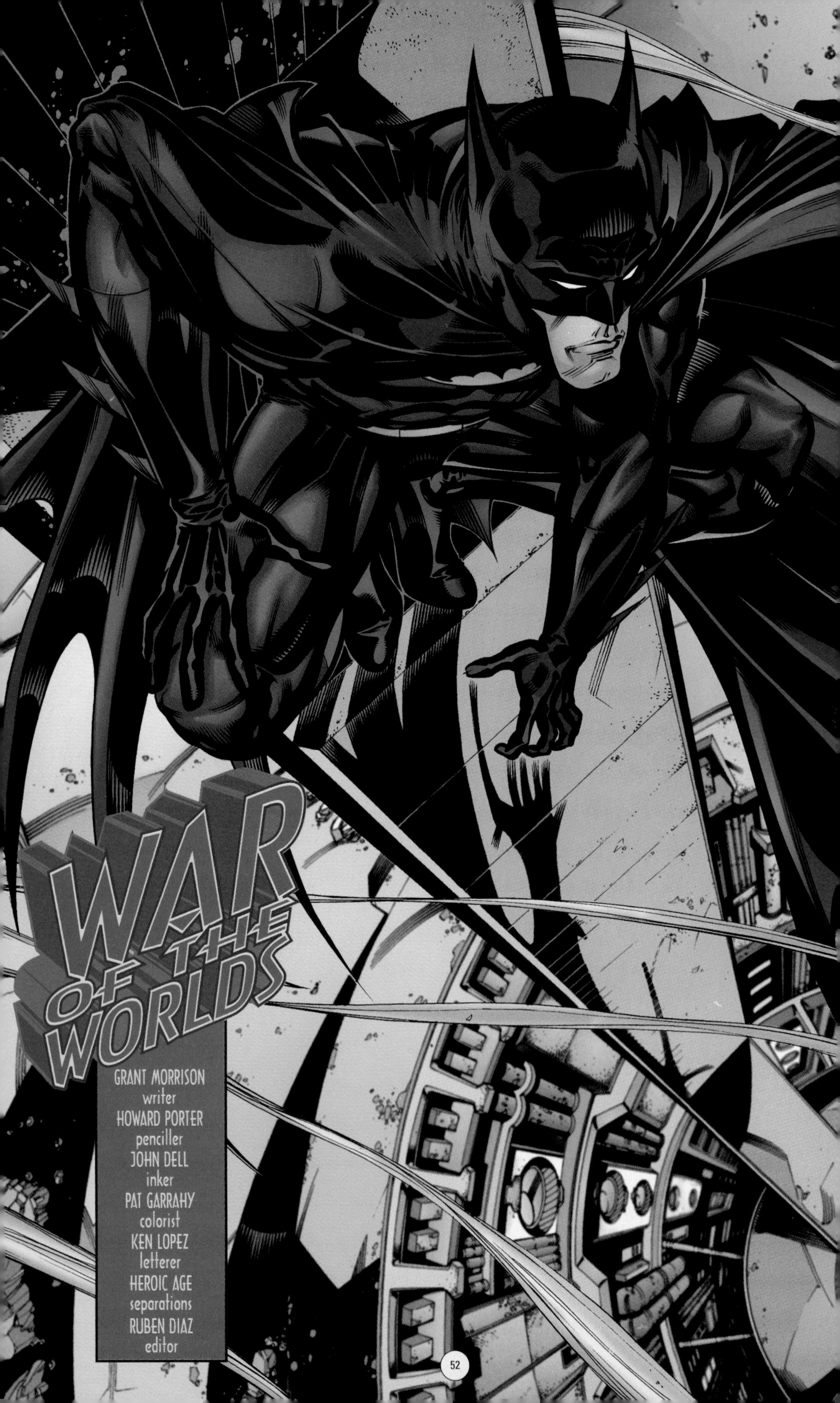
WAR OF THE WORLDS
GRANT MORRISON
writer
HOWARD PORTER
penciller
JOHN DELL
inker
PAT GARRAHY
colorist
KEN LOPEZ
letterer
HEROIC AGE
separations
RUBEN DIAZ
editor

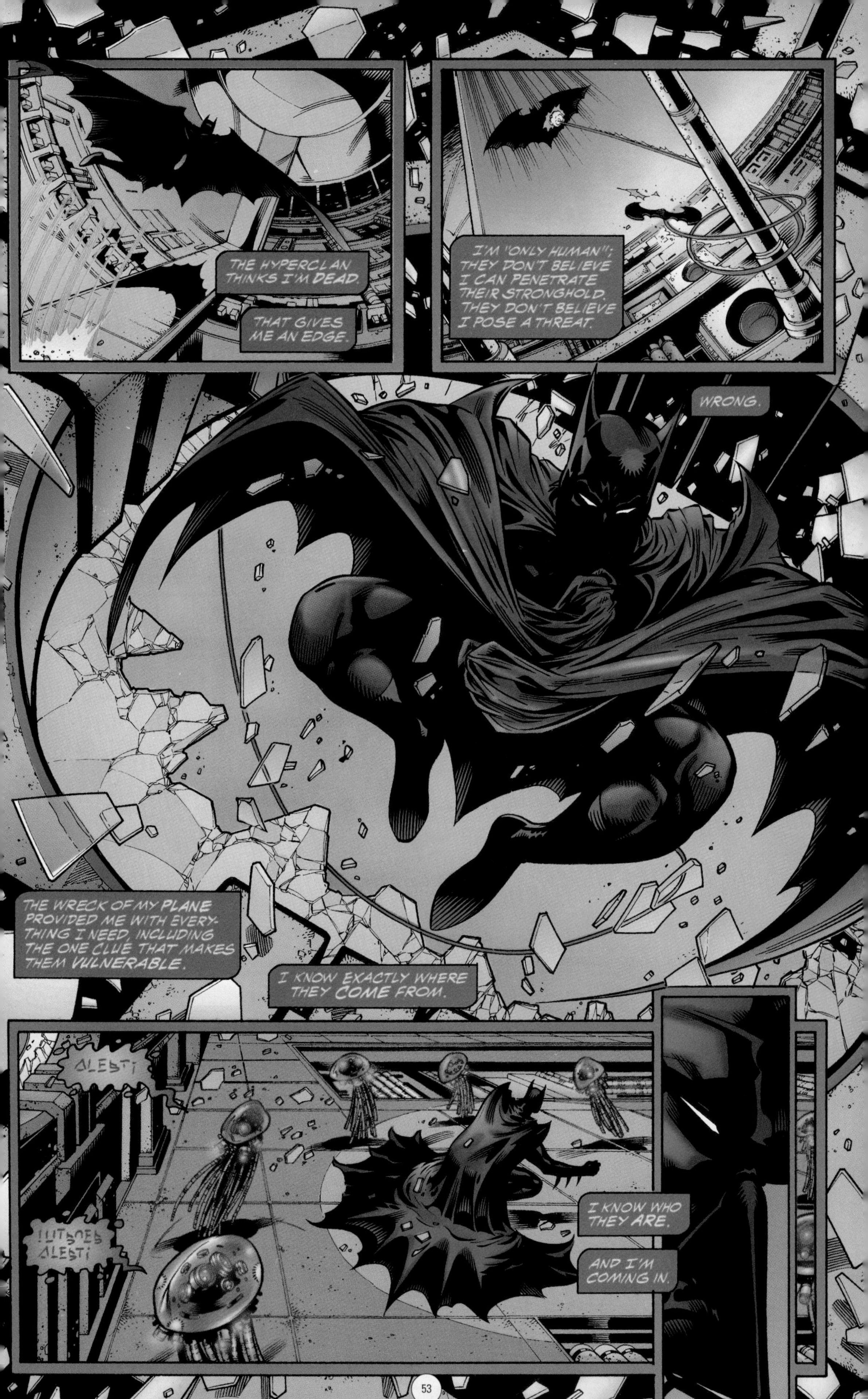
THE HYPERCLAN THINKS I'M DEAD.
THAT GIVES ME AN EDGE.
I'M "ONLY HUMAN"; THEY DON'T BELIEVE I CAN PENETRATE THEIR STRONGHOLD. THEY DON'T BELIEVE I POSE A THREAT.
WRONG.
THE WRECK OF MY PLANE PROVIDED ME WITH EVERYTHING I NEED, INCLUDING THE ONE CLUE THAT MAKES THEM VULNERABLE.
I KNOW EXACTLY WHERE THEY COME FROM.
I KNOW WHO THEY ARE.
AND I'M COMING IN.

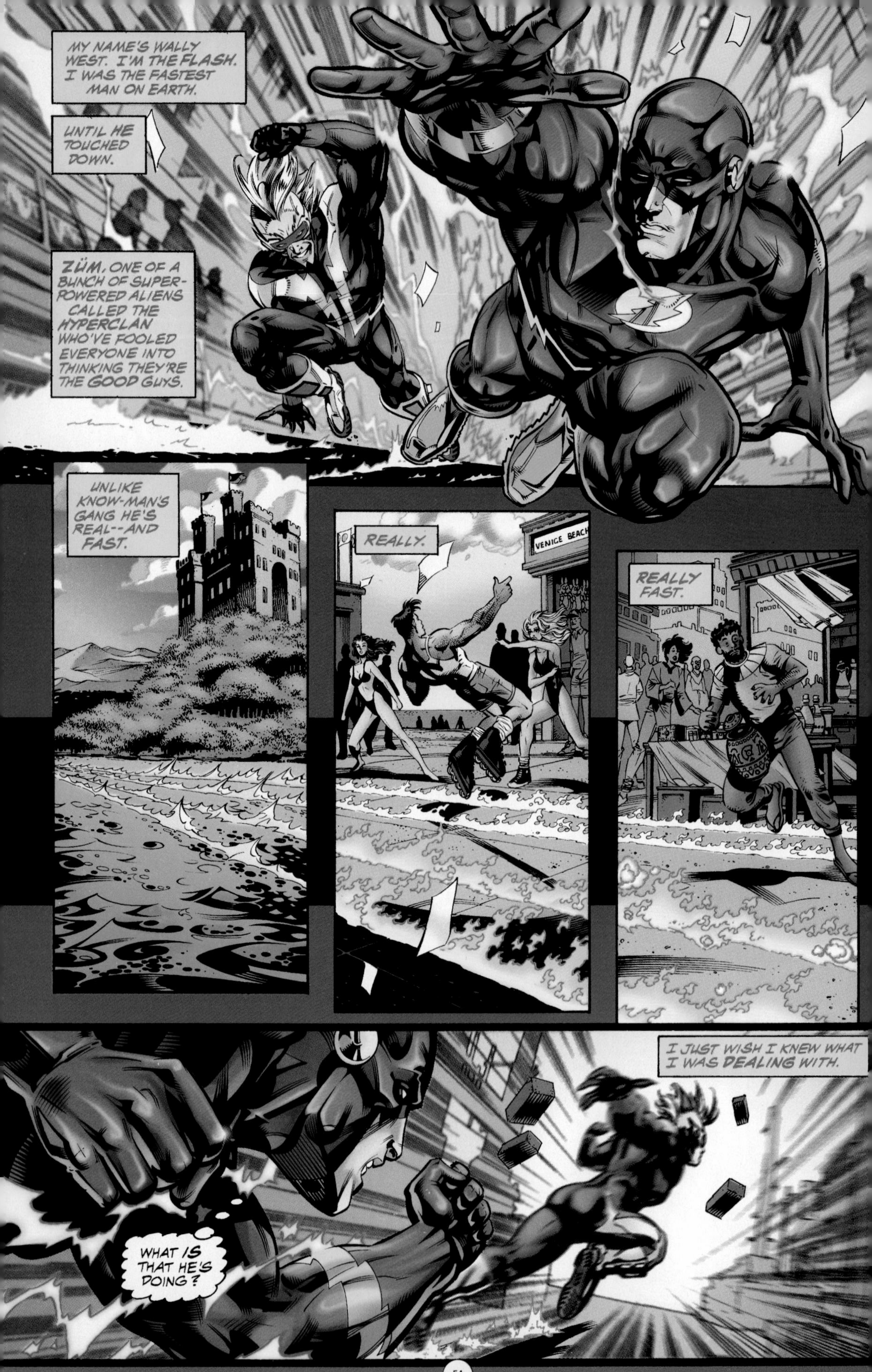
MY NAME'S WALLY WEST. I'M THE FLASH. I WAS THE FASTEST MAN ON EARTH.
UNTIL HE TOUCHED DOWN.
ZÜM, ONE OF A BUNCH OF SUPER-POWERED ALIENS CALLED THE HYPERCLAN WHO'VE FOOLED EVERYONE INTO THINKING THEY'RE THE GOOD GUYS.
UNLIKE KNOW-MAN'S GANG HE'S REAL--AND FAST.
REALLY.
VENICE BEACH
REALLY FAST.
I JUST WISH I KNEW WHAT I WAS DEALING WITH.
WHAT IS THAT HE'S DOING?

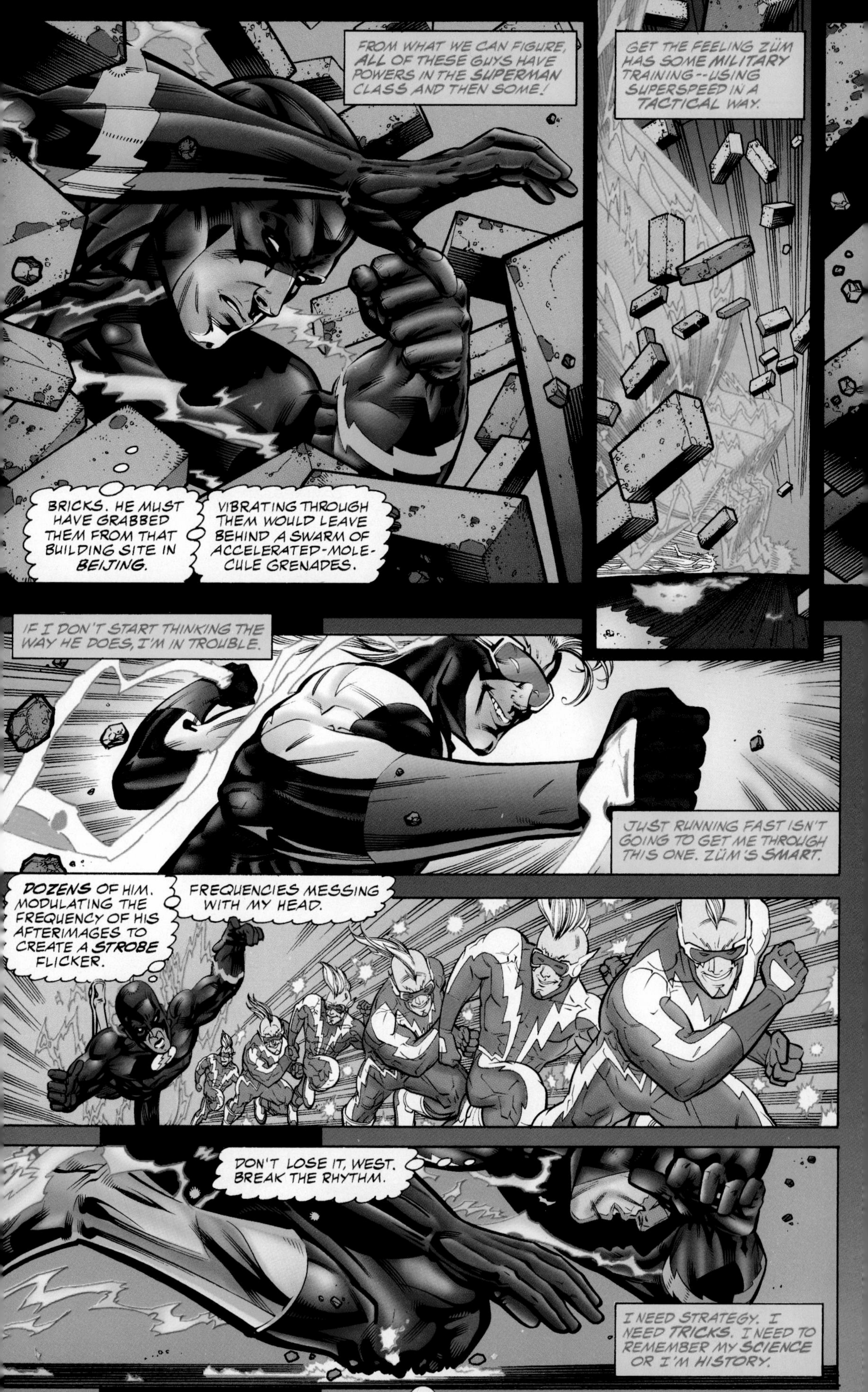
FROM WHAT WE CAN FIGURE, ALL OF THESE GUYS HAVE POWERS IN THE SUPERMAN CLASS AND THEN SOME!
GET THE FEELING ZÜM HAS SOME MILITARY TRAINING--USING SUPERSPEED IN A TACTICAL WAY.
BRICKS. HE MUST HAVE GRABBED THEM FROM THAT BUILDING SITE IN BEIJING.
VIBRATING THROUGH THEM WOULD LEAVE BEHIND A SWARM OF ACCELERATED-MOLECULE GRENADES.
IF I DON'T START THINKING THE WAY HE DOES, I'M IN TROUBLE.
JUST RUNNING FAST ISN'T GOING TO GET ME THROUGH THIS ONE. ZÜM'S SMART.
DOZENS OF HIM. MODULATING THE FREQUENCY OF HIS AFTERIMAGES TO CREATE A STROBE FLICKER.
FREQUENCIES MESSING WITH MY HEAD.
DON'T LOSE IT, WEST. BREAK THE RHYTHM.
I NEED STRATEGY. I NEED TRICKS. I NEED TO REMEMBER MY SCIENCE OR I'M HISTORY.

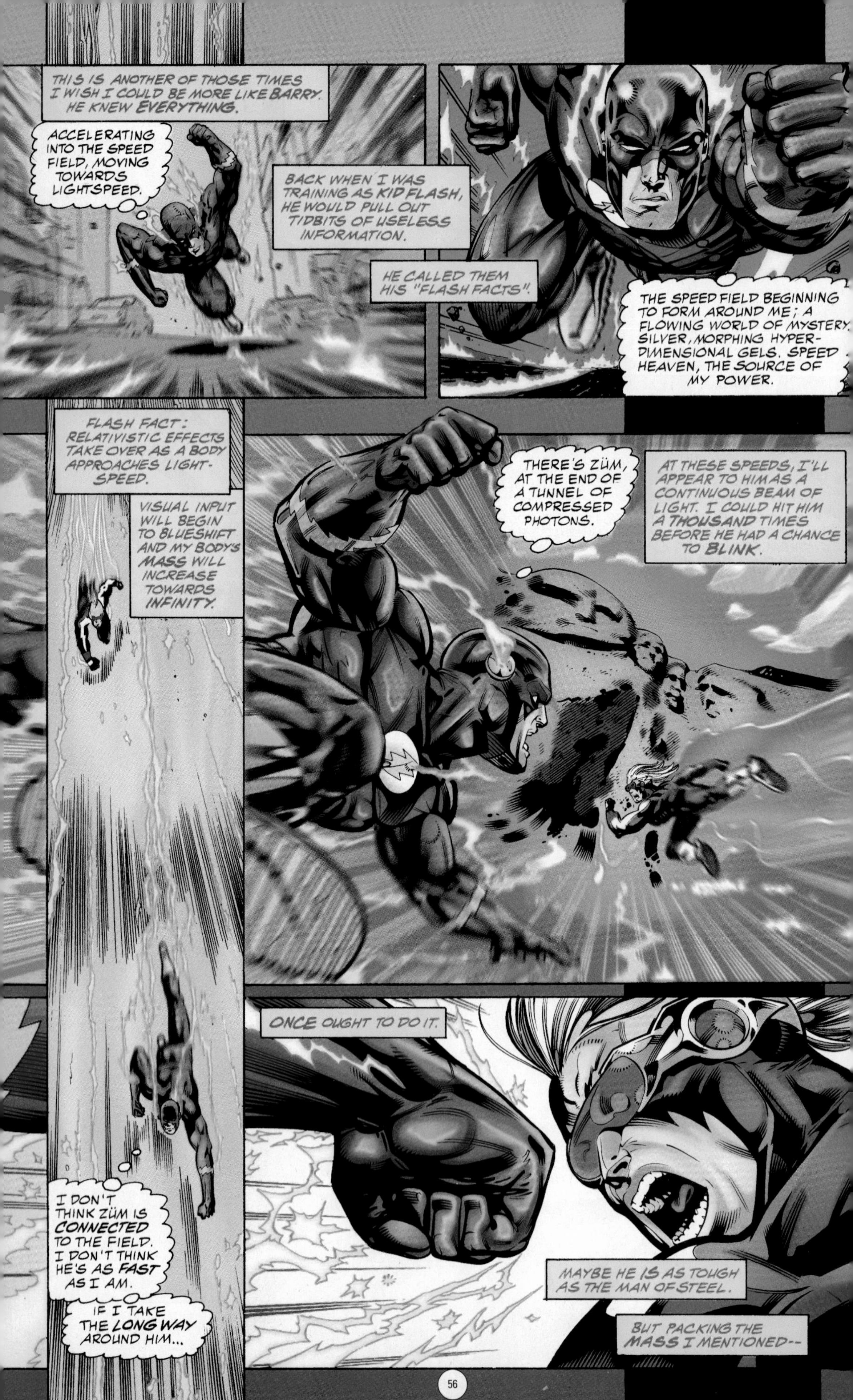

THIS IS ANOTHER OF THOSE TIMES I WISH I COULD BE MORE LIKE BARRY. HE KNEW EVERYTHING.
ACCELERATING INTO THE SPEED FIELD, MOVING TOWARDS LIGHTSPEED.
BACK WHEN I WAS TRAINING AS KID FLASH, HE WOULD PULL OUT TIDBITS OF USELESS INFORMATION.
HE CALLED THEM HIS "FLASH FACTS".
THE SPEED FIELD BEGINNING TO FORM AROUND ME; A FLOWING WORLD OF MYSTERY. SILVER, MORPHING HYPER-DIMENSIONAL GELS. SPEED HEAVEN, THE SOURCE OF MY POWER.
FLASH FACT: RELATIVISTIC EFFECTS TAKE OVER AS A BODY APPROACHES LIGHT-SPEED.
VISUAL INPUT WILL BEGIN TO BLUESHIFT AND MY BODY'S MASS WILL INCREASE TOWARDS INFINITY.
THERE'S ZÜM, AT THE END OF A TUNNEL OF COMPRESSED PHOTONS.
AT THESE SPEEDS, I'LL APPEAR TO HIM AS A CONTINUOUS BEAM OF LIGHT. I COULD HIT HIM A THOUSAND TIMES BEFORE HE HAD A CHANCE TO BLINK.
I DON'T THINK ZÜM IS CONNECTED TO THE FIELD. I DON'T THINK HE'S AS FAST AS I AM.
IF I TAKE THE LONG WAY AROUND HIM...
ONCE OUGHT TO DO IT.
MAYBE HE IS AS TOUGH AS THE MAN OF STEEL.
BUT PACKING THE MASS I MENTIONED--

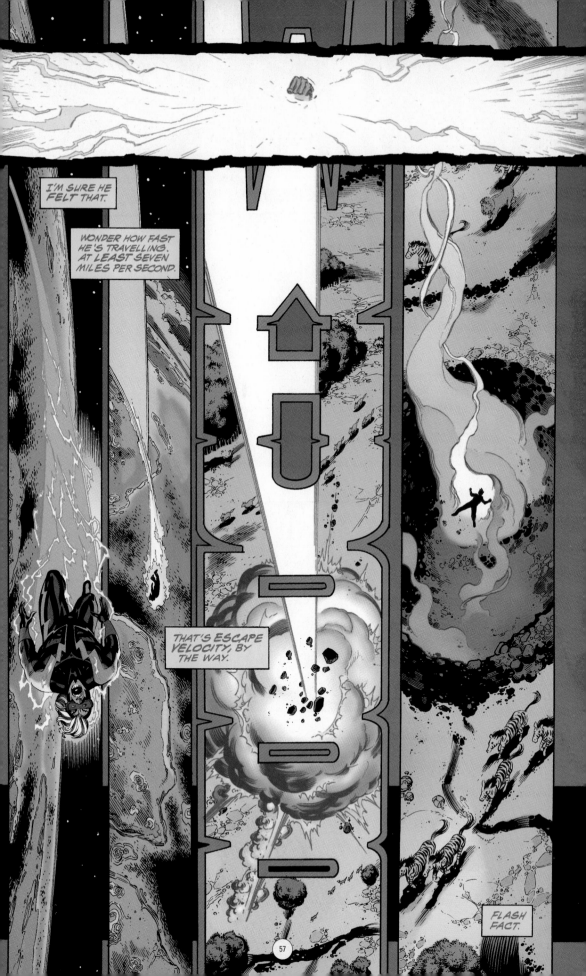

I'M SURE HE FELT THAT.

WONDER HOW FAST HE'S TRAVELLING. AT LEAST SEVEN MILES PER SECOND.

THAT'S ESCAPE VELOCITY, BY THE WAY.

FLASH FACT.

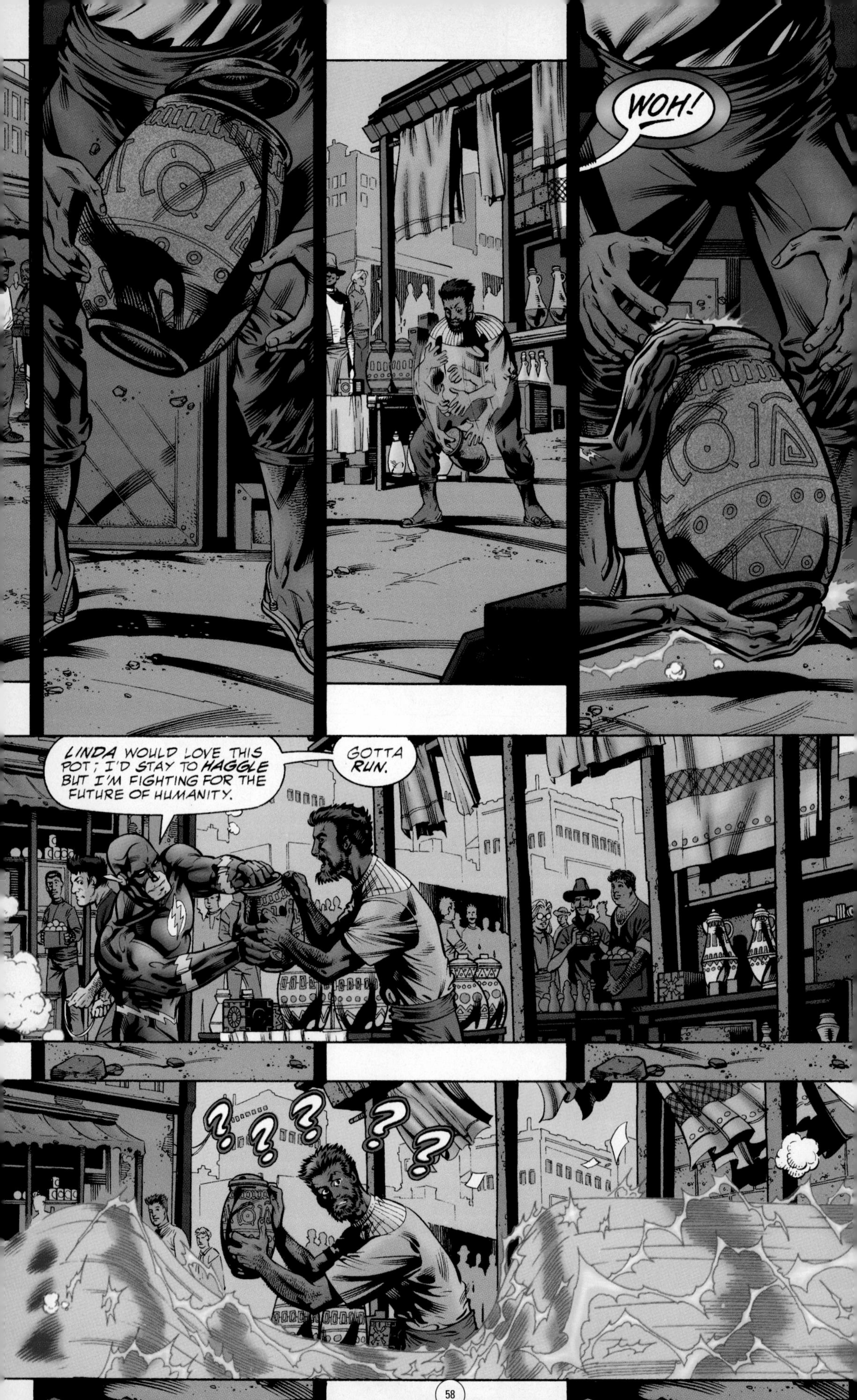
WOH!
LINDA WOULD LOVE THIS POT; I'D STAY TO HAGGLE BUT I'M FIGHTING FOR THE FUTURE OF HUMANITY.
GOTTA RUN.
? ? ? ? ?

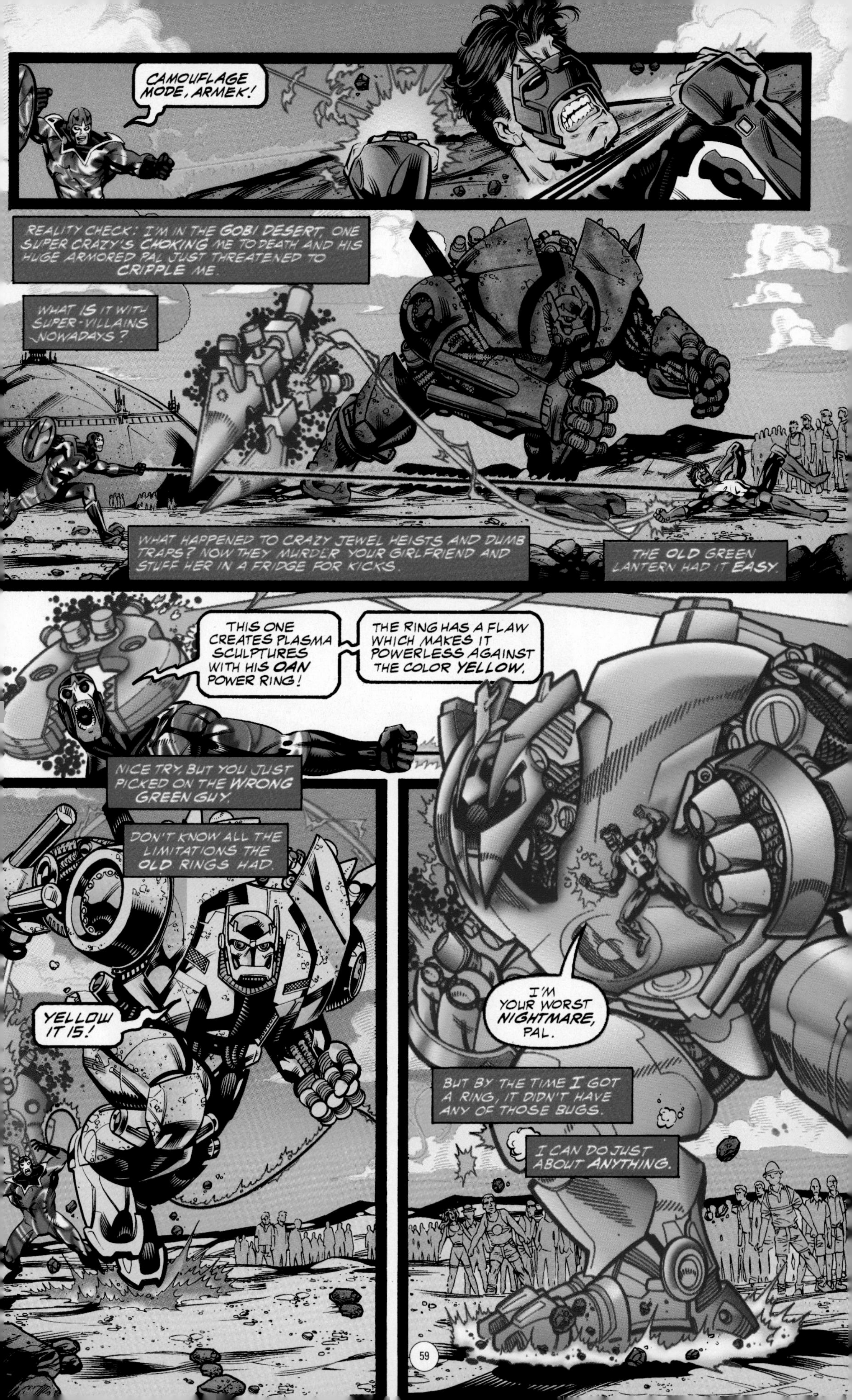
CAMOUFLAGE MODE, ARMEK!
REALITY CHECK: I'M IN THE GOBI DESERT, ONE SUPER CRAZY'S CHOKING ME TO DEATH AND HIS HUGE ARMORED PAL JUST THREATENED TO CRIPPLE ME.
WHAT IS IT WITH SUPER-VILLAINS NOWADAYS?
WHAT HAPPENED TO CRAZY JEWEL HEISTS AND DUMB TRAPS? NOW THEY MURDER YOUR GIRLFRIEND AND STUFF HER IN A FRIDGE FOR KICKS.
THE OLD GREEN LANTERN HAD IT EASY.
THIS ONE CREATES PLASMA SCULPTURES WITH HIS OAN POWER RING!
THE RING HAS A FLAW WHICH MAKES IT POWERLESS AGAINST THE COLOR YELLOW.
NICE TRY, BUT YOU JUST PICKED ON THE WRONG GREEN GUY.
DON'T KNOW ALL THE LIMITATIONS THE OLD RINGS HAD.
YELLOW IT IS!
I'M YOUR WORST NIGHTMARE, PAL.
BUT BY THE TIME I GOT A RING, IT DIDN'T HAVE ANY OF THOSE BUGS.
I CAN DO JUST ABOUT ANYTHING.

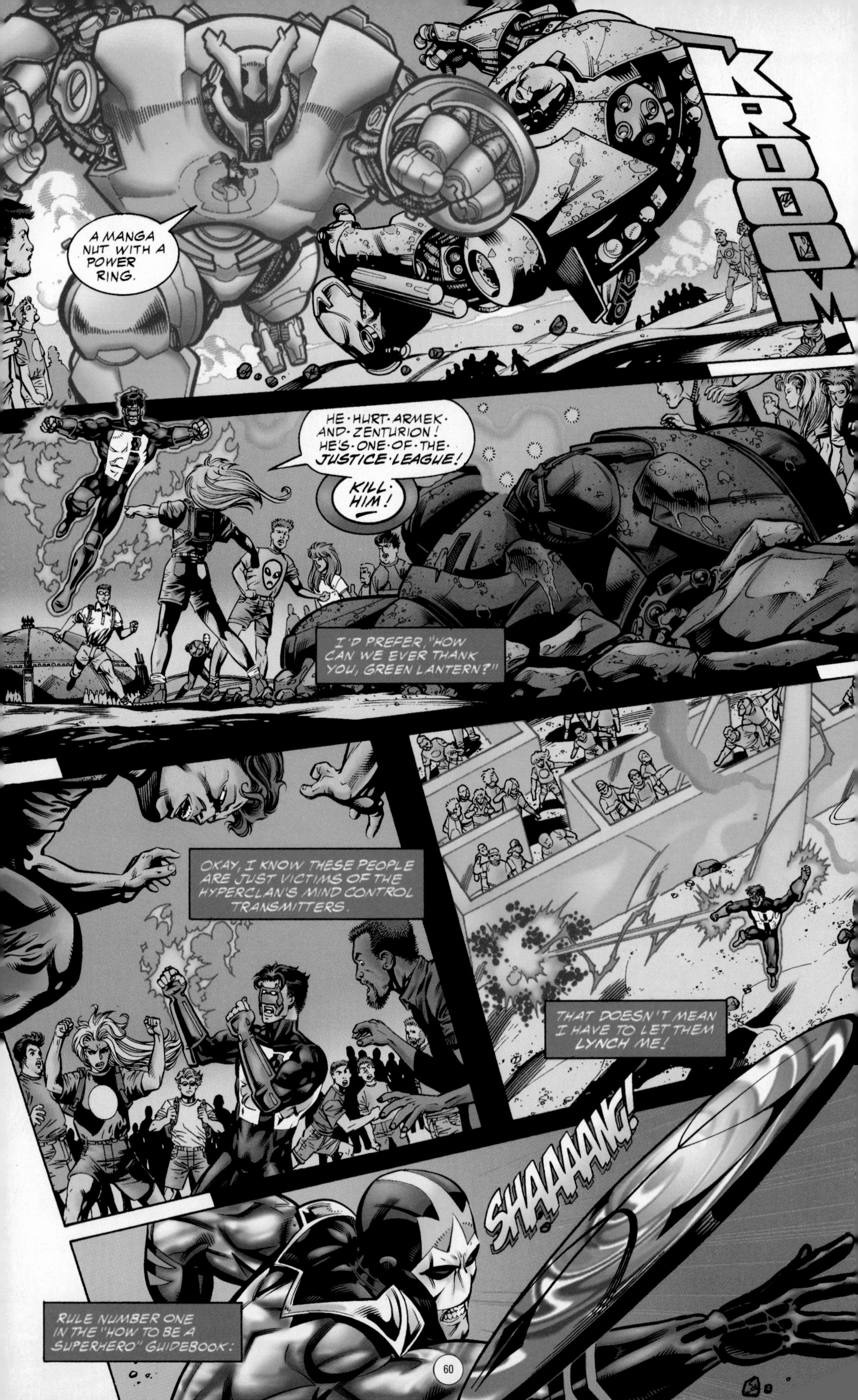
A MANGA NUT WITH A POWER RING.
KROOOM
HE·HURT·ARMEK· AND·ZENTURION! HE'S·ONE·OF·THE· JUSTICE·LEAGUE!
KILL· HIM!
I'D PREFER, "HOW CAN WE EVER THANK YOU, GREEN LANTERN?"
OKAY, I KNOW THESE PEOPLE ARE JUST VICTIMS OF THE HYPERCLAN'S MIND CONTROL TRANSMITTERS.
THAT DOESN'T MEAN I HAVE TO LET THEM LYNCH ME!
SHAAAANG!
RULE NUMBER ONE IN THE "HOW TO BE A SUPERHERO" GUIDEBOOK:

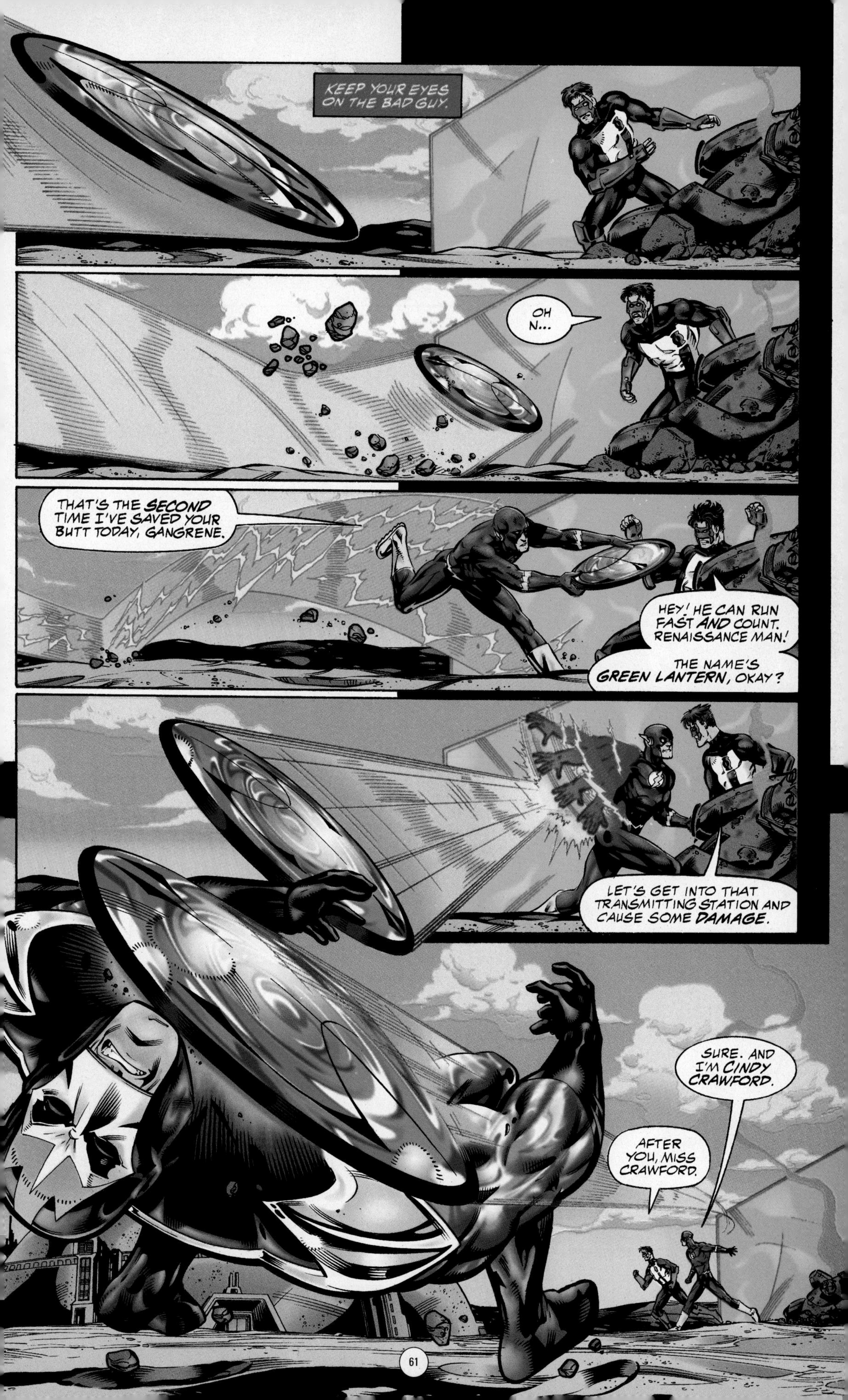
KEEP YOUR EYES ON THE BAD GUY.
OH N...
THAT'S THE SECOND TIME I'VE SAVED YOUR BUTT TODAY, GANGRENE.
HEY! HE CAN RUN FAST AND COUNT. RENAISSANCE MAN!
THE NAME'S GREEN LANTERN, OKAY?
LET'S GET INTO THAT TRANSMITTING STATION AND CAUSE SOME DAMAGE.
SURE. AND I'M CINDY CRAWFORD.
AFTER YOU, MISS CRAWFORD.

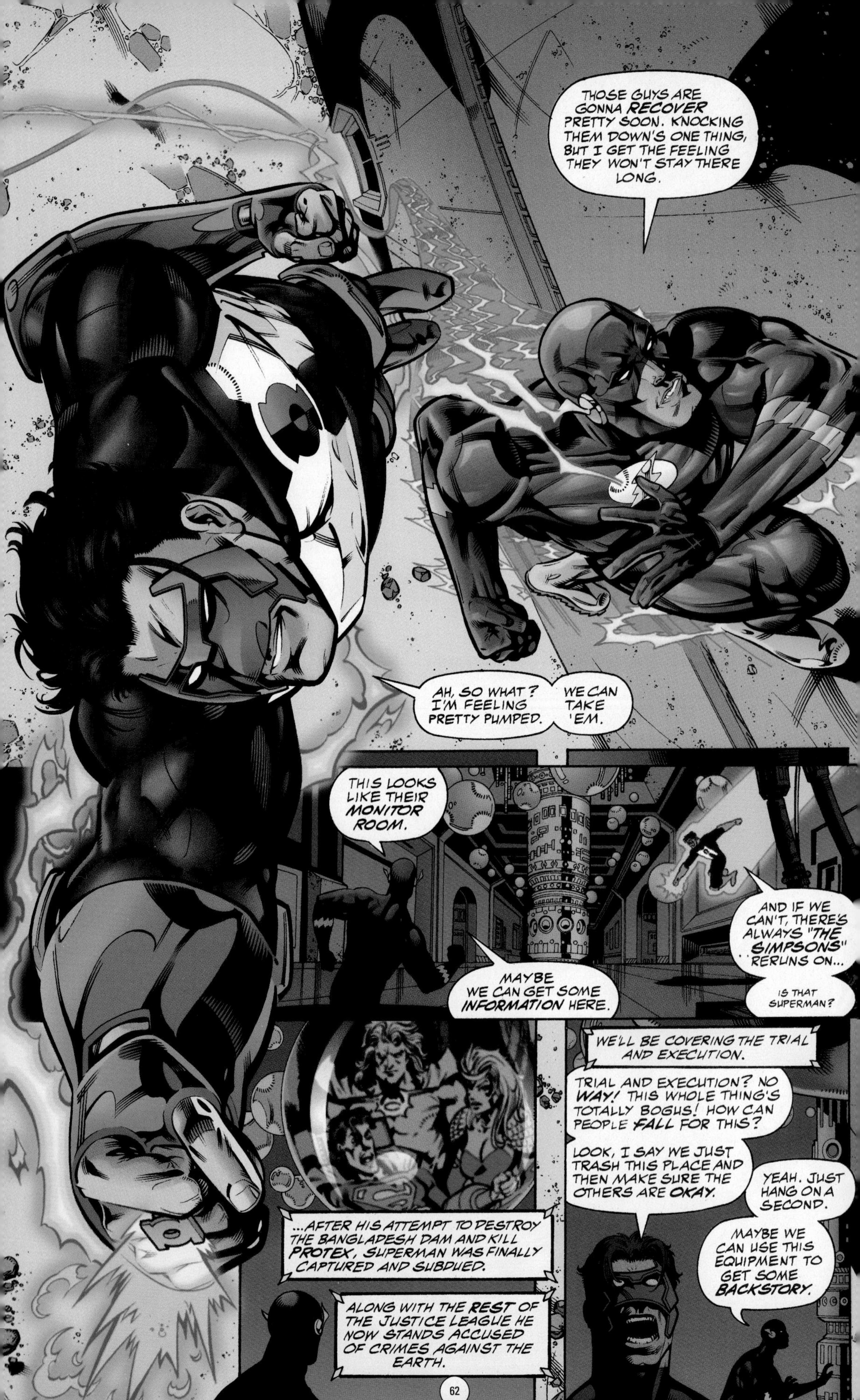
THOSE GUYS ARE GONNA RECOVER PRETTY SOON. KNOCKING THEM DOWN'S ONE THING, BUT I GET THE FEELING THEY WON'T STAY THERE LONG.
AH, SO WHAT? I'M FEELING PRETTY PUMPED.
WE CAN TAKE 'EM.
THIS LOOKS LIKE THEIR MONITOR ROOM.
MAYBE WE CAN GET SOME INFORMATION HERE.
AND IF WE CAN'T, THERE'S ALWAYS "THE SIMPSONS" RERUNS ON...
IS THAT SUPERMAN?
...AFTER HIS ATTEMPT TO DESTROY THE BANGLADESH DAM AND KILL PROTEX, SUPERMAN WAS FINALLY CAPTURED AND SUBDUED.
ALONG WITH THE REST OF THE JUSTICE LEAGUE HE NOW STANDS ACCUSED OF CRIMES AGAINST THE EARTH.
WE'LL BE COVERING THE TRIAL AND EXECUTION.
TRIAL AND EXECUTION? NO WAY! THIS WHOLE THING'S TOTALLY BOGUS! HOW CAN PEOPLE FALL FOR THIS?
LOOK, I SAY WE JUST TRASH THIS PLACE AND THEN MAKE SURE THE OTHERS ARE OKAY.
YEAH. JUST HANG ON A SECOND.
MAYBE WE CAN USE THIS EQUIPMENT TO GET SOME BACKSTORY.

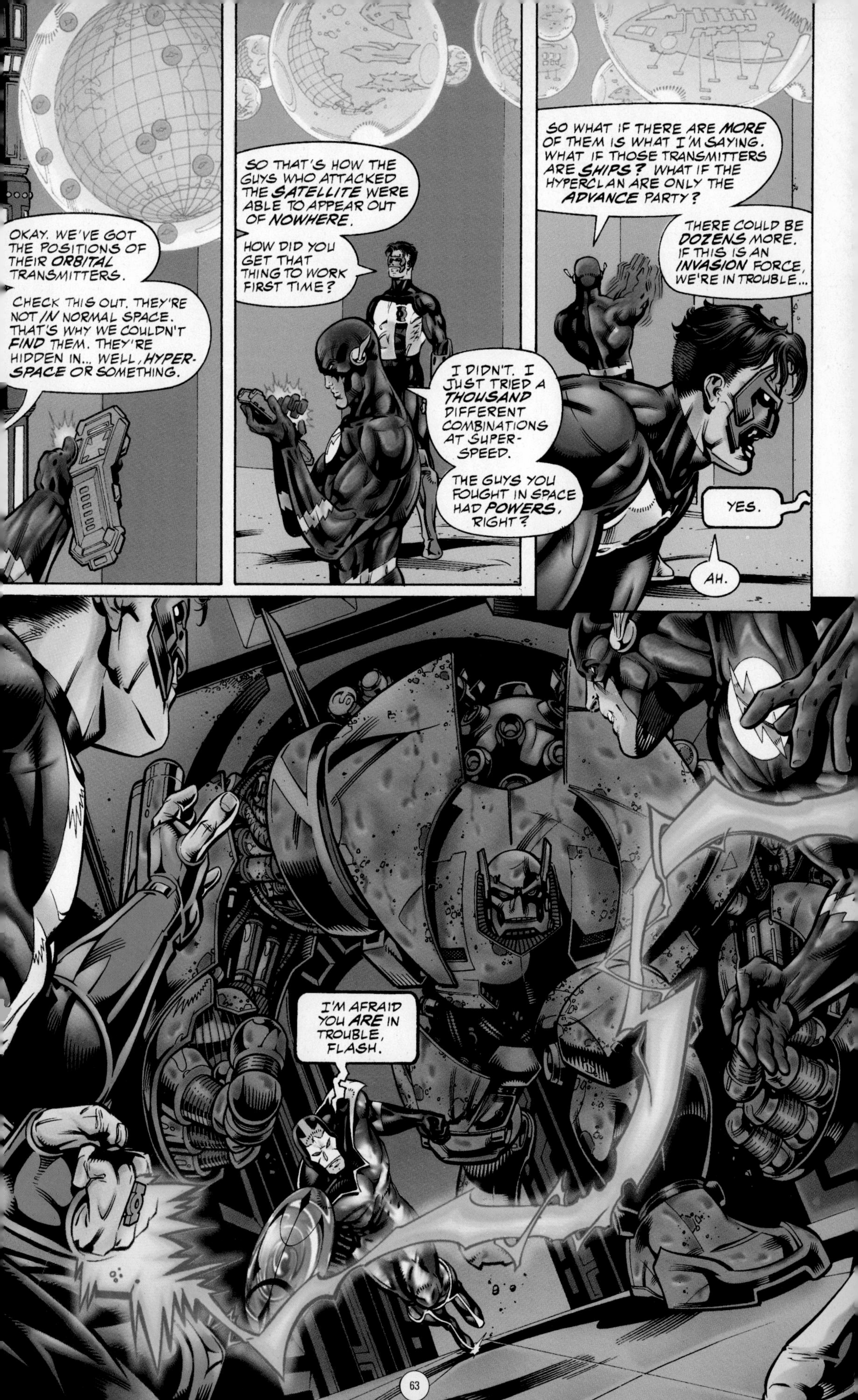
OKAY. WE'VE GOT THE POSITIONS OF THEIR ORBITAL TRANSMITTERS.
CHECK THIS OUT. THEY'RE NOT IN NORMAL SPACE. THAT'S WHY WE COULDN'T FIND THEM. THEY'RE HIDDEN IN... WELL, HYPER-SPACE OR SOMETHING.
SO THAT'S HOW THE GUYS WHO ATTACKED THE SATELLITE WERE ABLE TO APPEAR OUT OF NOWHERE.
HOW DID YOU GET THAT THING TO WORK FIRST TIME?
I DIDN'T. I JUST TRIED A THOUSAND DIFFERENT COMBINATIONS AT SUPER-SPEED.
THE GUYS YOU FOUGHT IN SPACE HAD POWERS, RIGHT?
SO WHAT IF THERE ARE MORE OF THEM IS WHAT I'M SAYING. WHAT IF THOSE TRANSMITTERS ARE SHIPS? WHAT IF THE HYPERCLAN ARE ONLY THE ADVANCE PARTY?
THERE COULD BE DOZENS MORE. IF THIS IS AN INVASION FORCE, WE'RE IN TROUBLE...
YES.
AH.
I'M AFRAID YOU ARE IN TROUBLE, FLASH.

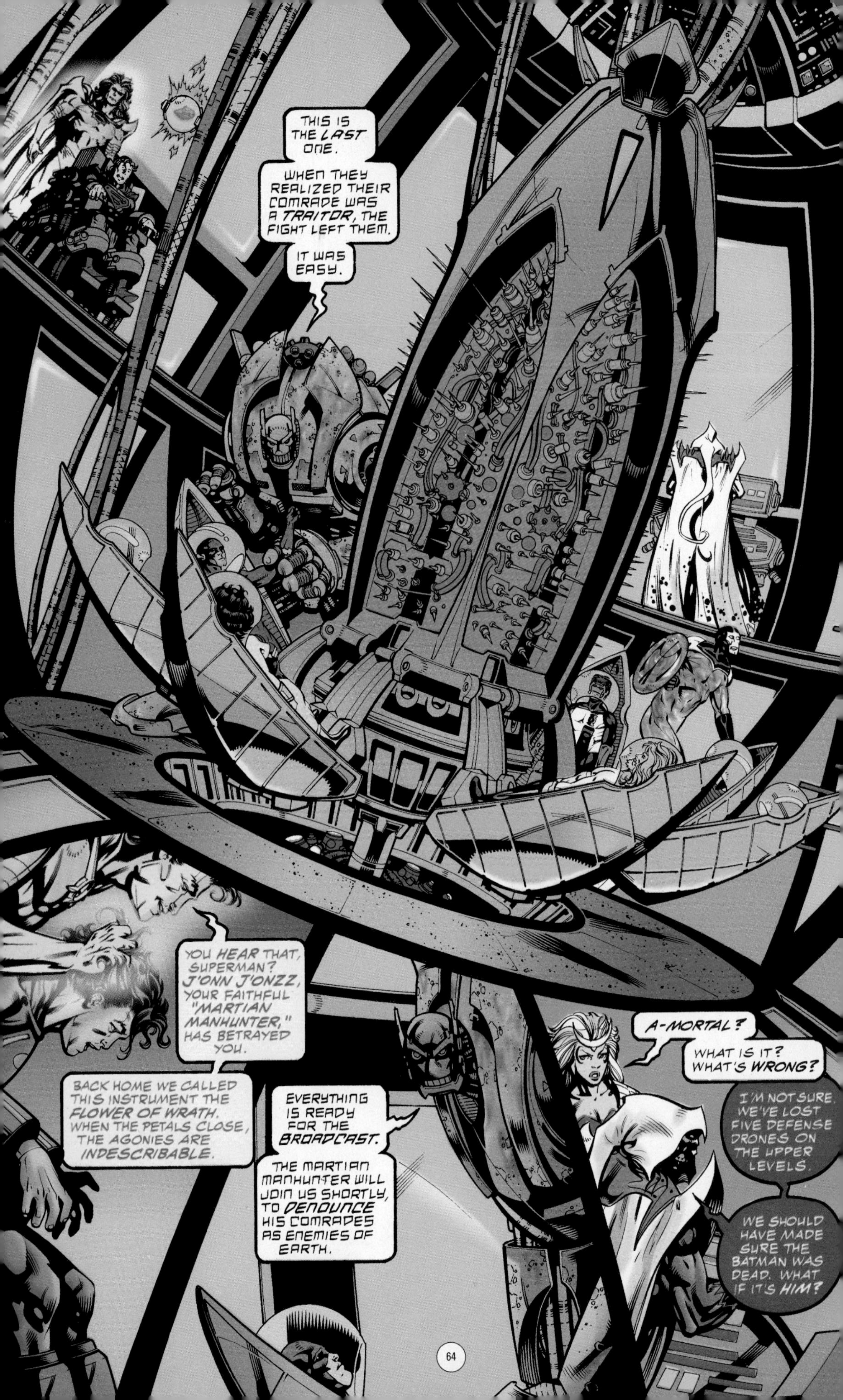
THIS IS THE LAST ONE.
WHEN THEY REALIZED THEIR COMRADE WAS A TRAITOR, THE FIGHT LEFT THEM.
IT WAS EASY.
YOU HEAR THAT, SUPERMAN? J'ONN J'ONZZ, YOUR FAITHFUL "MARTIAN MANHUNTER," HAS BETRAYED YOU.
BACK HOME WE CALLED THIS INSTRUMENT THE FLOWER OF WRATH. WHEN THE PETALS CLOSE, THE AGONIES ARE INDESCRIBABLE.
EVERYTHING IS READY FOR THE BROADCAST.
THE MARTIAN MANHUNTER WILL JOIN US SHORTLY, TO DENOUNCE HIS COMRADES AS ENEMIES OF EARTH.
A-MORTAL?
WHAT IS IT? WHAT'S WRONG?
I'M NOT SURE. WE'VE LOST FIVE DEFENSE DRONES ON THE UPPER LEVELS.
WE SHOULD HAVE MADE SURE THE BATMAN WAS DEAD. WHAT IF IT'S HIM?

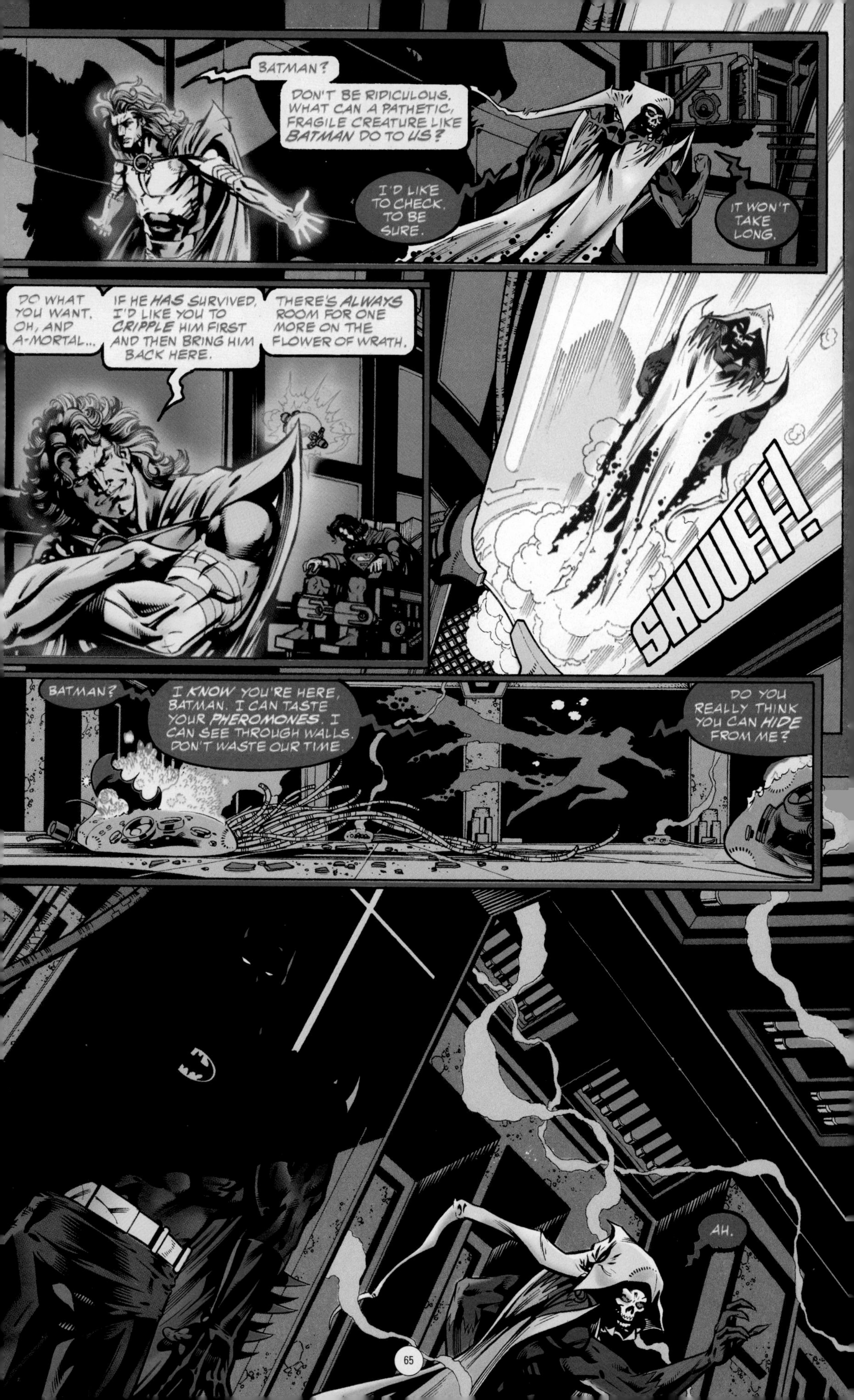
BATMAN?
DON'T BE RIDICULOUS. WHAT CAN A PATHETIC, FRAGILE CREATURE LIKE BATMAN DO TO US?
I'D LIKE TO CHECK, TO BE SURE.
IT WON'T TAKE LONG.
DO WHAT YOU WANT. OH, AND A-MORTAL...
IF HE HAS SURVIVED, I'D LIKE YOU TO CRIPPLE HIM FIRST AND THEN BRING HIM BACK HERE.
THERE'S ALWAYS ROOM FOR ONE MORE ON THE FLOWER OF WRATH.
SHUFF!
BATMAN?
I KNOW YOU'RE HERE, BATMAN. I CAN TASTE YOUR PHEROMONES. I CAN SEE THROUGH WALLS. DON'T WASTE OUR TIME.
DO YOU REALLY THINK YOU CAN HIDE FROM ME?
AH.

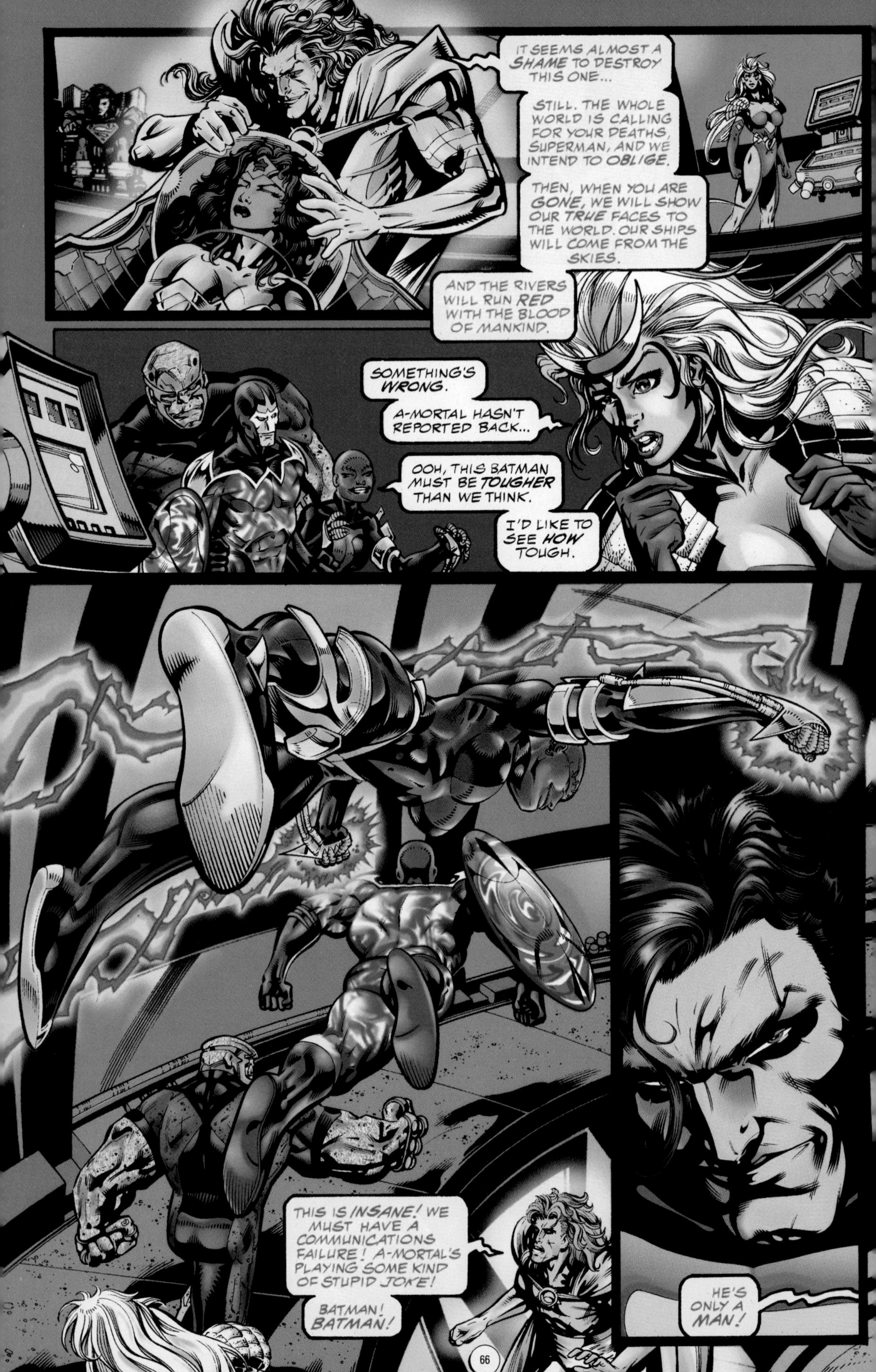

IT SEEMS ALMOST A SHAME TO DESTROY THIS ONE...
STILL. THE WHOLE WORLD IS CALLING FOR YOUR DEATHS, SUPERMAN, AND WE INTEND TO OBLIGE.
THEN, WHEN YOU ARE GONE, WE WILL SHOW OUR TRUE FACES TO THE WORLD. OUR SHIPS WILL COME FROM THE SKIES.
AND THE RIVERS WILL RUN RED WITH THE BLOOD OF MANKIND.
SOMETHING'S WRONG.
A-MORTAL HASN'T REPORTED BACK...
OOH, THIS BATMAN MUST BE TOUGHER THAN WE THINK.
I'D LIKE TO SEE HOW TOUGH.
THIS IS INSANE! WE MUST HAVE A COMMUNICATIONS FAILURE! A-MORTAL'S PLAYING SOME KIND OF STUPID JOKE!
BATMAN! BATMAN!
HE'S ONLY A MAN!

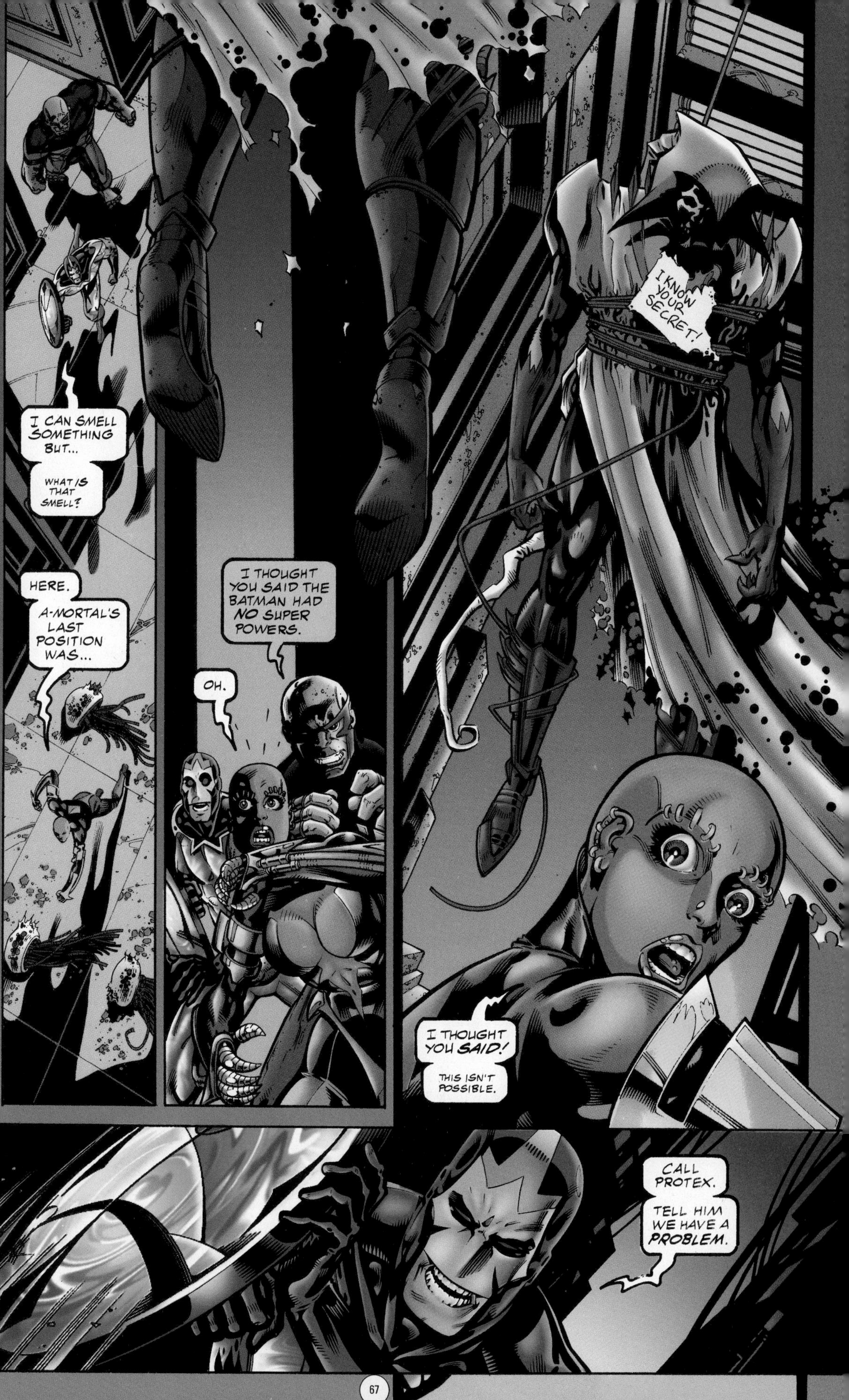

I KNOW YOUR SECRET!
I CAN SMELL SOMETHING BUT...
WHAT IS THAT SMELL?
HERE.
A-MORTAL'S LAST POSITION WAS...
I THOUGHT YOU SAID THE BATMAN HAD NO SUPER POWERS.
OH.
I THOUGHT YOU SAID!
THIS ISN'T POSSIBLE.
CALL PROTEX.
TELL HIM WE HAVE A PROBLEM.

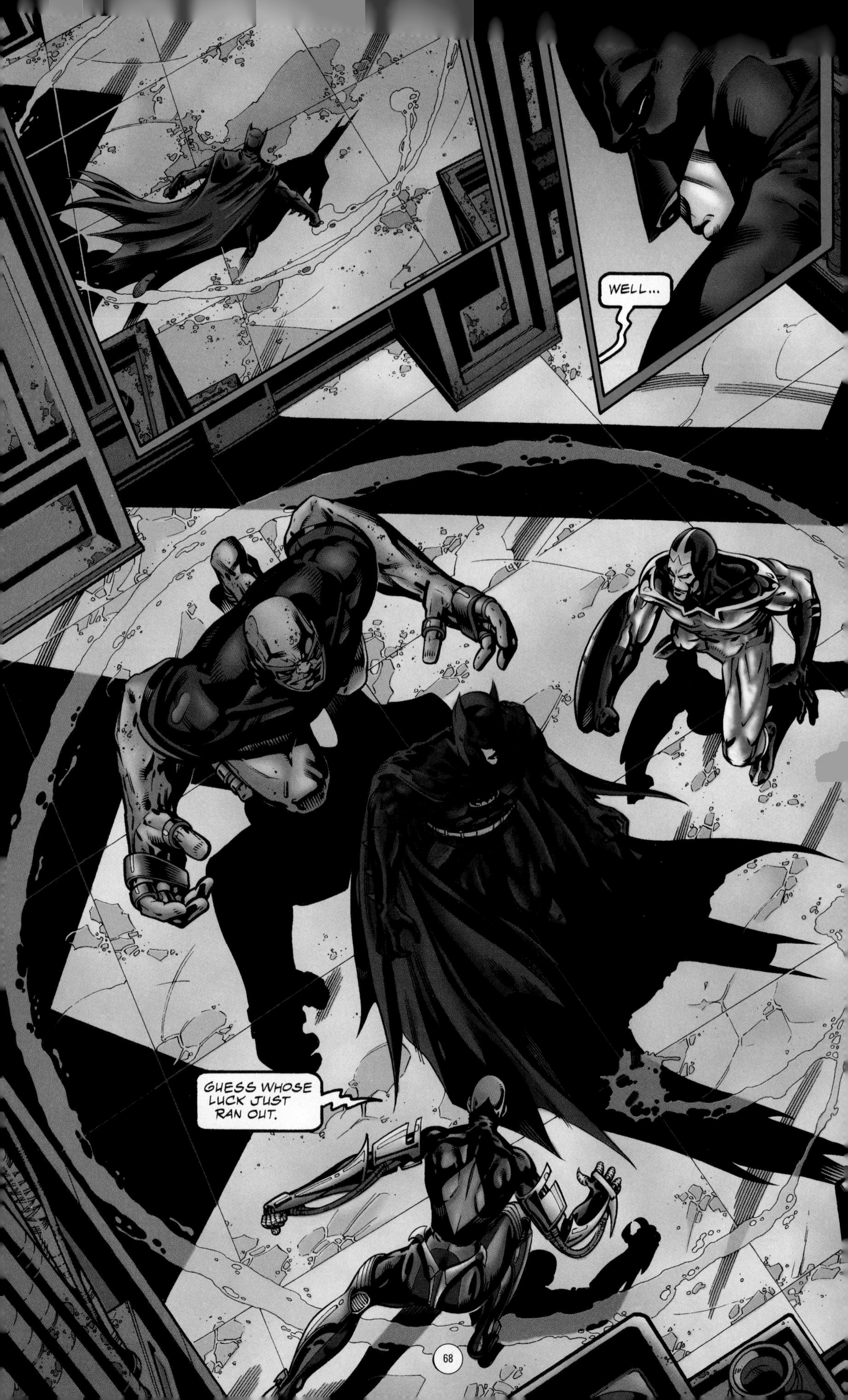
WELL...
GUESS WHOSE LUCK JUST RAN OUT.

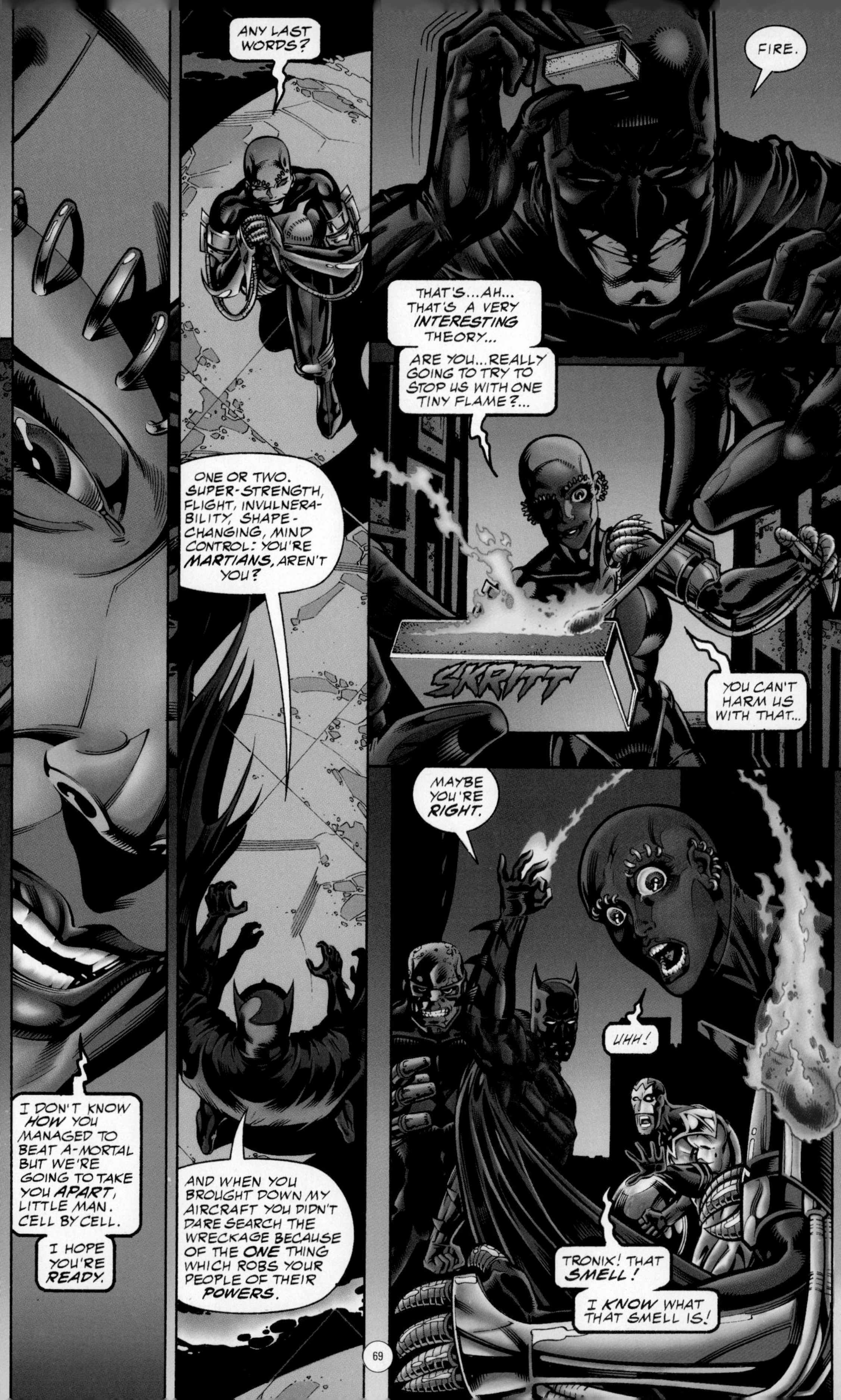
ANY LAST WORDS?
FIRE.
THAT'S...AH... THAT'S A VERY INTERESTING THEORY...
ARE YOU...REALLY GOING TO TRY TO STOP US WITH ONE TINY FLAME?...
ONE OR TWO. SUPER-STRENGTH, FLIGHT, INVULNERA-BILITY, SHAPE-CHANGING, MIND CONTROL: YOU'RE MARTIANS, AREN'T YOU?
SKRITT
YOU CAN'T HARM US WITH THAT...
I DON'T KNOW HOW YOU MANAGED TO BEAT A-MORTAL BUT WE'RE GOING TO TAKE YOU APART, LITTLE MAN. CELL BY CELL.
I HOPE YOU'RE READY.
AND WHEN YOU BROUGHT DOWN MY AIRCRAFT YOU DIDN'T DARE SEARCH THE WRECKAGE BECAUSE OF THE ONE THING WHICH ROBS YOUR PEOPLE OF THEIR POWERS.
MAYBE YOU'RE RIGHT.
UHH!
TRONIX! THAT SMELL!
I KNOW WHAT THAT SMELL IS!

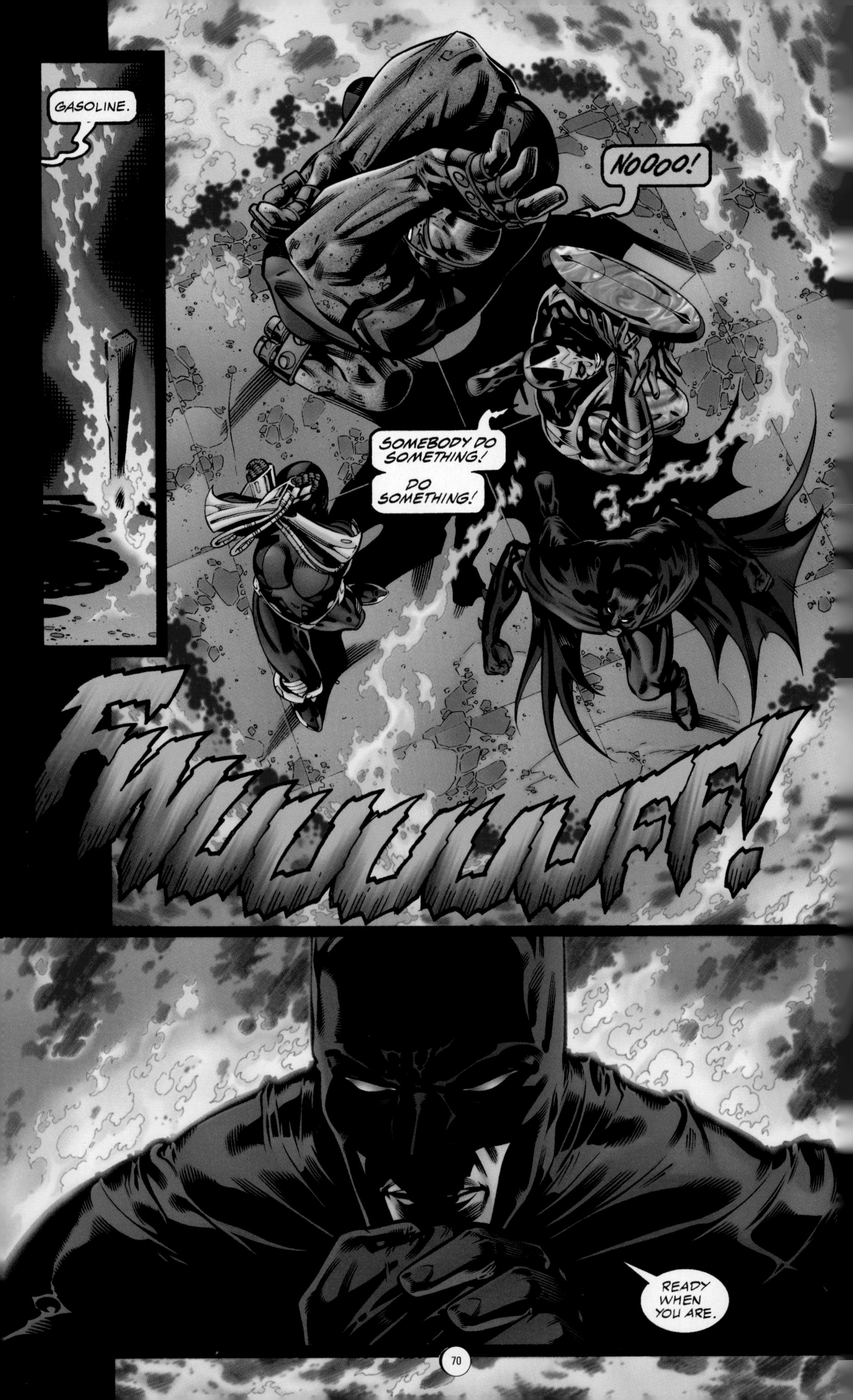
GASOLINE.
NOOOO!
SOMEBODY DO SOMETHING!
DO SOMETHING!
FWUUUUFF!
READY WHEN YOU ARE.

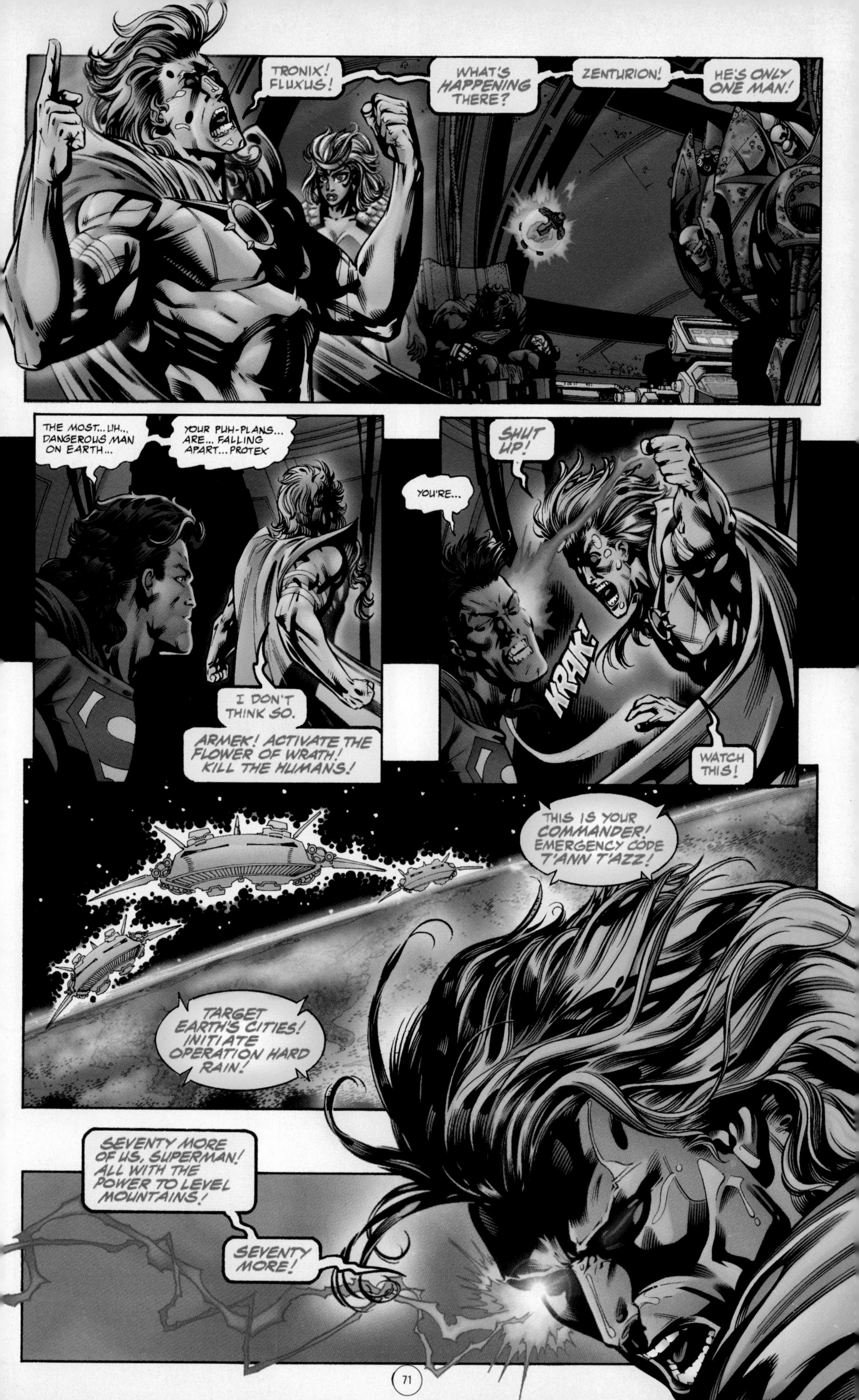
TRONIX! FLUXUS!
WHAT'S HAPPENING THERE?
ZENTURION!
HE'S ONLY ONE MAN!
THE MOST... UH... DANGEROUS MAN ON EARTH...
YOUR PUH-PLANS... ARE... FALLING APART... PROTEX
I DON'T THINK SO.
ARMEK! ACTIVATE THE FLOWER OF WRATH! KILL THE HUMANS!
SHUT UP!
YOU'RE...
KRAK!
WATCH THIS!
THIS IS YOUR COMMANDER! EMERGENCY CODE T'ANN T'AZZ!
TARGET EARTH'S CITIES! INITIATE OPERATION HARD RAIN!
SEVENTY MORE OF US, SUPERMAN! ALL WITH THE POWER TO LEVEL MOUNTAINS!
SEVENTY MORE!

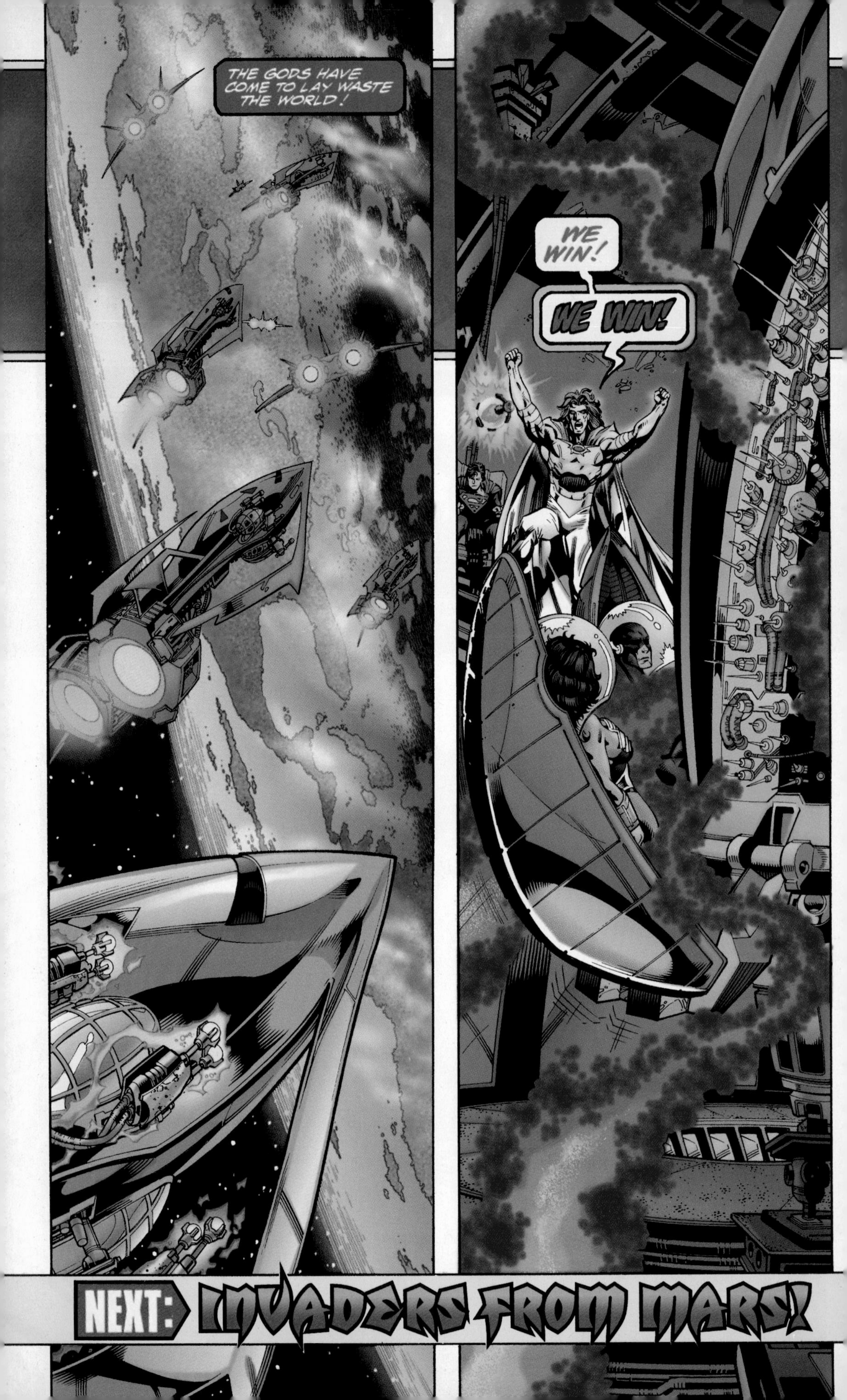
THE GODS HAVE COME TO LAY WASTE THE WORLD!
WE WIN!
WE WIN!
NEXT: INVADERS FROM MARS!

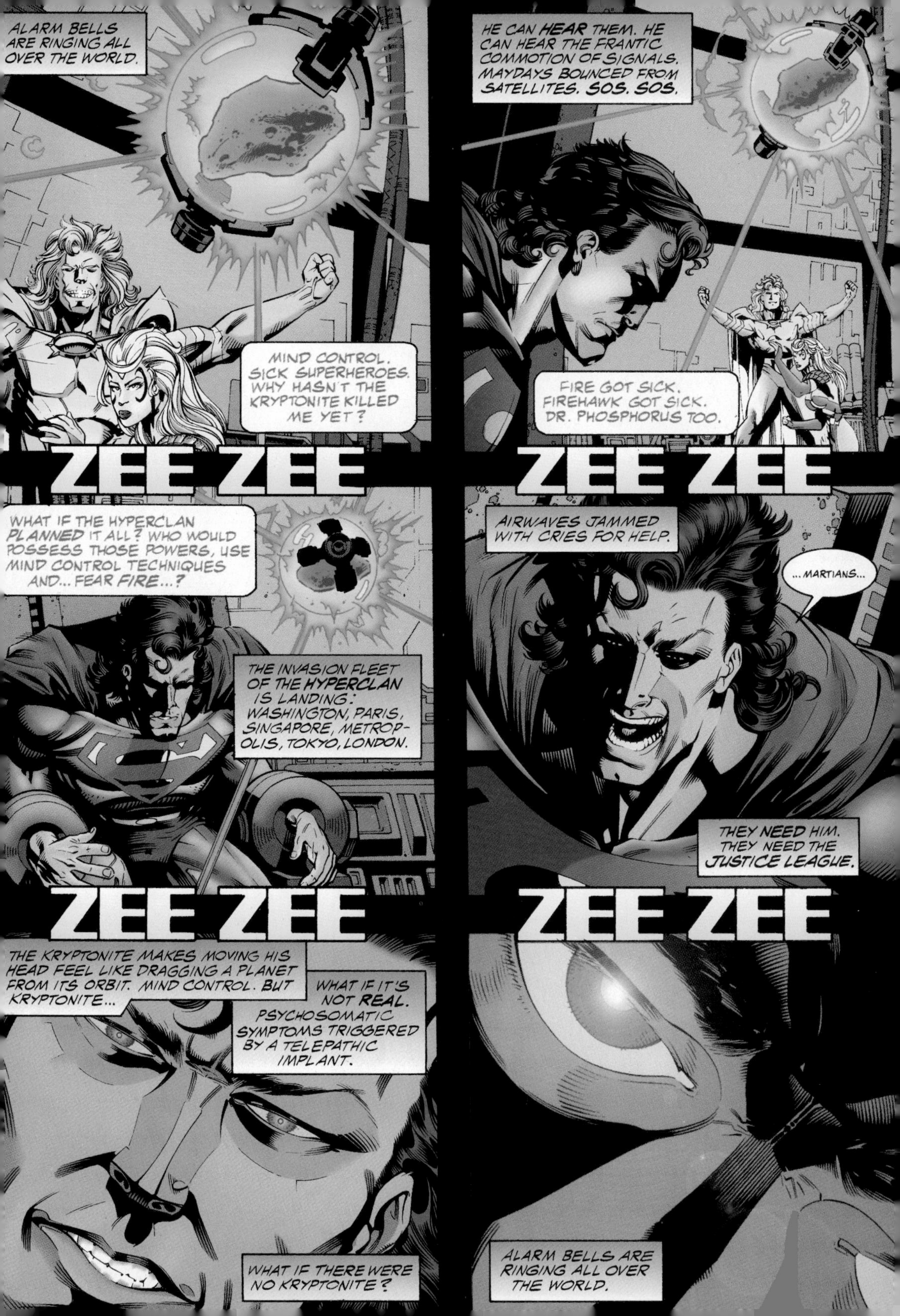
ALARM BELLS ARE RINGING ALL OVER THE WORLD.
MIND CONTROL. SICK SUPERHEROES. WHY HASN'T THE KRYPTONITE KILLED ME YET?
HE CAN HEAR THEM. HE CAN HEAR THE FRANTIC COMMOTION OF SIGNALS. MAYDAYS BOUNCED FROM SATELLITES. SOS. SOS.
FIRE GOT SICK. FIREHAWK GOT SICK. DR. PHOSPHORUS TOO.
ZEE ZEE
ZEE ZEE
WHAT IF THE HYPERCLAN PLANNED IT ALL? WHO WOULD POSSESS THOSE POWERS, USE MIND CONTROL TECHNIQUES AND... FEAR FIRE...?
THE INVASION FLEET OF THE HYPERCLAN IS LANDING: WASHINGTON, PARIS, SINGAPORE, METROPOLIS, TOKYO, LONDON.
AIRWAVES JAMMED WITH CRIES FOR HELP.
...MARTIANS...
THEY NEED HIM. THEY NEED THE JUSTICE LEAGUE.
ZEE ZEE
ZEE ZEE
THE KRYPTONITE MAKES MOVING HIS HEAD FEEL LIKE DRAGGING A PLANET FROM ITS ORBIT. MIND CONTROL. BUT KRYPTONITE...
WHAT IF IT'S NOT REAL. PSYCHOSOMATIC SYMPTOMS TRIGGERED BY A TELEPATHIC IMPLANT.
WHAT IF THERE WERE NO KRYPTONITE?
ALARM BELLS ARE RINGING ALL OVER THE WORLD.

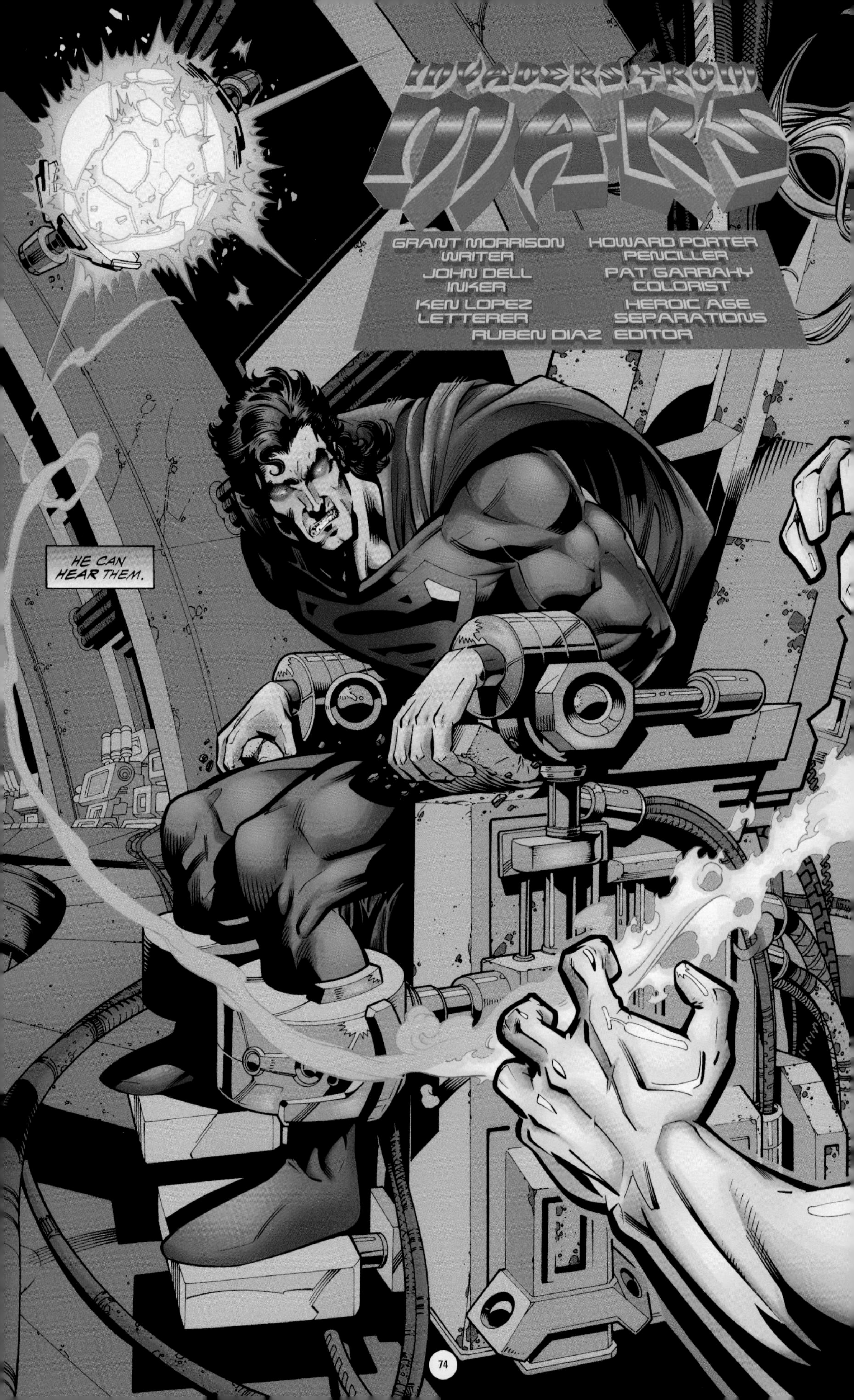
INVADERS FROM
MARS
GRANT MORRISON WRITER
HOWARD PORTER PENCILLER
JOHN DELL INKER
PAT GARRAHY COLORIST
KEN LOPEZ LETTERER
HEROIC AGE SEPARATIONS
RUBEN DIAZ EDITOR
HE CAN HEAR THEM.

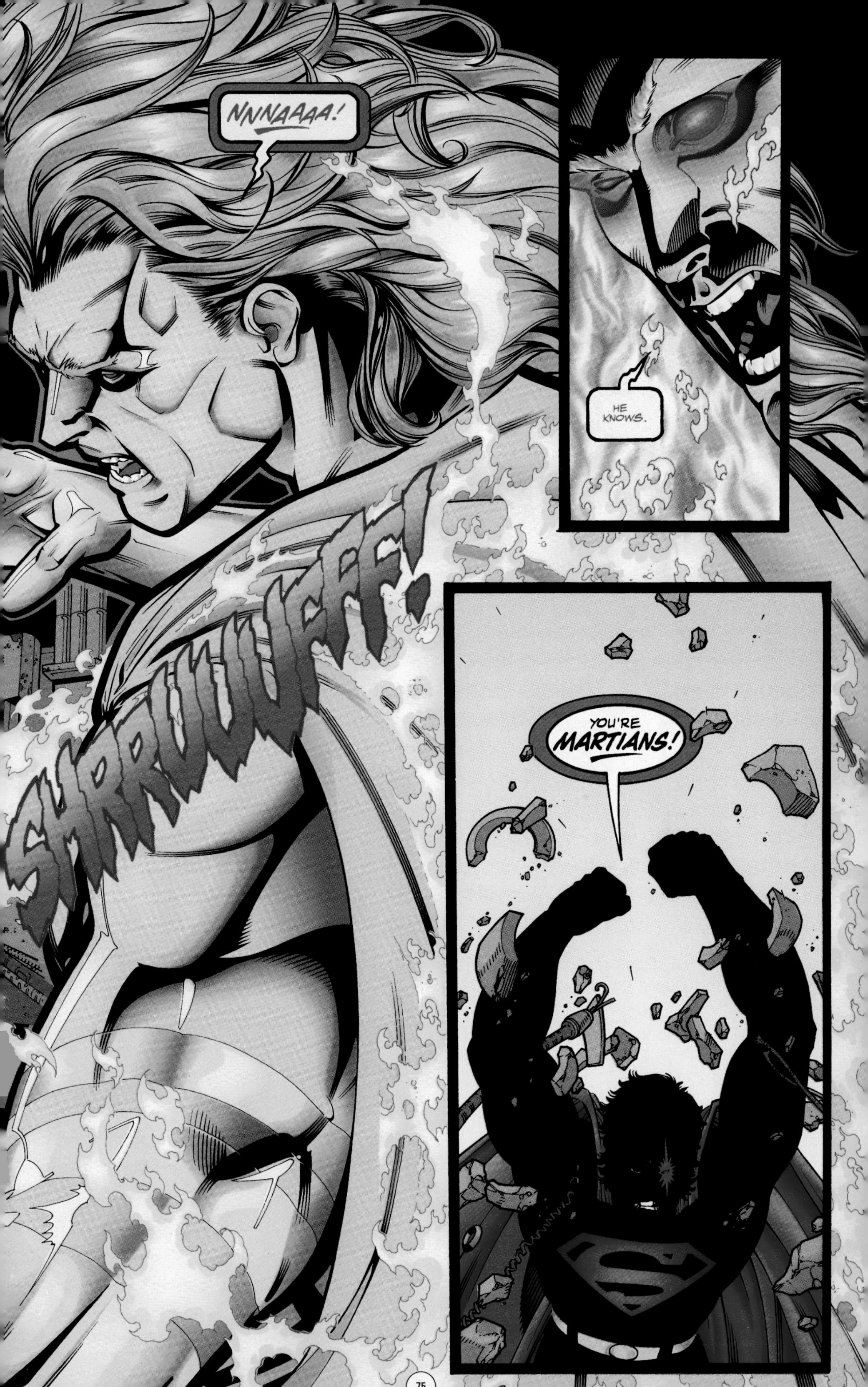
NNNAAAA!
HE KNOWS.
SHRRUUUUFFF!
YOU'RE MARTIANS!

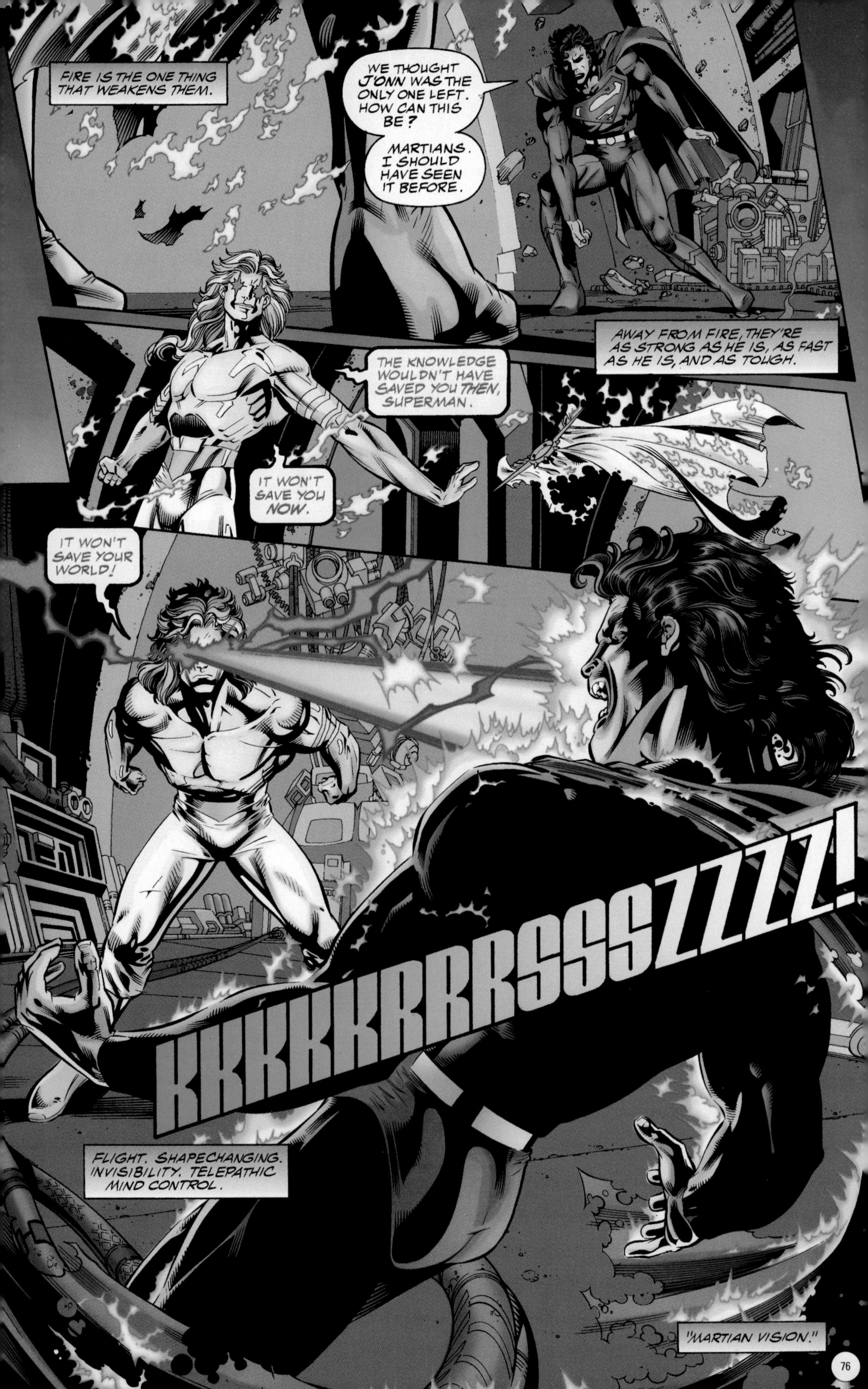
FIRE IS THE ONE THING THAT WEAKENS THEM.
WE THOUGHT J'ONN WAS THE ONLY ONE LEFT. HOW CAN THIS BE?
MARTIANS. I SHOULD HAVE SEEN IT BEFORE.
AWAY FROM FIRE, THEY'RE AS STRONG AS HE IS, AS FAST AS HE IS, AND AS TOUGH.
THE KNOWLEDGE WOULDN'T HAVE SAVED YOU THEN, SUPERMAN.
IT WON'T SAVE YOU NOW.
IT WON'T SAVE YOUR WORLD!
KKKKKRRRRSSSSZZZZ!
FLIGHT. SHAPECHANGING. INVISIBILITY. TELEPATHIC MIND CONTROL.
"MARTIAN VISION."

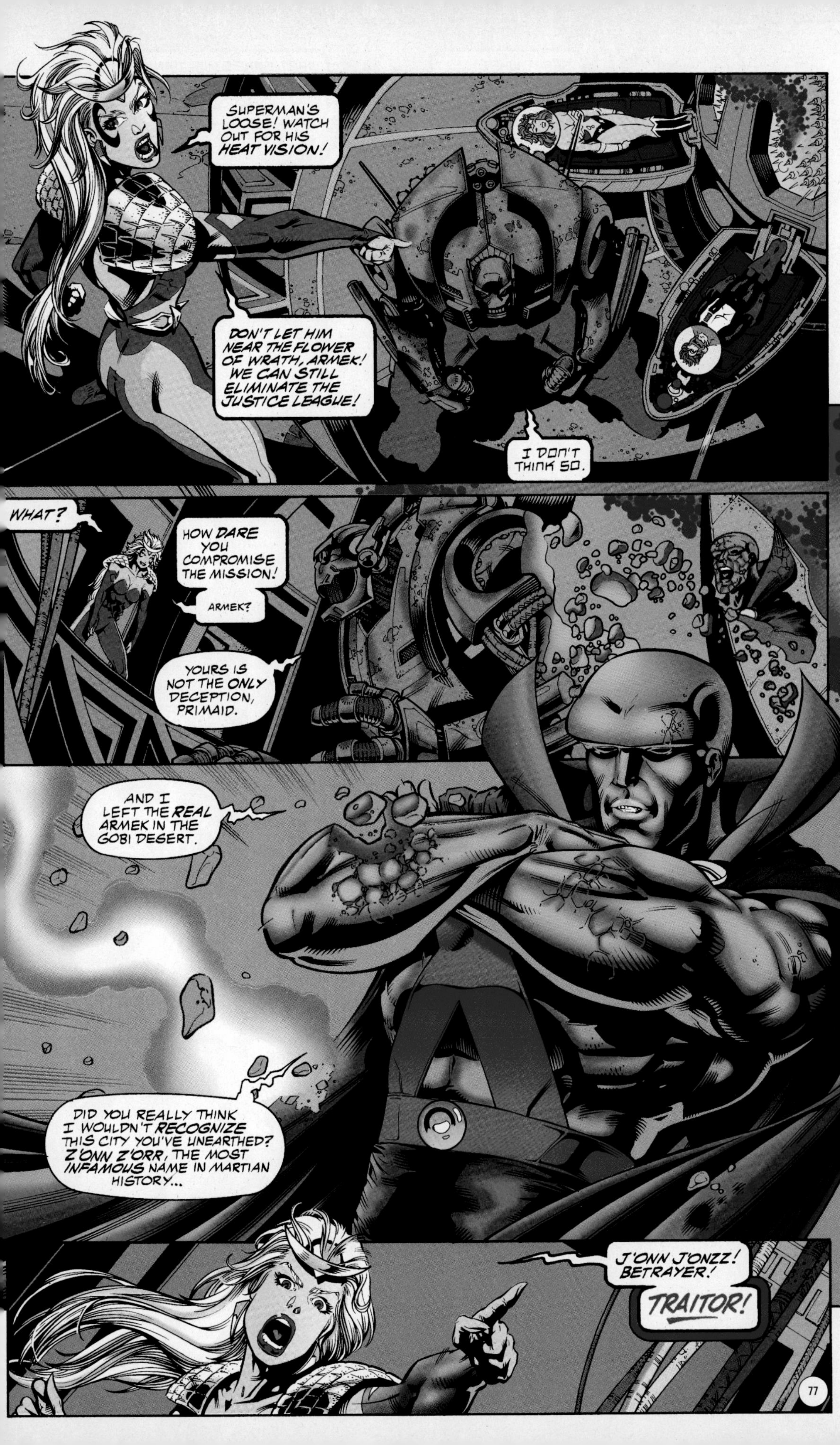
SUPERMAN'S LOOSE! WATCH OUT FOR HIS HEAT VISION!
DON'T LET HIM NEAR THE FLOWER OF WRATH, ARMEK! WE CAN STILL ELIMINATE THE JUSTICE LEAGUE!
I DON'T THINK SO.
WHAT?
HOW DARE YOU COMPROMISE THE MISSION!
ARMEK?
YOURS IS NOT THE ONLY DECEPTION, PRIMAID.
AND I LEFT THE REAL ARMEK IN THE GOBI DESERT.
DID YOU REALLY THINK I WOULDN'T RECOGNIZE THIS CITY YOU'VE UNEARTHED? Z'ONN Z'ORR, THE MOST INFAMOUS NAME IN MARTIAN HISTORY...
J'ONN J'ONZZ! BETRAYER!
TRAITOR!

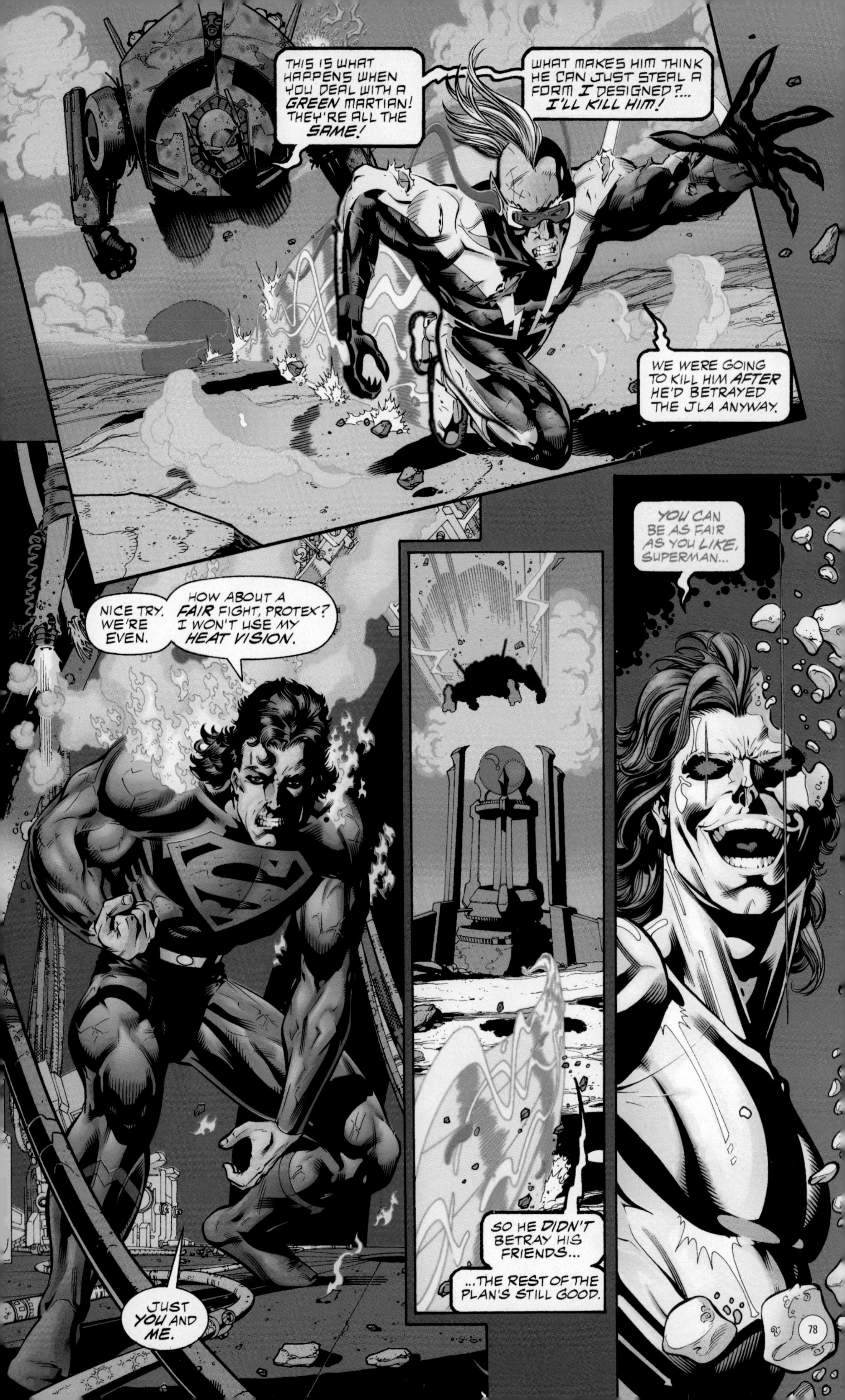

THIS IS WHAT HAPPENS WHEN YOU DEAL WITH A GREEN MARTIAN! THEY'RE ALL THE SAME!
WHAT MAKES HIM THINK HE CAN JUST STEAL A FORM I DESIGNED?... I'LL KILL HIM!
WE WERE GOING TO KILL HIM AFTER HE'D BETRAYED THE JLA ANYWAY.
NICE TRY. WE'RE EVEN.
HOW ABOUT A FAIR FIGHT, PROTEX? I WON'T USE MY HEAT VISION.
JUST YOU AND ME.
SO HE DIDN'T BETRAY HIS FRIENDS...
...THE REST OF THE PLAN'S STILL GOOD.
YOU CAN BE AS FAIR AS YOU LIKE, SUPERMAN...

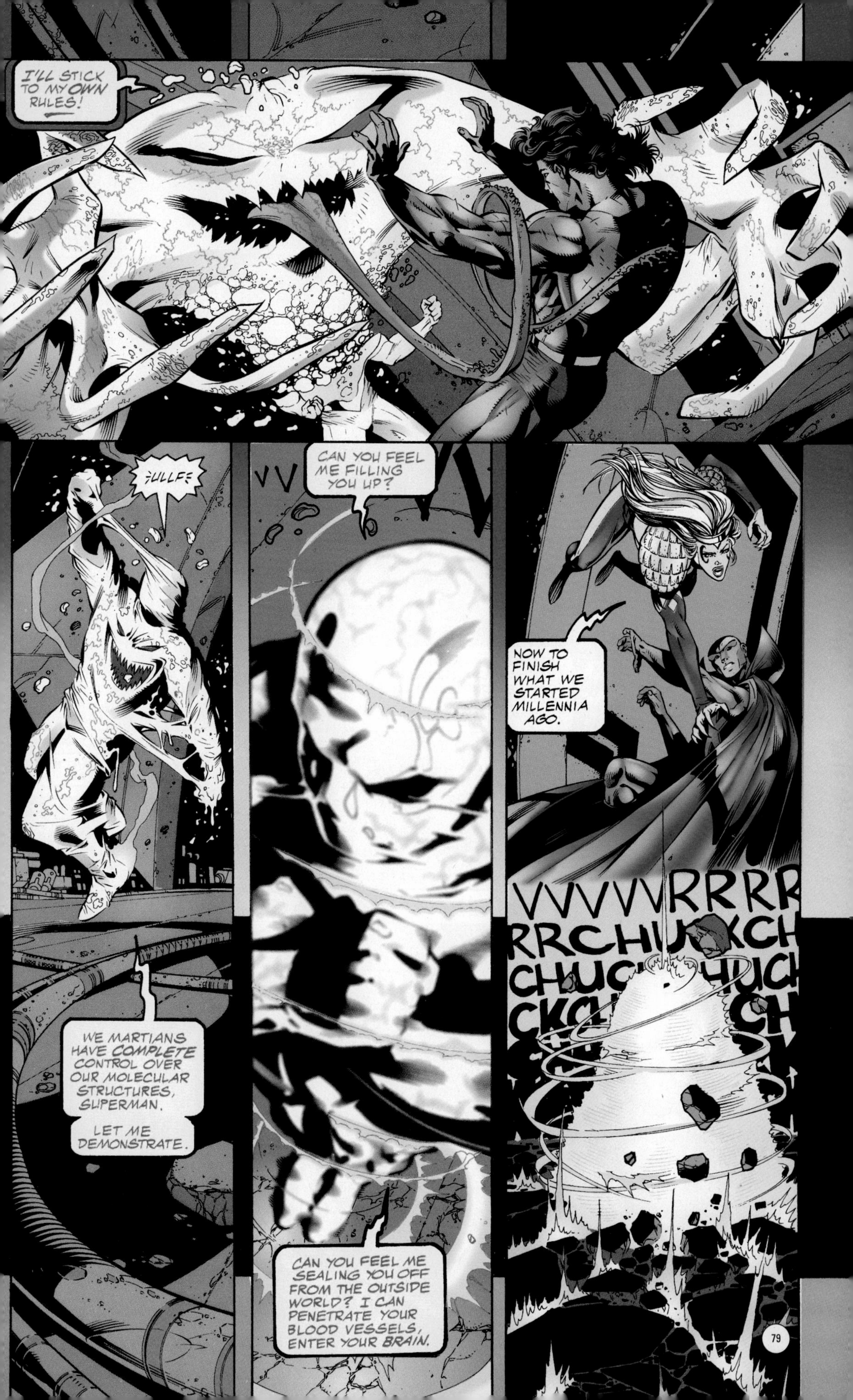
I'LL STICK TO MY OWN RULES!
ЉULLF≥
VV
CAN YOU FEEL ME FILLING YOU UP?
NOW TO FINISH WHAT WE STARTED MILLENNIA AGO.
WE MARTIANS HAVE COMPLETE CONTROL OVER OUR MOLECULAR STRUCTURES, SUPERMAN.
LET ME DEMONSTRATE.
CAN YOU FEEL ME SEALING YOU OFF FROM THE OUTSIDE WORLD? I CAN PENETRATE YOUR BLOOD VESSELS, ENTER YOUR BRAIN.
VVVVVVRRRR RRCHUCKCH CHUCHUCK CKCH CH

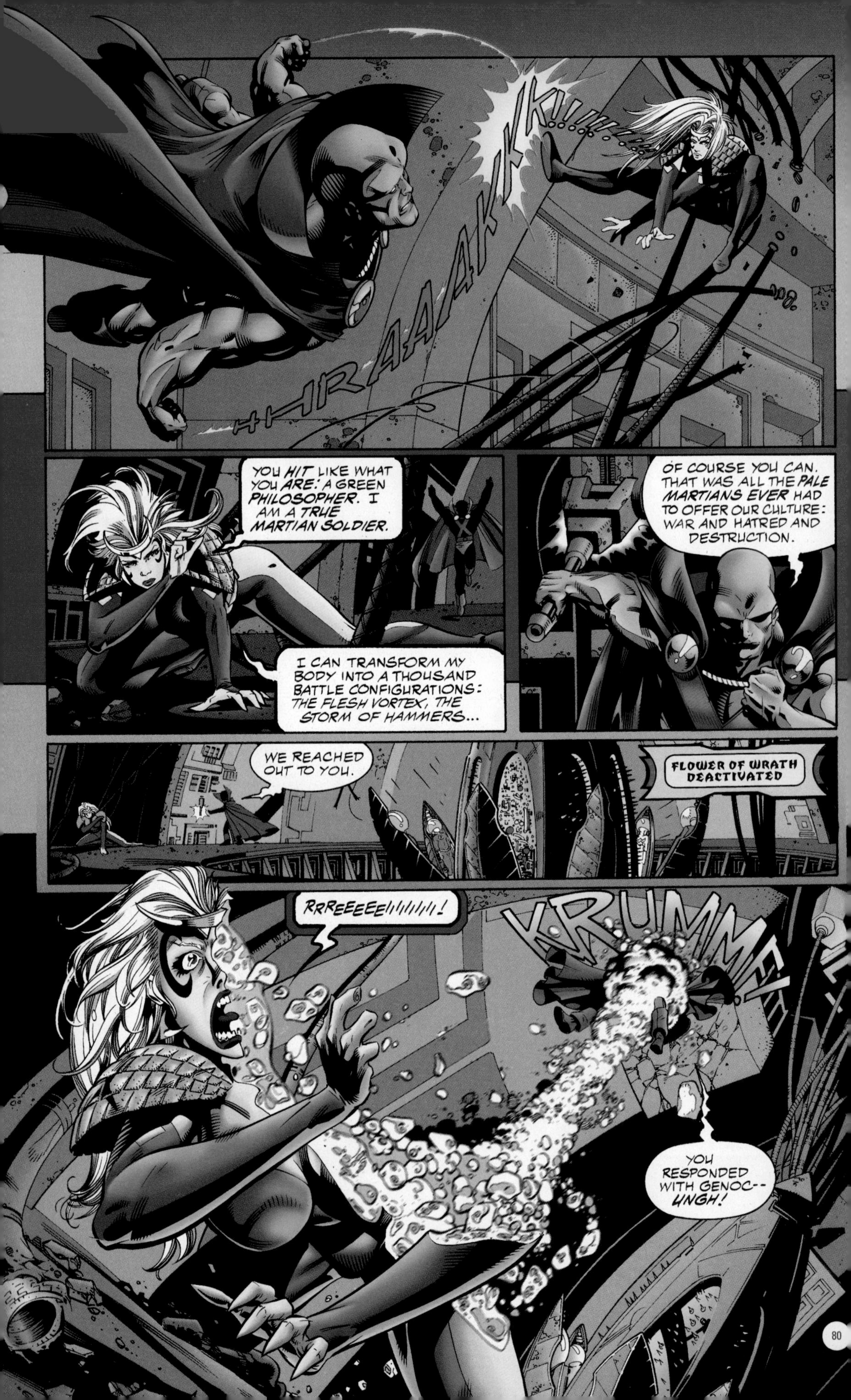
HHRAAAAKKK!!!!...
YOU HIT LIKE WHAT YOU ARE: A GREEN PHILOSOPHER. I AM A TRUE MARTIAN SOLDIER.
I CAN TRANSFORM MY BODY INTO A THOUSAND BATTLE CONFIGURATIONS: THE FLESH VORTEX, THE STORM OF HAMMERS...
OF COURSE YOU CAN. THAT WAS ALL THE PALE MARTIANS EVER HAD TO OFFER OUR CULTURE: WAR AND HATRED AND DESTRUCTION.
WE REACHED OUT TO YOU.
FLOWER OF WRATH DEACTIVATED
RRREEEEEE!!!!!!!!!
KRUMM
YOU RESPONDED WITH GENOC-- UNGH!

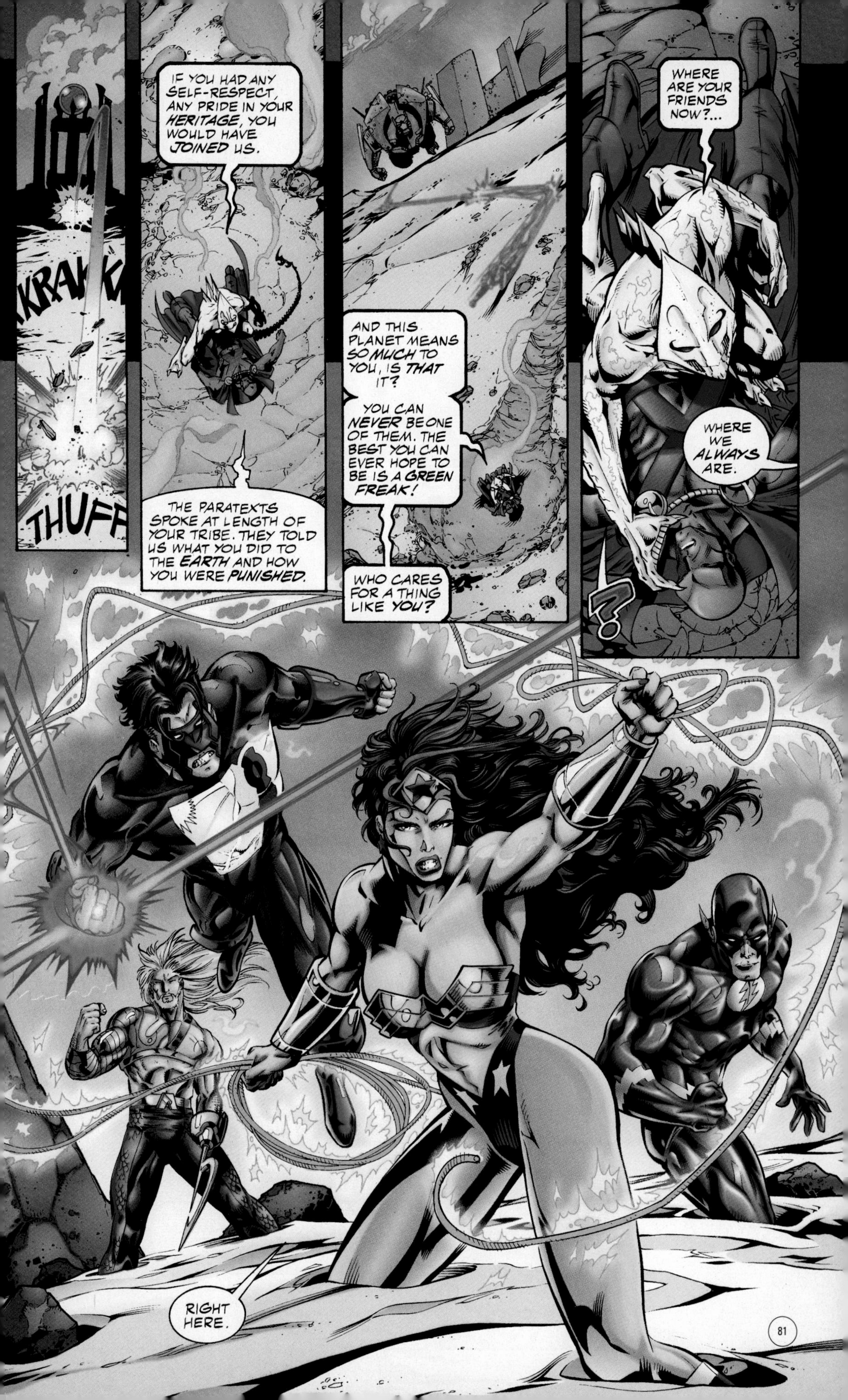
KRAKK
THUFF
IF YOU HAD ANY SELF-RESPECT, ANY PRIDE IN YOUR HERITAGE, YOU WOULD HAVE JOINED US.
THE PARATEXTS SPOKE AT LENGTH OF YOUR TRIBE. THEY TOLD US WHAT YOU DID TO THE EARTH AND HOW YOU WERE PUNISHED.
AND THIS PLANET MEANS SO MUCH TO YOU, IS THAT IT?
YOU CAN NEVER BE ONE OF THEM. THE BEST YOU CAN EVER HOPE TO BE IS A GREEN FREAK!
WHO CARES FOR A THING LIKE YOU?
WHERE ARE YOUR FRIENDS NOW?...
WHERE WE ALWAYS ARE.
?
RIGHT HERE.

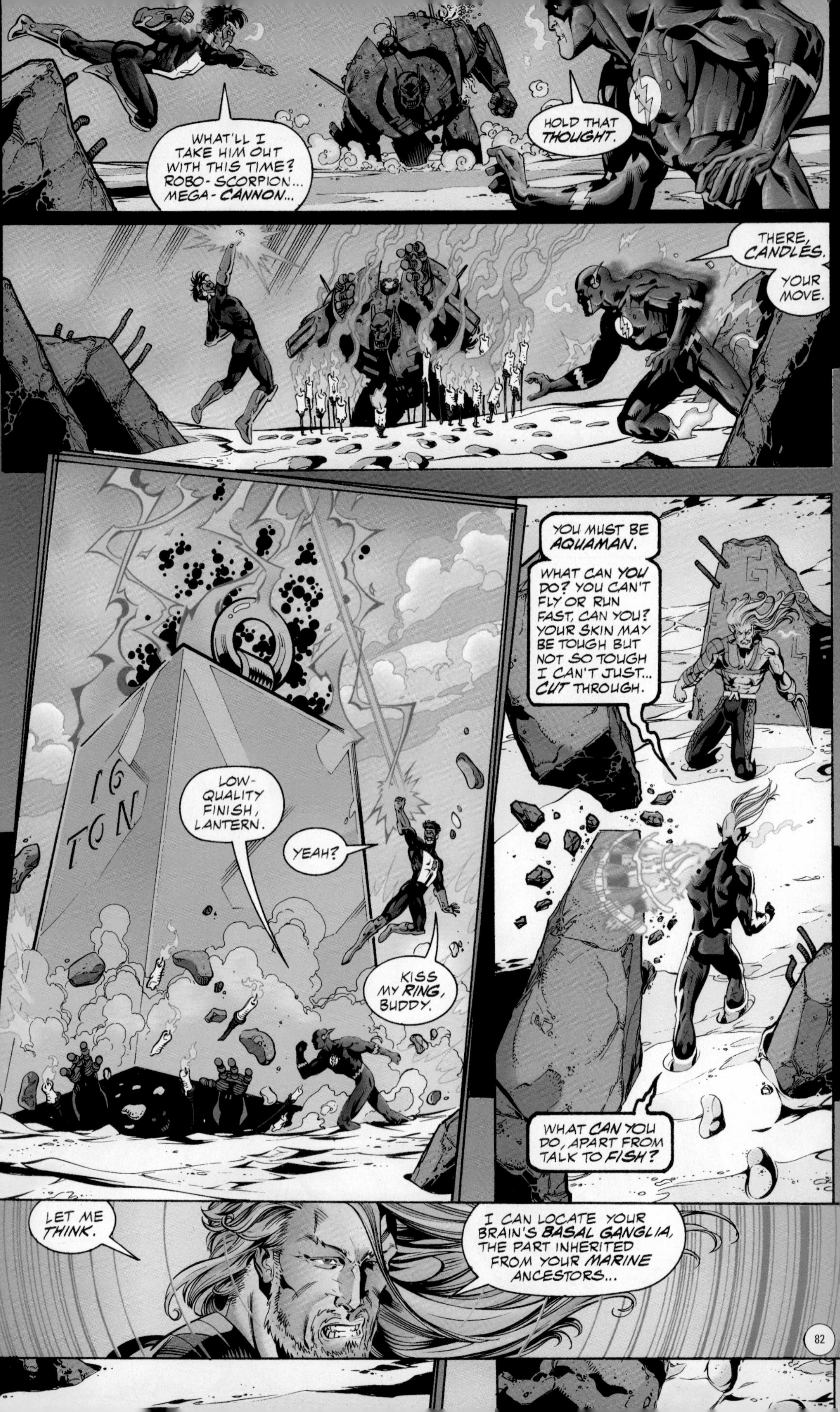
WHAT'LL I TAKE HIM OUT WITH THIS TIME? ROBO-SCORPION... MEGA-CANNON...
HOLD THAT THOUGHT.
THERE, CANDLES.
YOUR MOVE.
LOW-QUALITY FINISH, LANTERN.
YEAH?
KISS MY RING, BUDDY.
16 TON
YOU MUST BE AQUAMAN.
WHAT CAN YOU DO? YOU CAN'T FLY OR RUN FAST, CAN YOU? YOUR SKIN MAY BE TOUGH BUT NOT SO TOUGH I CAN'T JUST... CUT THROUGH.
WHAT CAN YOU DO, APART FROM TALK TO FISH?
LET ME THINK.
I CAN LOCATE YOUR BRAIN'S BASAL GANGLIA, THE PART INHERITED FROM YOUR MARINE ANCESTORS...

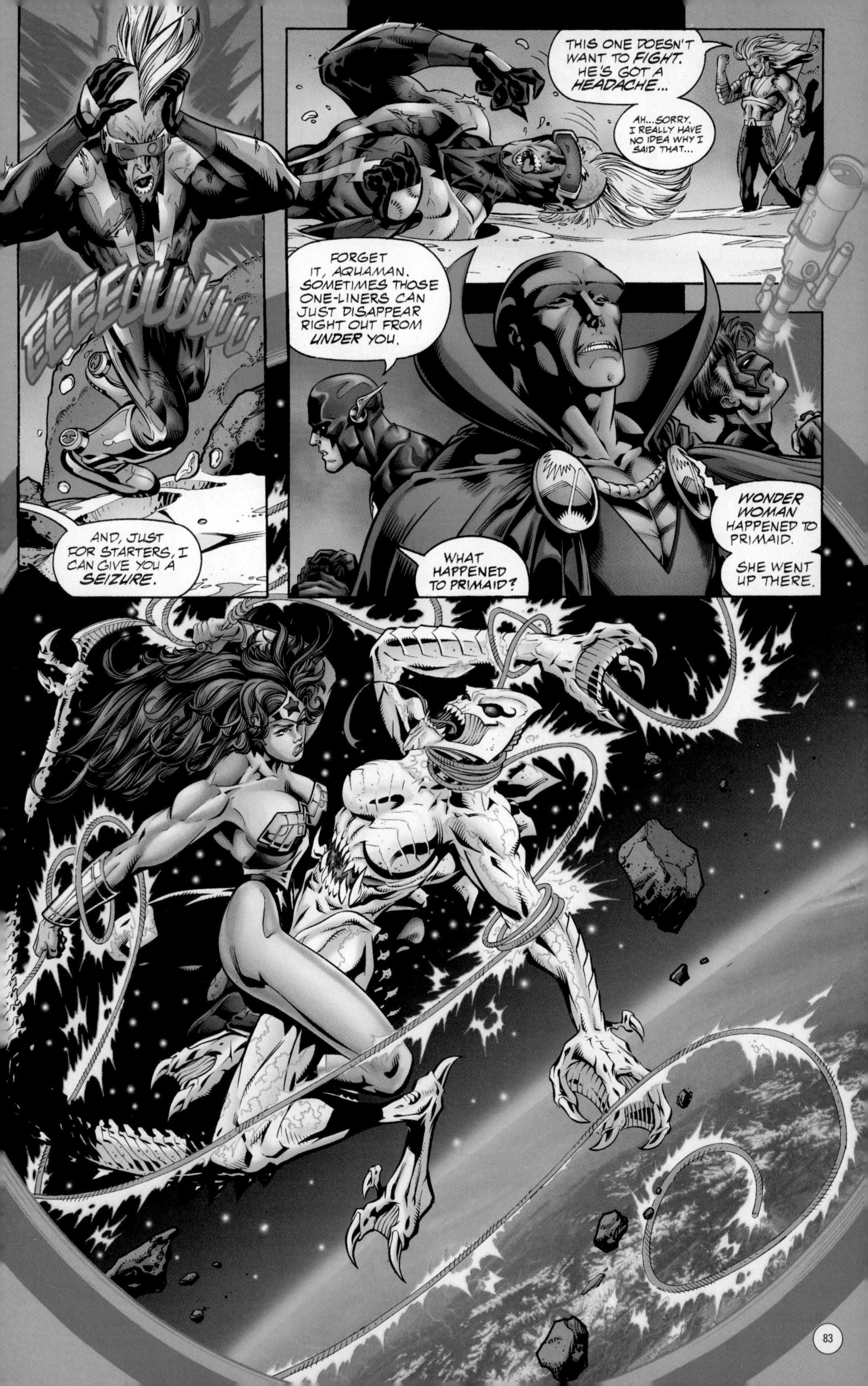
EEEEUUUUUU
AND, JUST FOR STARTERS, I CAN GIVE YOU A SEIZURE.
THIS ONE DOESN'T WANT TO FIGHT. HE'S GOT A HEADACHE...
AH...SORRY. I REALLY HAVE NO IDEA WHY I SAID THAT...
FORGET IT, AQUAMAN. SOMETIMES THOSE ONE-LINERS CAN JUST DISAPPEAR RIGHT OUT FROM UNDER YOU.
WHAT HAPPENED TO PRIMAID?
WONDER WOMAN HAPPENED TO PRIMAID.
SHE WENT UP THERE.

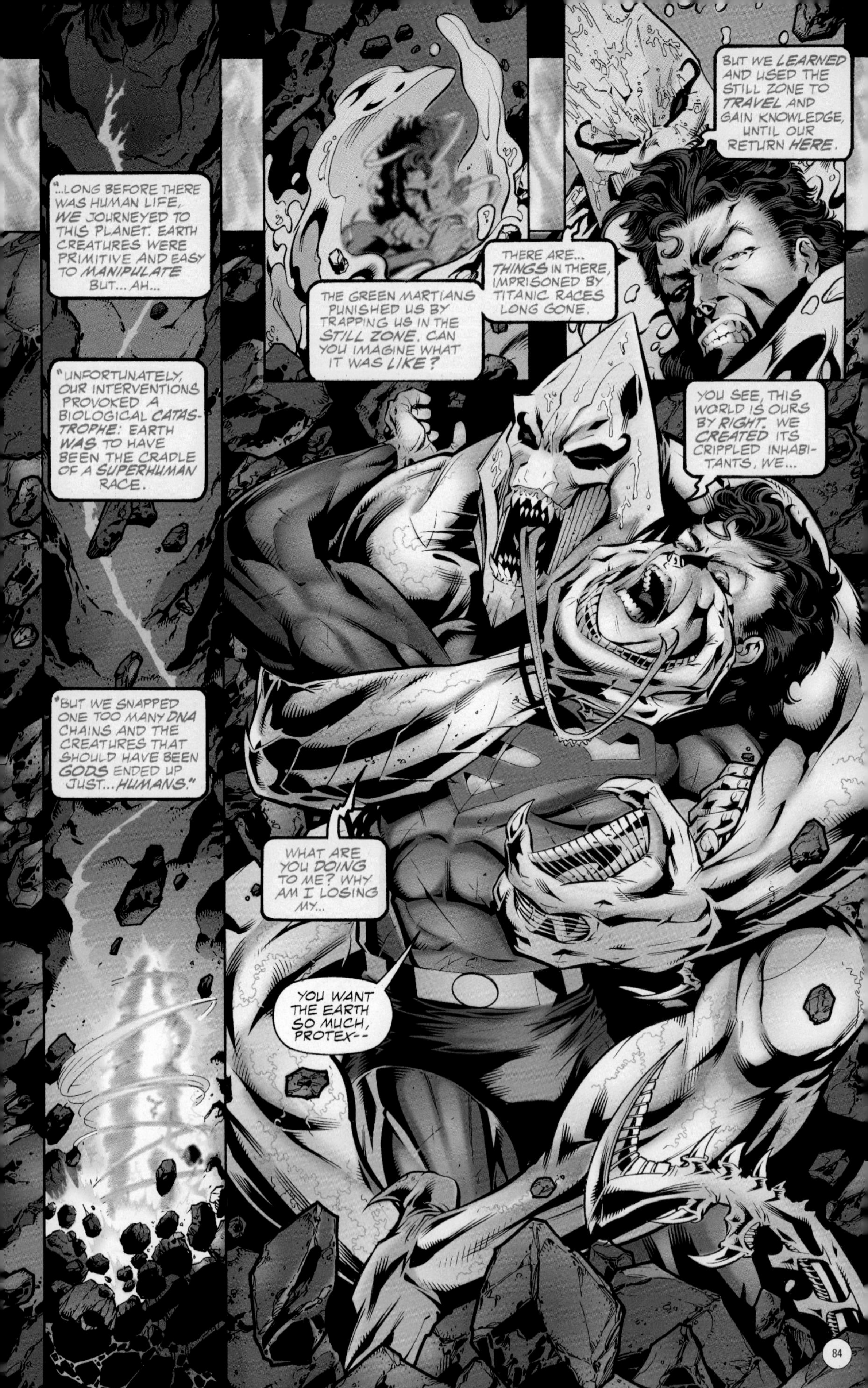

"...LONG BEFORE THERE WAS HUMAN LIFE, WE JOURNEYED TO THIS PLANET. EARTH CREATURES WERE PRIMITIVE AND EASY TO MANIPULATE BUT... AH...
"UNFORTUNATELY, OUR INTERVENTIONS PROVOKED A BIOLOGICAL CATASTROPHE: EARTH WAS TO HAVE BEEN THE CRADLE OF A SUPERHUMAN RACE.
"BUT WE SNAPPED ONE TOO MANY DNA CHAINS AND THE CREATURES THAT SHOULD HAVE BEEN GODS ENDED UP JUST... HUMANS."
THE GREEN MARTIANS PUNISHED US BY TRAPPING US IN THE STILL ZONE. CAN YOU IMAGINE WHAT IT WAS LIKE?
THERE ARE... THINGS IN THERE, IMPRISONED BY TITANIC RACES LONG GONE.
BUT WE LEARNED AND USED THE STILL ZONE TO TRAVEL AND GAIN KNOWLEDGE, UNTIL OUR RETURN HERE.
YOU SEE, THIS WORLD IS OURS BY RIGHT. WE CREATED ITS CRIPPLED INHABITANTS, WE...
WHAT ARE YOU DOING TO ME? WHY AM I LOSING MY...
YOU WANT THE EARTH SO MUCH, PROTEX--

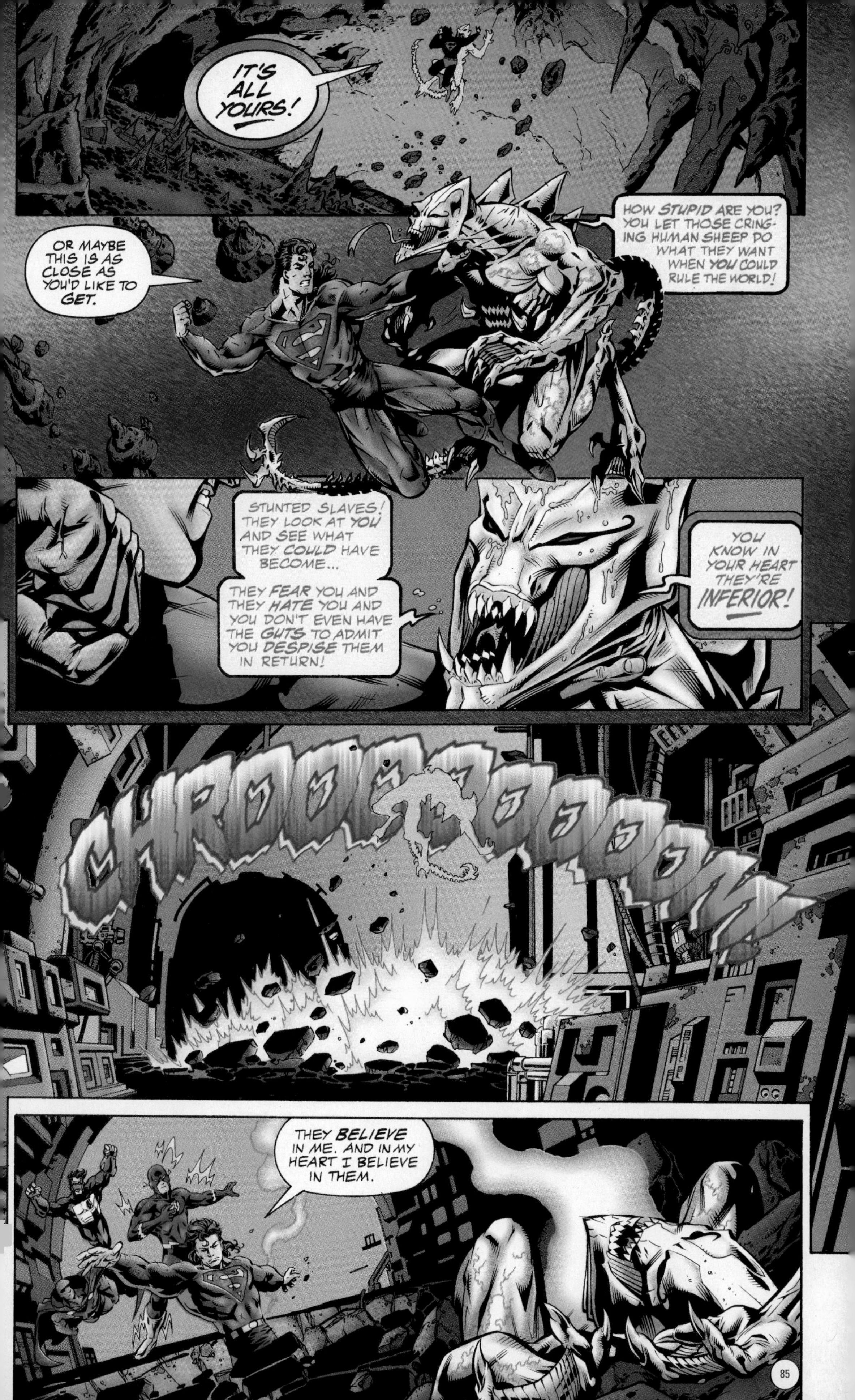

IT'S ALL YOURS!
OR MAYBE THIS IS AS CLOSE AS YOU'D LIKE TO GET.
HOW STUPID ARE YOU? YOU LET THOSE CRING-ING HUMAN SHEEP DO WHAT THEY WANT WHEN YOU COULD RULE THE WORLD!
STUNTED SLAVES! THEY LOOK AT YOU AND SEE WHAT THEY COULD HAVE BECOME...
THEY FEAR YOU AND THEY HATE YOU AND YOU DON'T EVEN HAVE THE GUTS TO ADMIT YOU DESPISE THEM IN RETURN!
YOU KNOW IN YOUR HEART THEY'RE INFERIOR!
CHROOOOOOOOM
THEY BELIEVE IN ME. AND IN MY HEART I BELIEVE IN THEM.

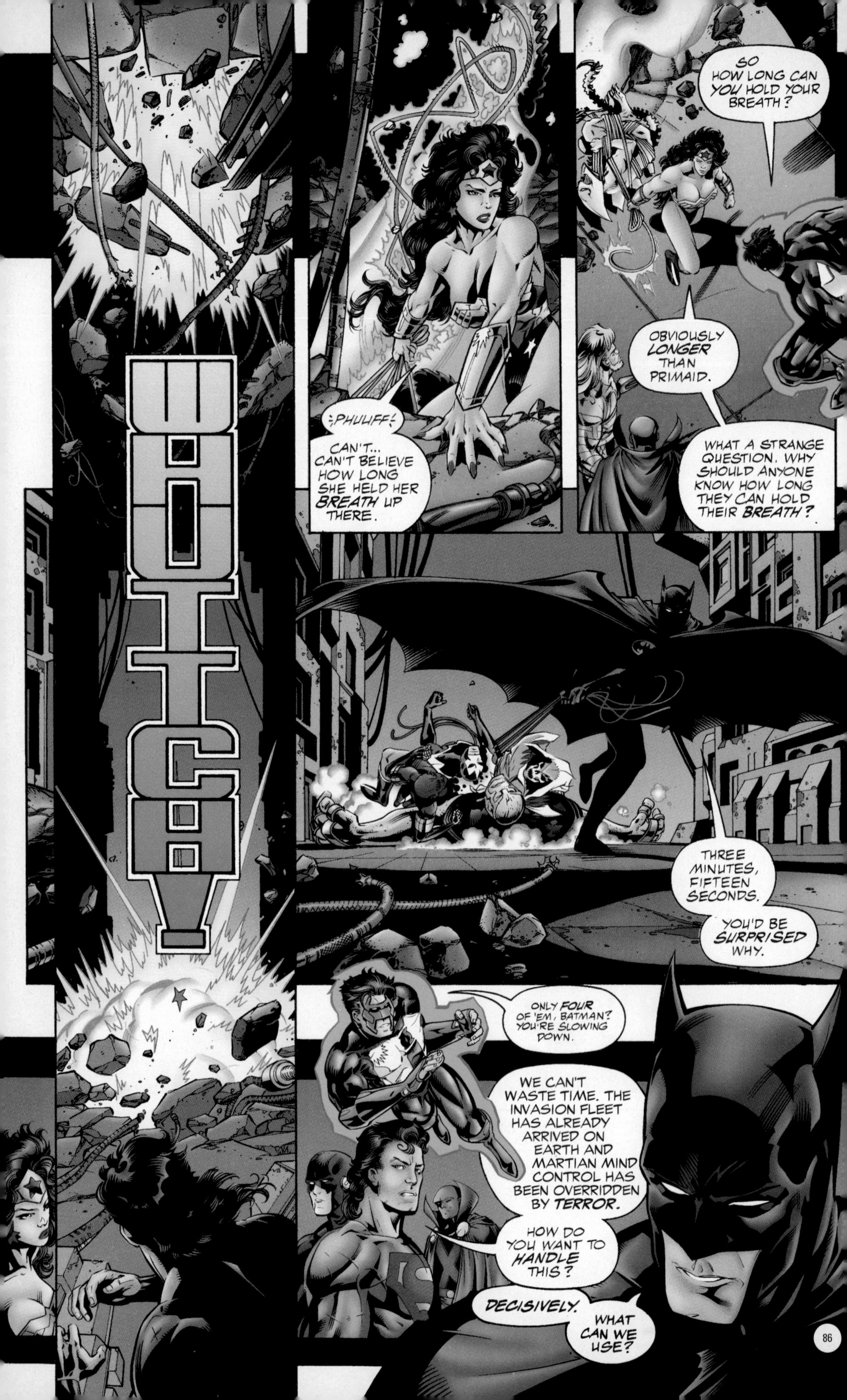
WHUTCHAV
PHUUFF
CAN'T... CAN'T BELIEVE HOW LONG SHE HELD HER BREATH UP THERE.
SO HOW LONG CAN YOU HOLD YOUR BREATH?
OBVIOUSLY LONGER THAN PRIMAID.
WHAT A STRANGE QUESTION. WHY SHOULD ANYONE KNOW HOW LONG THEY CAN HOLD THEIR BREATH?
THREE MINUTES, FIFTEEN SECONDS.
YOU'D BE SURPRISED WHY.
ONLY FOUR OF 'EM, BATMAN? YOU'RE SLOWING DOWN.
WE CAN'T WASTE TIME. THE INVASION FLEET HAS ALREADY ARRIVED ON EARTH AND MARTIAN MIND CONTROL HAS BEEN OVERRIDDEN BY TERROR.
HOW DO YOU WANT TO HANDLE THIS?
DECISIVELY.
WHAT CAN WE USE?

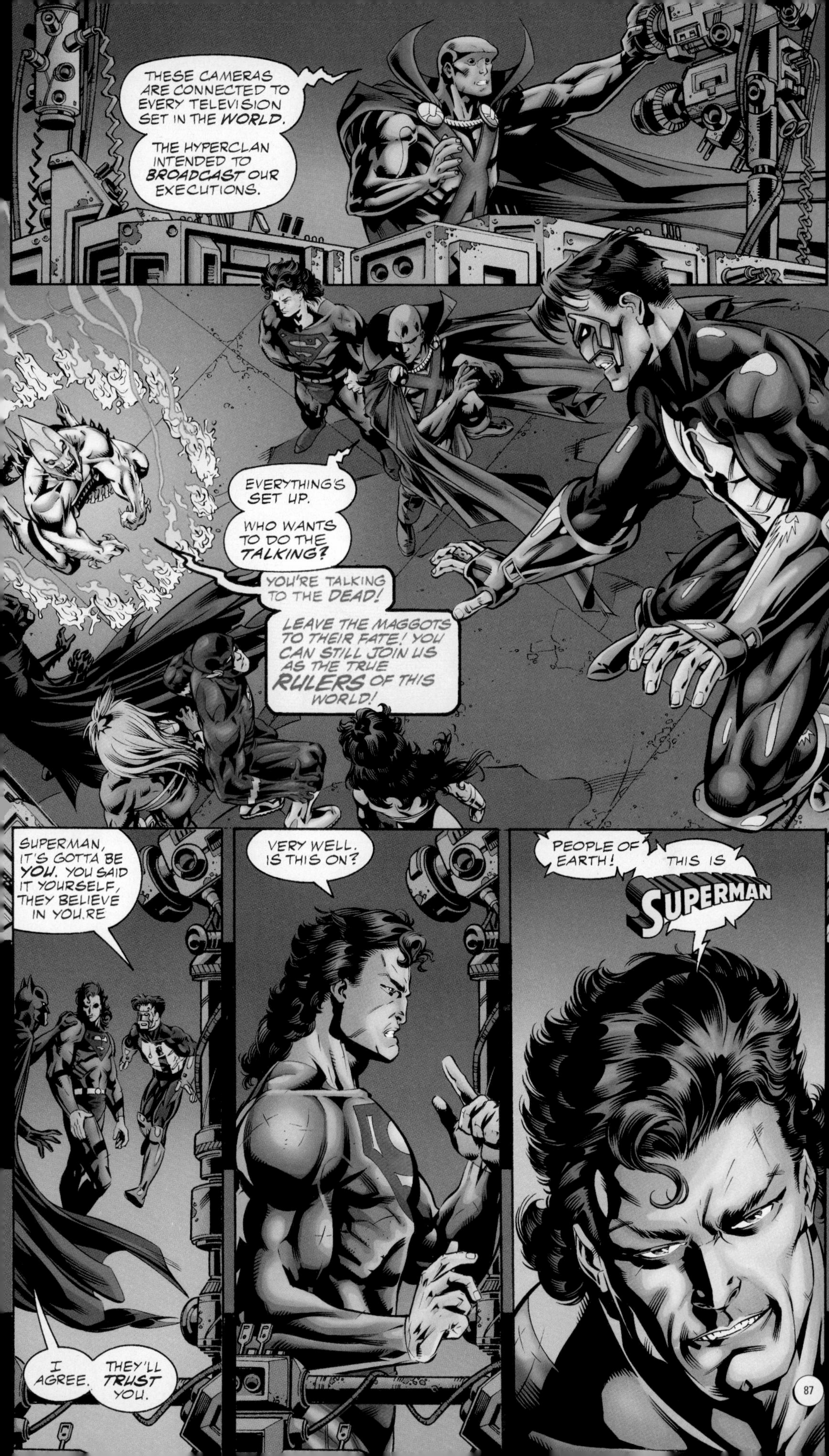
THESE CAMERAS ARE CONNECTED TO EVERY TELEVISION SET IN THE WORLD.
THE HYPERCLAN INTENDED TO BROADCAST OUR EXECUTIONS.
EVERYTHING'S SET UP.
WHO WANTS TO DO THE TALKING?
YOU'RE TALKING TO THE DEAD!
LEAVE THE MAGGOTS TO THEIR FATE! YOU CAN STILL JOIN US AS THE TRUE RULERS OF THIS WORLD!
SUPERMAN, IT'S GOTTA BE YOU. YOU SAID IT YOURSELF, THEY BELIEVE IN YOU.RE
I AGREE.
THEY'LL TRUST YOU.
VERY WELL. IS THIS ON?
PEOPLE OF EARTH!
THIS IS
SUPERMAN

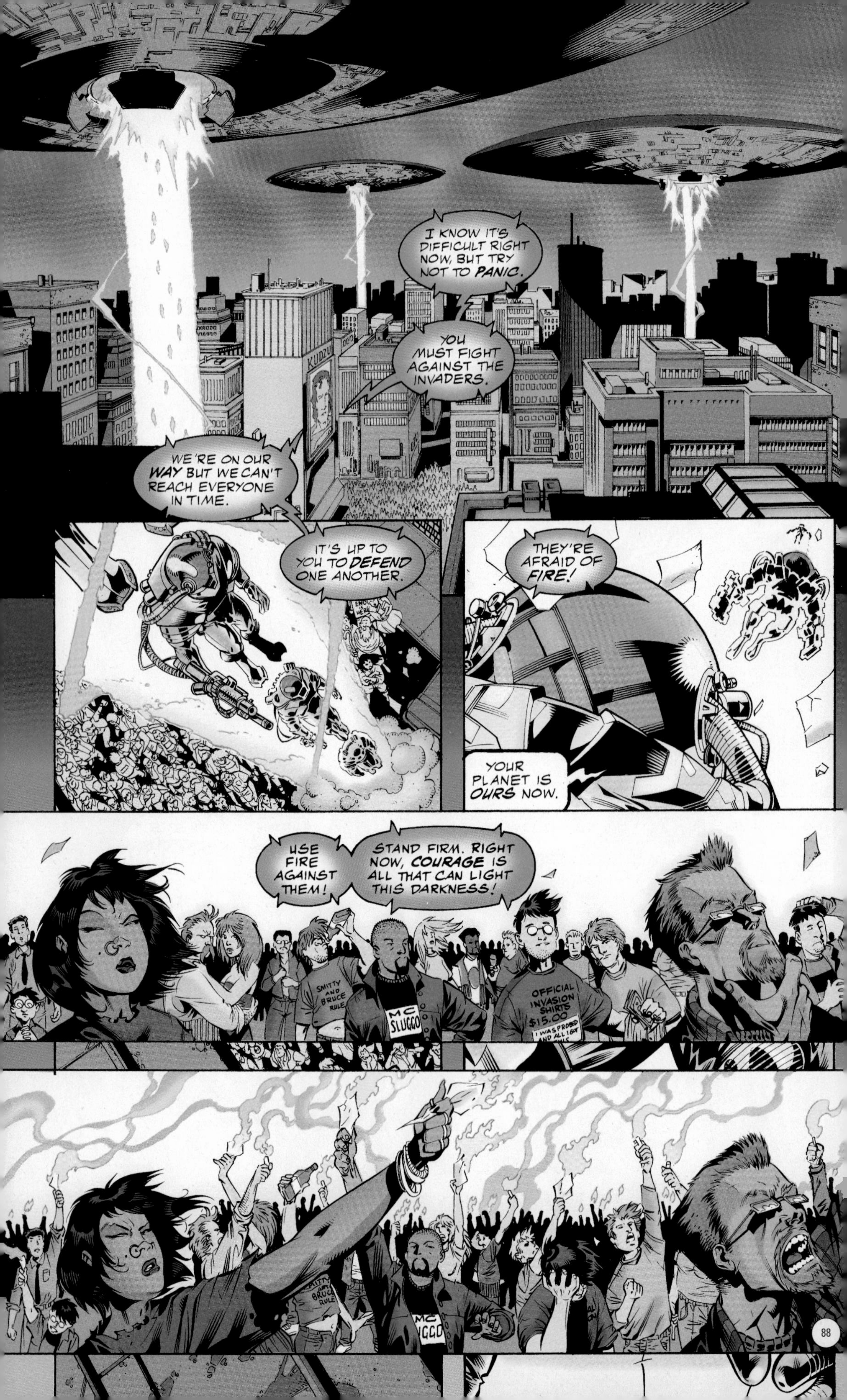
I KNOW IT'S DIFFICULT RIGHT NOW, BUT TRY NOT TO PANIC.
KUDZU
YOU MUST FIGHT AGAINST THE INVADERS.
WE'RE ON OUR WAY BUT WE CAN'T REACH EVERYONE IN TIME.
IT'S UP TO YOU TO DEFEND ONE ANOTHER.
THEY'RE AFRAID OF FIRE!
YOUR PLANET IS OURS NOW.
USE FIRE AGAINST THEM!
STAND FIRM. RIGHT NOW, COURAGE IS ALL THAT CAN LIGHT THIS DARKNESS!
SMITTY AND BRUCE RULE
MC SLUGGO
OFFICIAL INVASION SHIRTS $15.00

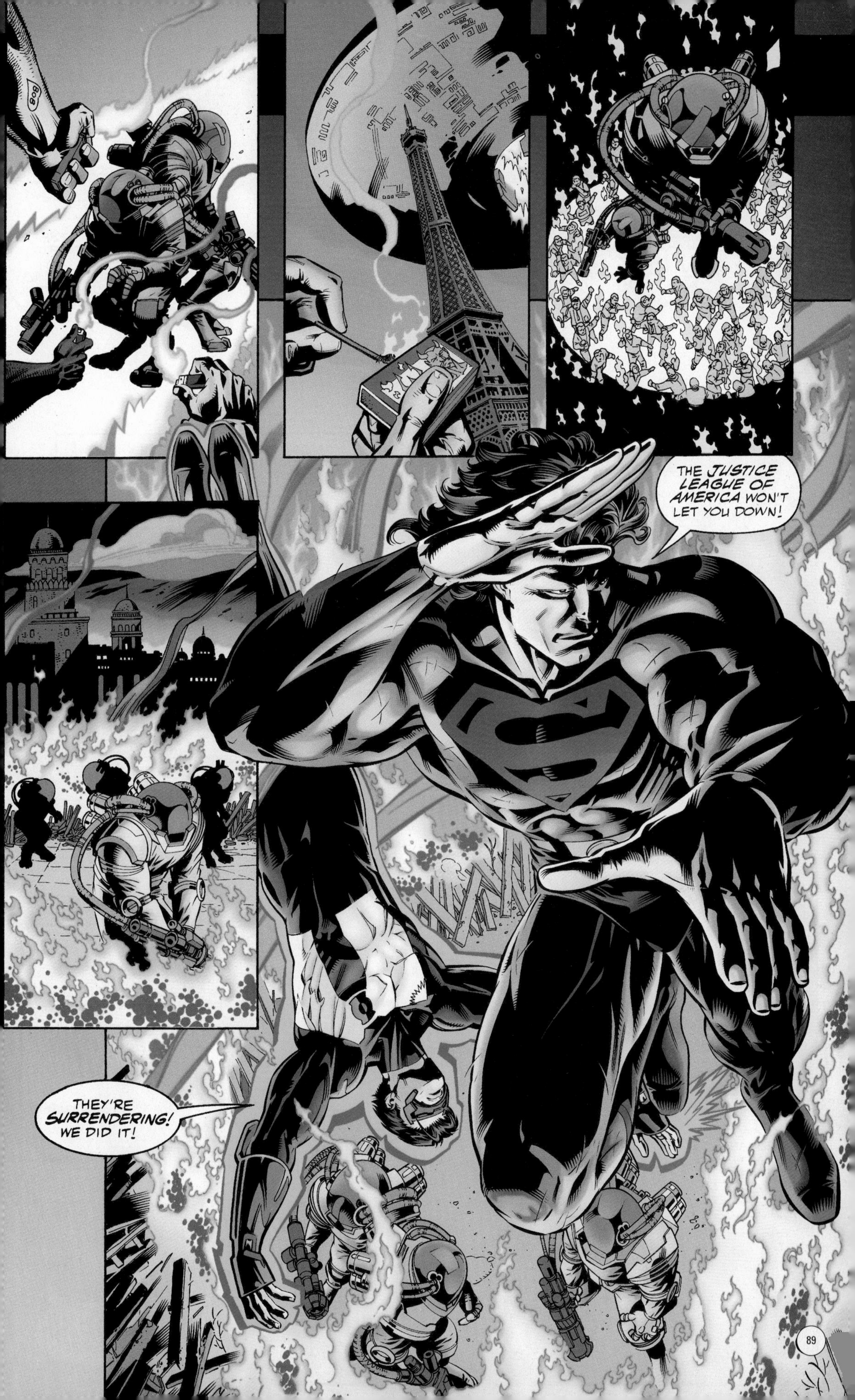
THE JUSTICE LEAGUE OF AMERICA WON'T LET YOU DOWN!
THEY'RE SURRENDERING! WE DID IT!

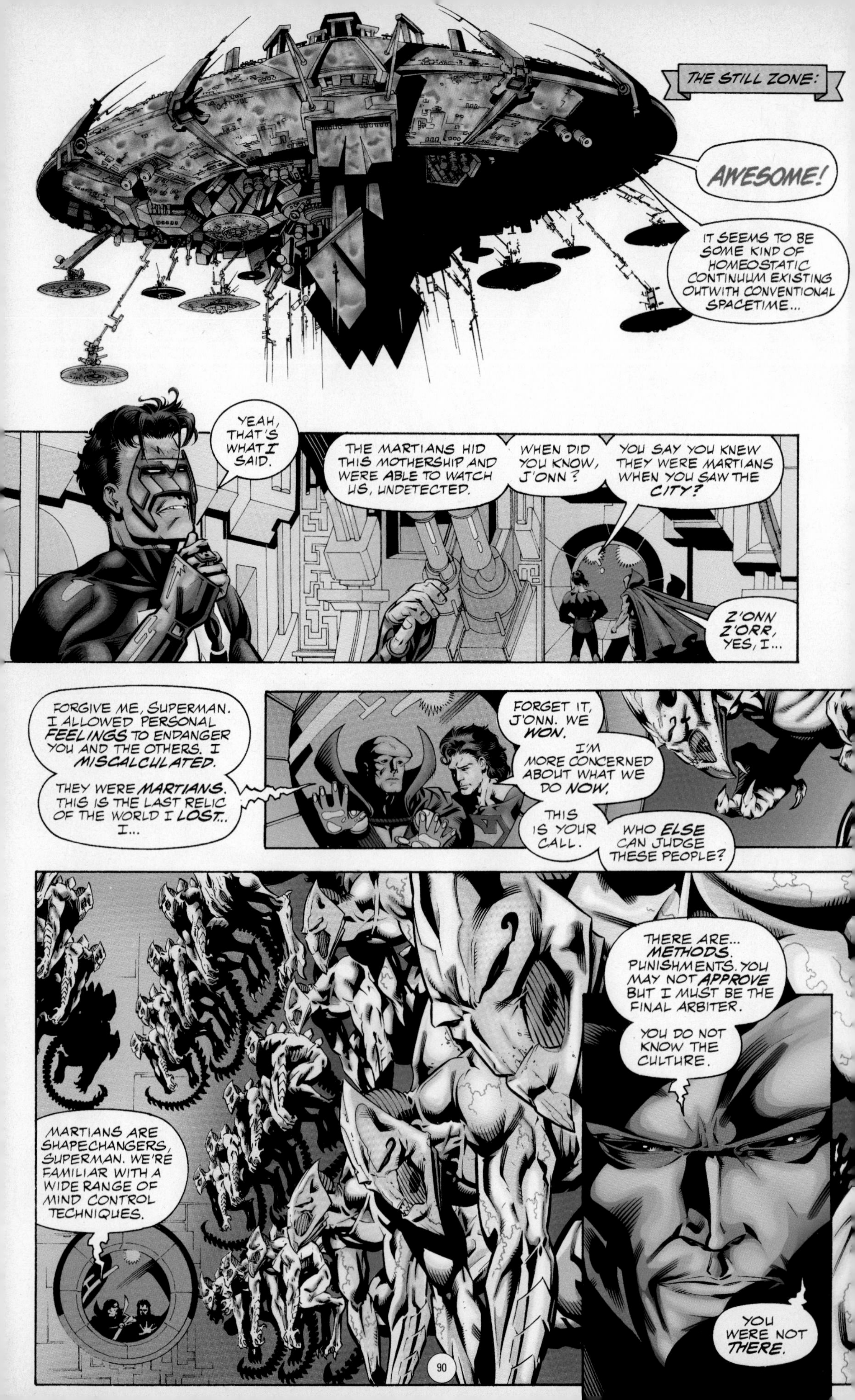
THE STILL ZONE:
AWESOME!
IT SEEMS TO BE SOME KIND OF HOMEOSTATIC CONTINUUM EXISTING OUTWITH CONVENTIONAL SPACETIME...
YEAH, THAT'S WHAT I SAID.
THE MARTIANS HID THIS MOTHERSHIP AND WERE ABLE TO WATCH US, UNDETECTED.
WHEN DID YOU KNOW, J'ONN?
YOU SAY YOU KNEW THEY WERE MARTIANS WHEN YOU SAW THE CITY?
Z'ONN Z'ORR, YES, I...
FORGIVE ME, SUPERMAN. I ALLOWED PERSONAL FEELINGS TO ENDANGER YOU AND THE OTHERS. I MISCALCULATED.
THEY WERE MARTIANS. THIS IS THE LAST RELIC OF THE WORLD I LOST... I...
FORGET IT, J'ONN. WE WON.
I'M MORE CONCERNED ABOUT WHAT WE DO NOW.
THIS IS YOUR CALL.
WHO ELSE CAN JUDGE THESE PEOPLE?
MARTIANS ARE SHAPECHANGERS, SUPERMAN. WE'RE FAMILIAR WITH A WIDE RANGE OF MIND CONTROL TECHNIQUES.
THERE ARE... METHODS. PUNISHMENTS. YOU MAY NOT APPROVE BUT I MUST BE THE FINAL ARBITER.
YOU DO NOT KNOW THE CULTURE.
YOU WERE NOT THERE.

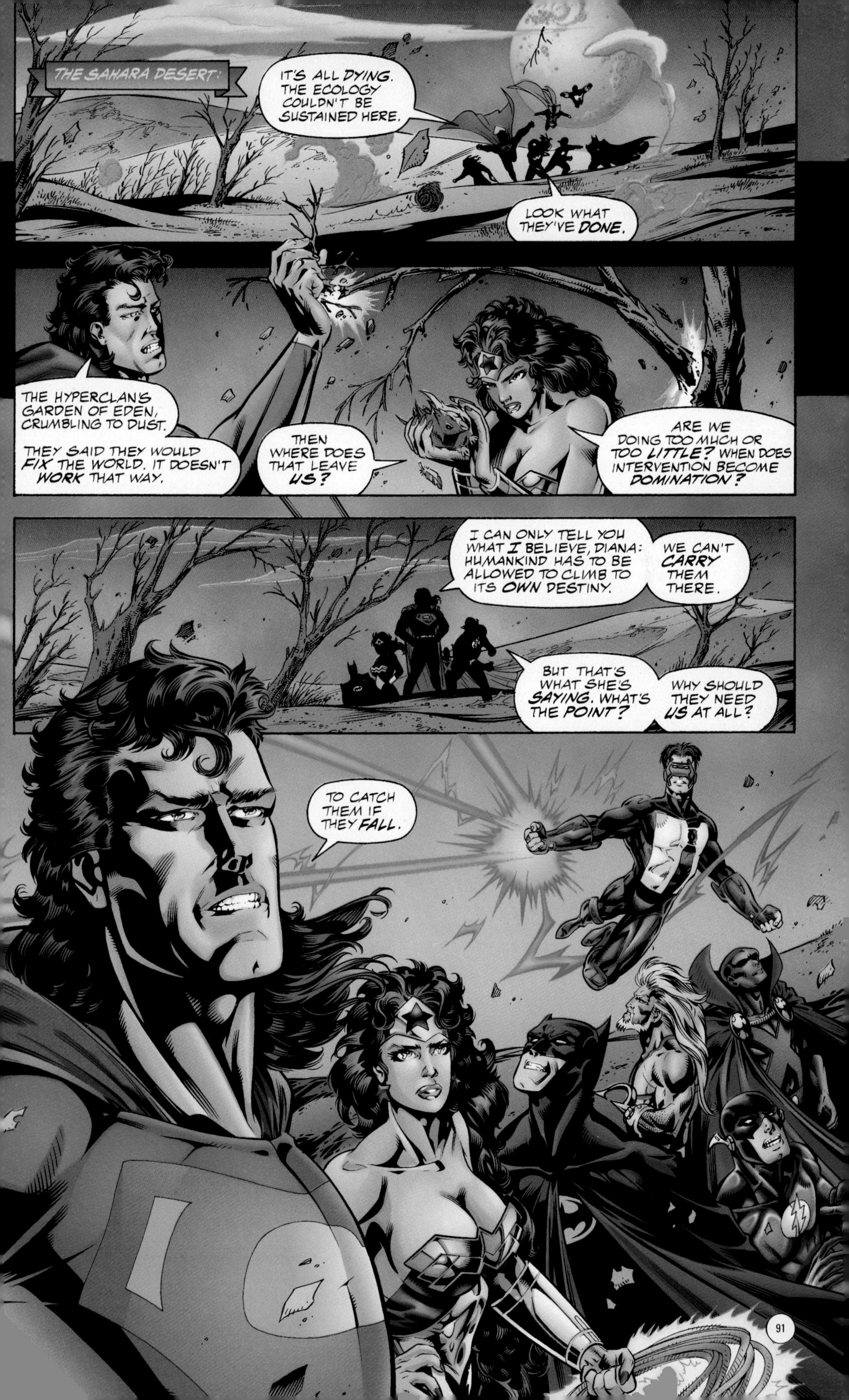
THE SAHARA DESERT:
IT'S ALL DYING. THE ECOLOGY COULDN'T BE SUSTAINED HERE.
LOOK WHAT THEY'VE DONE.
THE HYPERCLAN'S GARDEN OF EDEN, CRUMBLING TO DUST.
THEY SAID THEY WOULD FIX THE WORLD. IT DOESN'T WORK THAT WAY.
THEN WHERE DOES THAT LEAVE US?
ARE WE DOING TOO MUCH OR TOO LITTLE? WHEN DOES INTERVENTION BECOME DOMINATION?
I CAN ONLY TELL YOU WHAT I BELIEVE, DIANA: HUMANKIND HAS TO BE ALLOWED TO CLIMB TO ITS OWN DESTINY.
WE CAN'T CARRY THEM THERE.
BUT THAT'S WHAT SHE'S SAYING. WHAT'S THE POINT?
WHY SHOULD THEY NEED US AT ALL?
TO CATCH THEM IF THEY FALL.

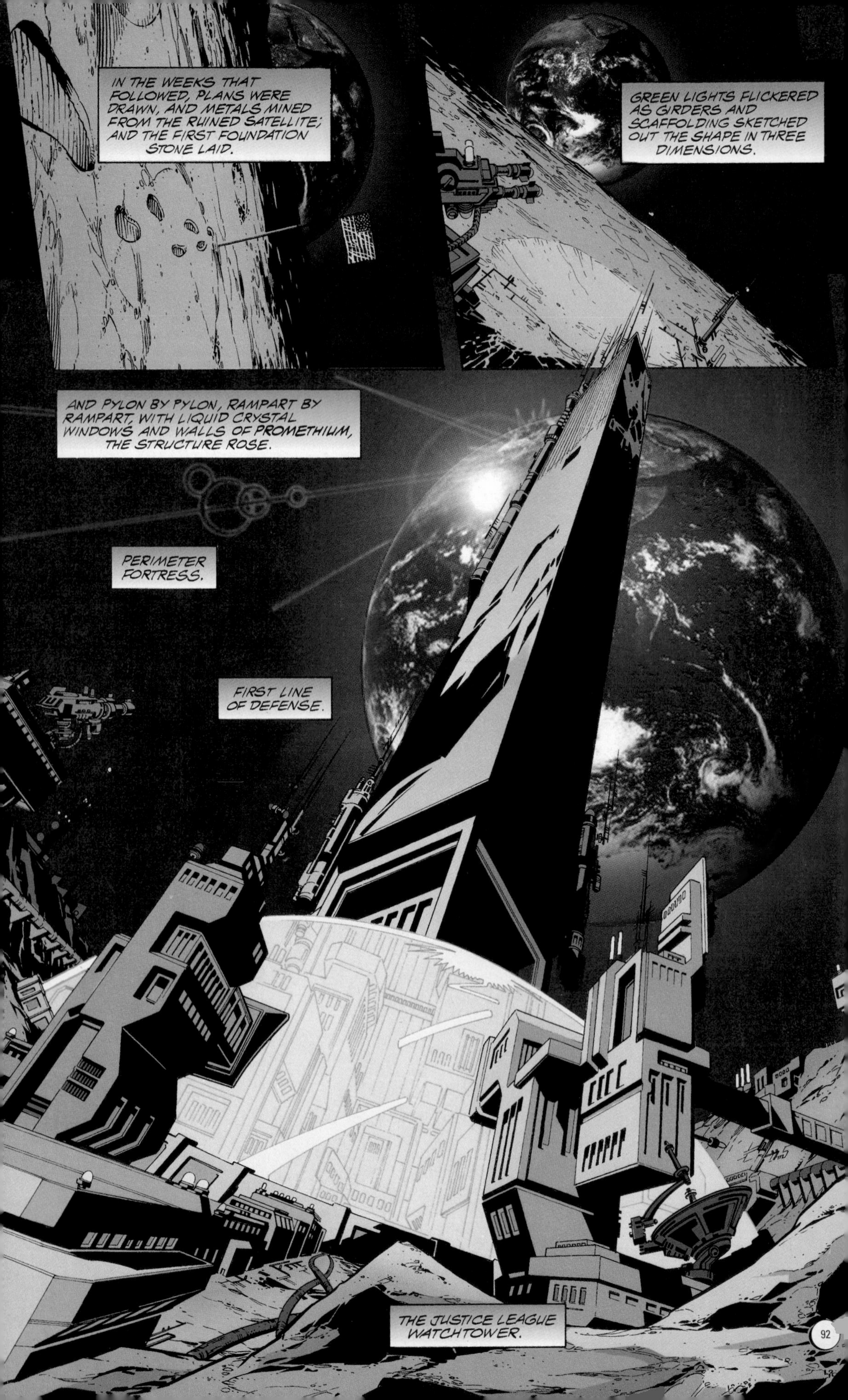
IN THE WEEKS THAT FOLLOWED, PLANS WERE DRAWN, AND METALS MINED FROM THE RUINED SATELLITE; AND THE FIRST FOUNDATION STONE LAID.
GREEN LIGHTS FLICKERED AS GIRDERS AND SCAFFOLDING SKETCHED OUT THE SHAPE IN THREE DIMENSIONS.
AND PYLON BY PYLON, RAMPART BY RAMPART, WITH LIQUID CRYSTAL WINDOWS AND WALLS OF PROMETHIUM, THE STRUCTURE ROSE.
PERIMETER FORTRESS.
FIRST LINE OF DEFENSE.
THE JUSTICE LEAGUE WATCHTOWER.

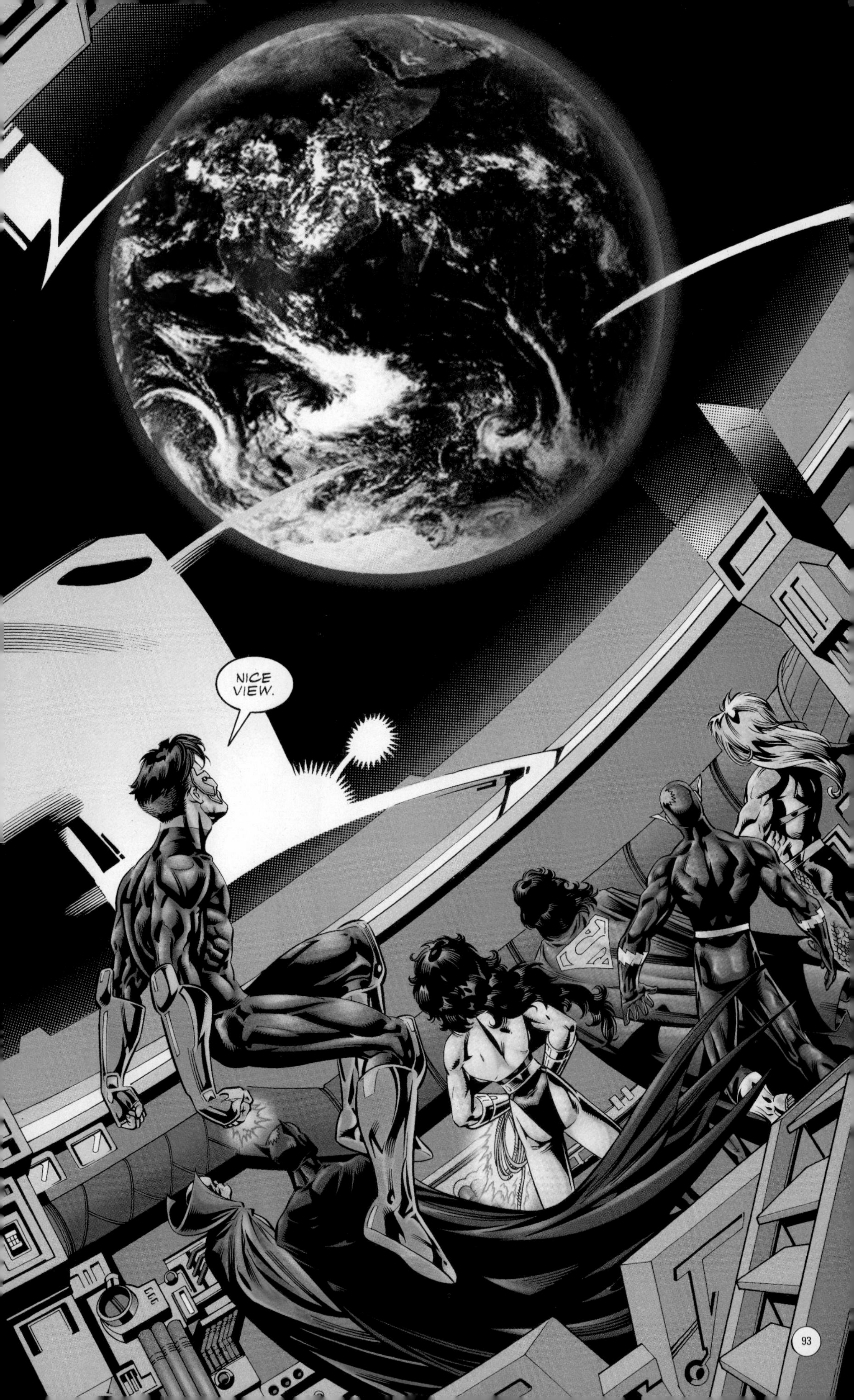
NICE VIEW.

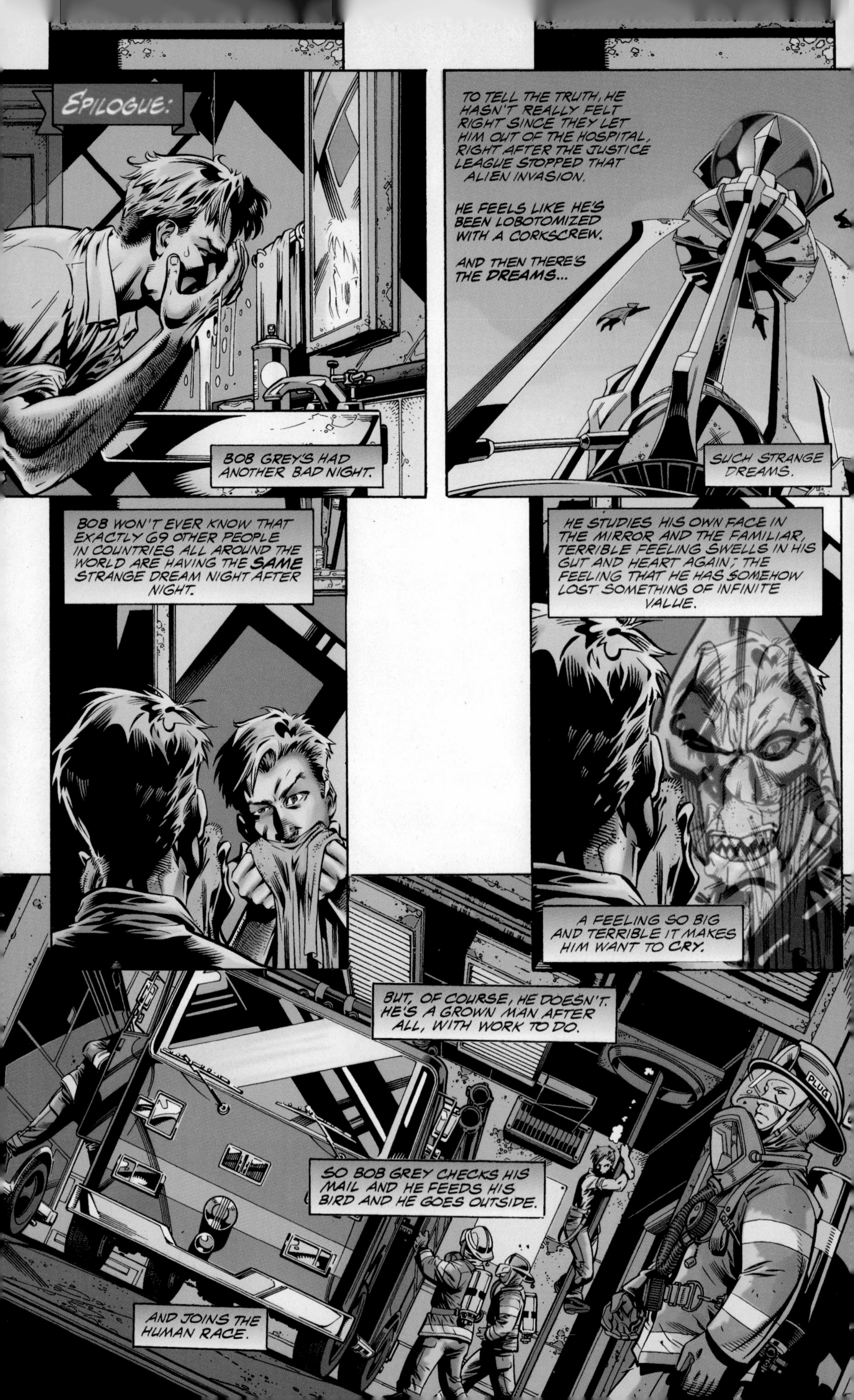
EPILOGUE:
BOB GREY'S HAD ANOTHER BAD NIGHT.
TO TELL THE TRUTH, HE HASN'T REALLY FELT RIGHT SINCE THEY LET HIM OUT OF THE HOSPITAL, RIGHT AFTER THE JUSTICE LEAGUE STOPPED THAT ALIEN INVASION.
HE FEELS LIKE HE'S BEEN LOBOTOMIZED WITH A CORKSCREW.
AND THEN THERE'S THE DREAMS...
SUCH STRANGE DREAMS.
BOB WON'T EVER KNOW THAT EXACTLY 69 OTHER PEOPLE IN COUNTRIES ALL AROUND THE WORLD ARE HAVING THE SAME STRANGE DREAM NIGHT AFTER NIGHT.
HE STUDIES HIS OWN FACE IN THE MIRROR AND THE FAMILIAR, TERRIBLE FEELING SWELLS IN HIS GUT AND HEART AGAIN; THE FEELING THAT HE HAS SOMEHOW LOST SOMETHING OF INFINITE VALUE.
A FEELING SO BIG AND TERRIBLE IT MAKES HIM WANT TO CRY.
BUT, OF COURSE, HE DOESN'T. HE'S A GROWN MAN AFTER ALL, WITH WORK TO DO.
SO BOB GREY CHECKS HIS MAIL AND HE FEEDS HIS BIRD AND HE GOES OUTSIDE.
PLUG
AND JOINS THE HUMAN RACE.

COVER GALLERY

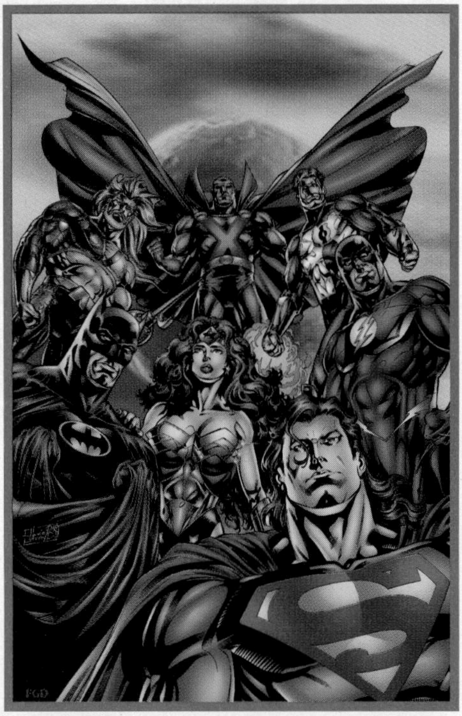

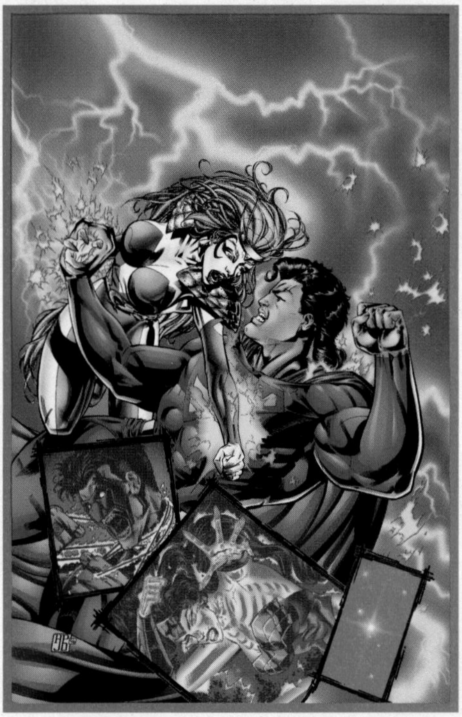

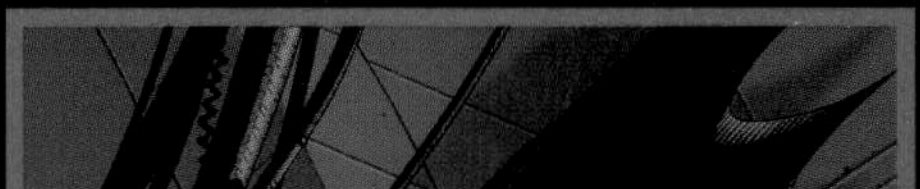

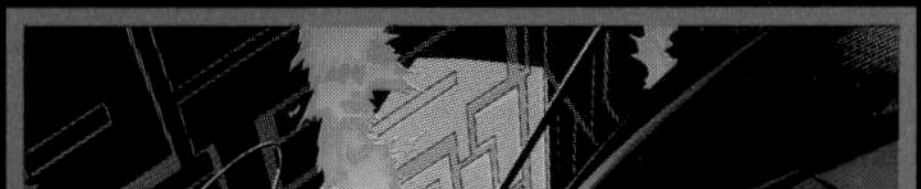

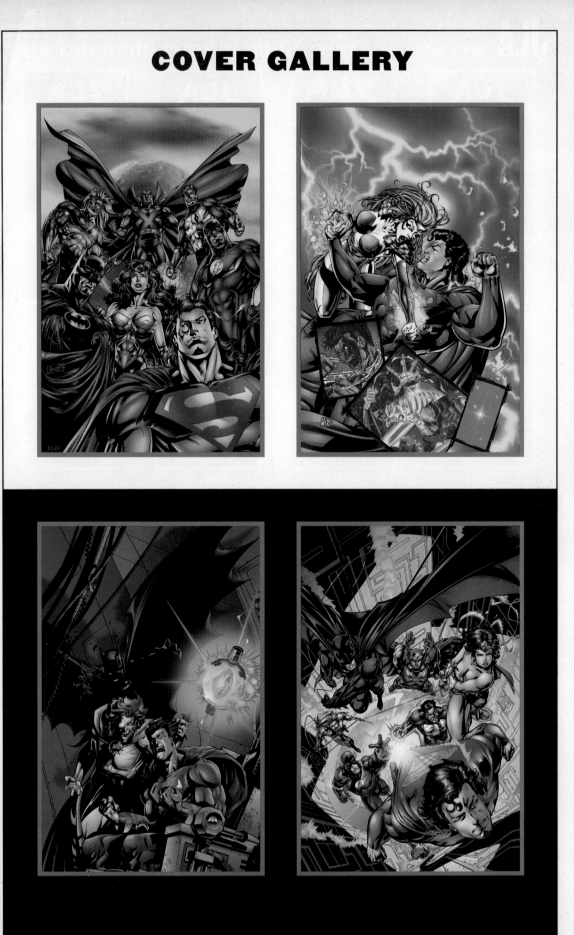

JLA DON'T MISS A SINGLE VOLUME FEATURING THE WORLD'S GREATEST SUPER-HEROES

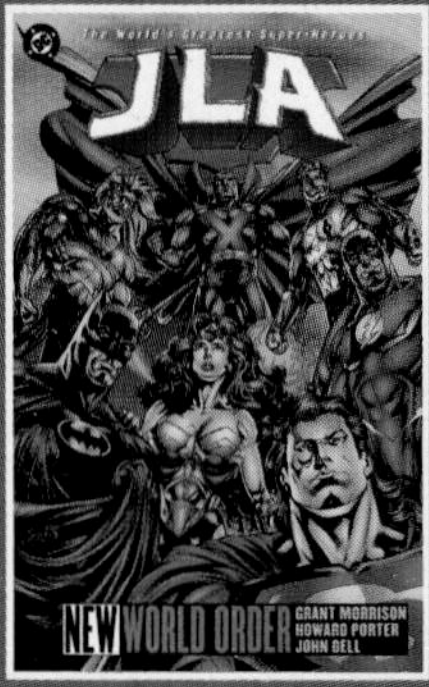
JLA
NEW WORLD ORDER
GRANT MORRISON
HOWARD PORTER
JOHN DELL

VOLUME 1:
NEW WORLD ORDER
Morrison/Porter/Dell

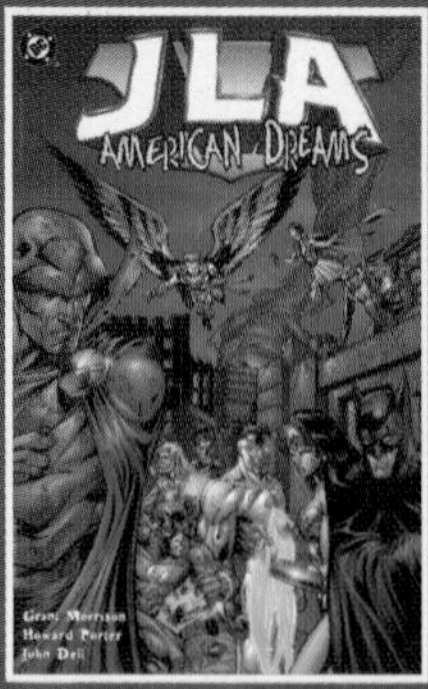
JLA
AMERICAN DREAMS
Grant Morrison
Howard Porter
John Dell

VOLUME 2:
AMERICAN DREAMS
Morrison/Porter/Dell/various

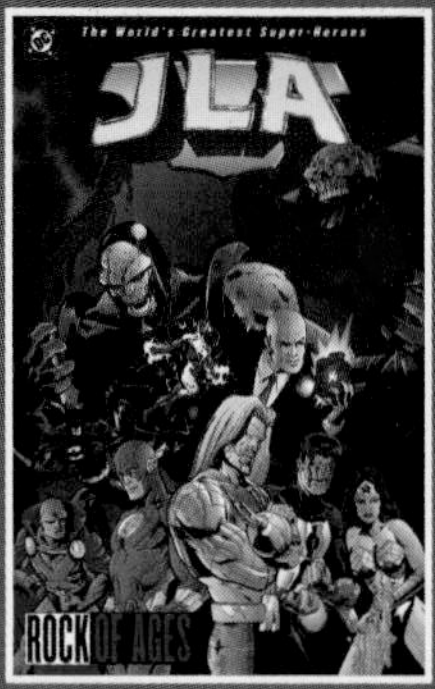
The World's Greatest Super-Heroes
JLA
ROCK OF AGES

VOLUME 3:
ROCK OF AGES
Morrison/Porter/Dell/various

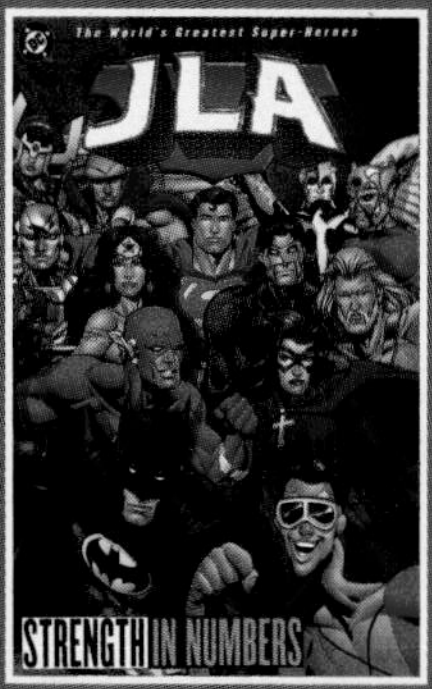
The World's Greatest Super-Heroes
JLA
STRENGTH IN NUMBERS

VOLUME 4:
STRENGTH IN NUMBERS
Morrison/Porter/Dell/various

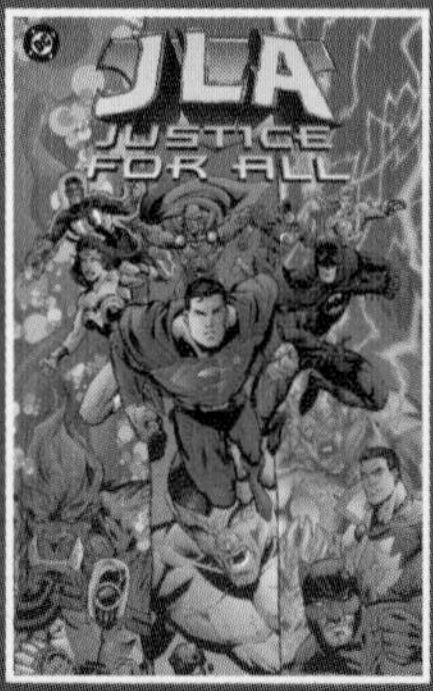
JLA
JUSTICE FOR ALL

VOLUME 5:
JUSTICE FOR ALL
Morrison/Waid/Porter/various

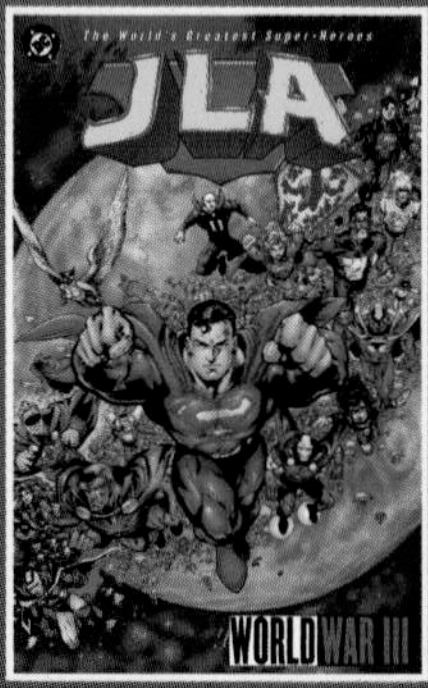
The World's Greatest Super-Heroes
JLA
WORLD WAR III

VOLUME 6:
WORLD WAR III
Morrison/DeMatteis/Porter/various

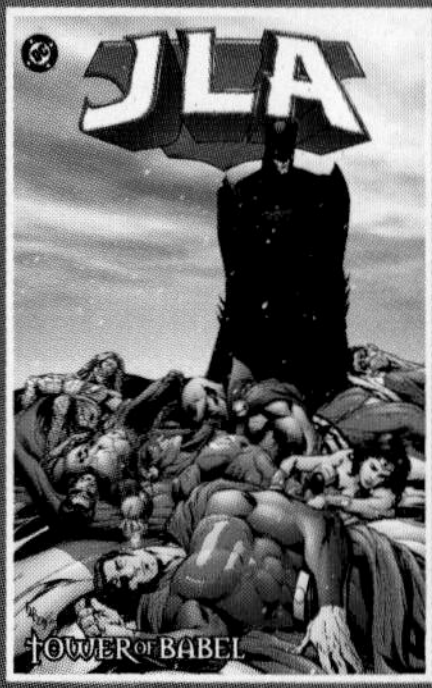
JLA
TOWER OF BABEL

VOLUME 7:
TOWER OF BABEL
Waid/Porter/Dell/various

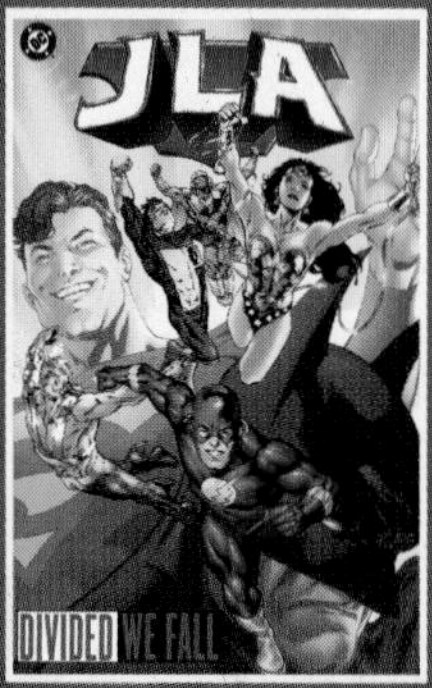
JLA
DIVIDED WE FALL

VOLUME 8:
DIVIDED WE FALL
Waid/Hitch/Neary/various

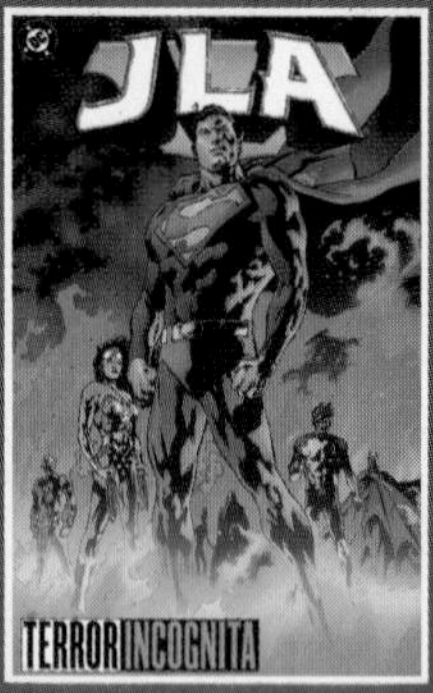
JLA
TERROR INCOGNITA

VOLUME 9:
TERROR INCOGNITA
Waid/Dixon/Beatty/Hitch/various

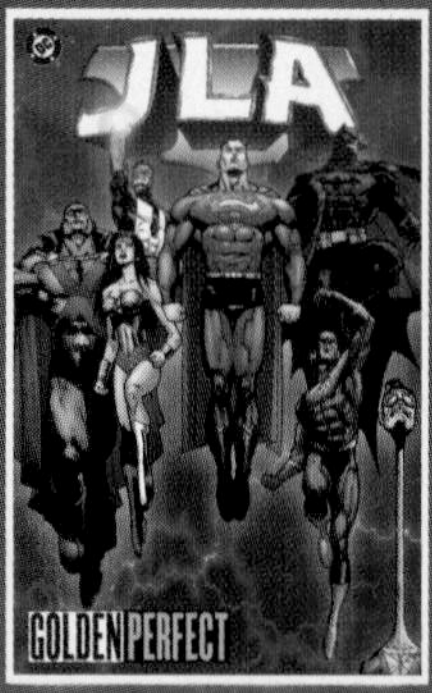
JLA
GOLDEN PERFECT

VOLUME 10:
GOLDEN PERFECT
Kelly/Mahnke/Nguyen

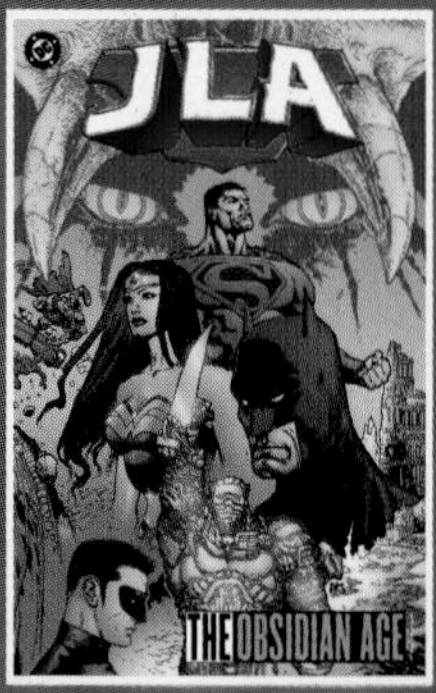
JLA
THE OBSIDIAN AGE

VOLUME 11:
OBSIDIAN AGE BOOK 1
Kelly/Mahnke/Guichet/Nguyen/Propst

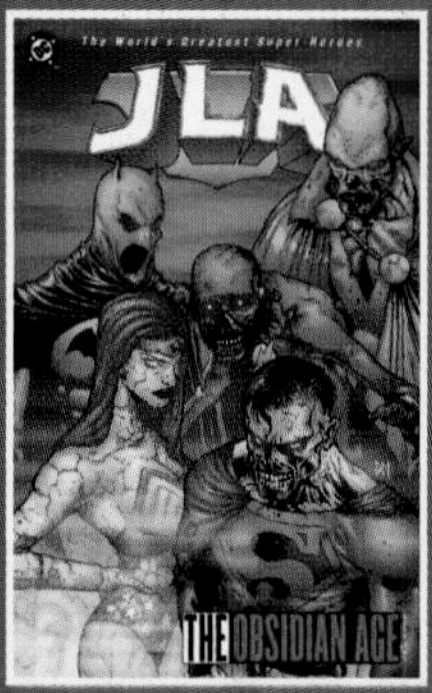
The World's Greatest Super-Heroes
JLA
THE OBSIDIAN AGE

VOLUME 12:
OBSIDIAN AGE BOOK 2
Kelly/Mahnke/Guichet/Larossa/Nguyen/Propst/Milgrom

JLA Volume 13: Rules of Engagement
Kelly/Mahnke/Nguyen/various

JLA: Earth 2
Morrison/Quitely

JLA: A League of One

JLA: One Million
Morrison/Semeiks/various

JLA: Riddle of the Beast
A. Grant/various

JLA: World Without Grown-Ups

JLA: Year One
Waid/Augustyn/Kitson/Bair/various

JLA/JSA: Virtue & Vice
Goyer/Johns/Pacheco/Merino

JLA/The Titans: The Technis Imperative
Grayson/Jimenez/Pelletier/various

Justice League: A Midsummer's Nightmare
Waid/Nicieza/various

Justice League of America: The Nail
Davis/Farmer